D0193706

teach®
yourself

korean
mark vincent and
jaehoon yeon

For over 60 years, more than
40 million people have learnt over
750 subjects the **teach yourself**
way, with impressive results.

be where you want to be
with **teach yourself**

For UK order enquiries: please contact Bookpoint Ltd, 130 Milton Park, Abingdon, Oxon OX14 4SB. Telephone: +44 (0) 1235 827720. Fax: +44 (0) 1235 400454. Lines are open 09.00–18.00, Monday to Saturday, with a 24-hour message answering service. Details about our titles and how to order are available at www.teachyourself.co.uk

For USA order enquiries: please contact McGraw-Hill Customer Services, PO Box 545, Blacklick, OH 43004-0545, USA. Telephone: 1-800-722-4726. Fax: 1-614-755-5645.

For Canada order enquiries: please contact McGraw-Hill Ryerson Ltd, 300 Water St, Whitby, Ontario L1N 9B6, Canada. Telephone: 905 430 5000. Fax: 905 430 5020.

Long renowned as the authoritative source for self-guided learning – with more than 40 million copies sold worldwide – the **teach yourself** series includes over 300 titles in the fields of languages, crafts, hobbies, business, computing and education.

British Library Cataloguing in Publication Data: a catalogue record for this title is available from the British Library.

Library of Congress Catalog Card Number: on file.

First published in UK 1997 by Hodder Education, 338 Euston Road, London, NW1 3BH.

First published in US 1997 by Contemporary Books, a Division of the McGraw-Hill Companies, 1 Prudential Plaza, 130 East Randolph Street, Chicago, IL 60601 USA.

This edition published 2003.

The **teach yourself** name is a registered trade mark of Hodder Headline.

Typeset by Graphicraft Limited, Hong Kong

Printed in Great Britain for Hodder Education, a division of Hodder Headline, 338 Euston Road, London NW1 3BH, by Cox & Wyman Ltd, Reading, Berkshire.

Hodder Headline's policy is to use papers that are natural, renewable and recyclable products and made from wood grown in sustainable forests. The logging and manufacturing processes are expected to conform to the environmental regulations of the country of origin.

Impression number	10					
Year	2010	2009	2008	2007	2006	2005

contents

foreword

There are now several introductory Korean courses on the market, and our aim has been to make this one stand out in the following ways. First, it focuses on real-life situations, with dialogues which feature authentic Korean as it is spoken on the street. We have tried to make the book be led by the dialogues, while maintaining a logical progression through the basics of the grammar. Apart from the first few units, in which we have deliberately simplified things, the dialogues contain real Korean with colloquial phrases and idiomatic expressions left in and explained.

Our second aim has been to make the lesson notes as clear as possible – drawing comparisons with English to illustrate how Korean is both similar and different, rather than introducing a lot of grammatical terminology. We have tried to explain in detail the crucial grammar points, and also provide a taster for a few more advanced matters, without letting these intrude. Much non-essential grammar has been omitted to put the focus on what is especially important. The exercises have been designed to test the essential grammar thoroughly, and to give lots of practice with practical language use.

The book is a collaboration, despite the authors being 6,000 miles apart for some of its production! The content of the dialogues was jointly planned, and then became Jaehoon Yeon's responsibility. The grammar content was also jointly planned, and the notes were written by Mark Vincent and then checked by Jaehoon Yeon. The exercises were created by Mark Vincent and then checked by Jaehoon Yeon.

We are grateful to those before us who have written books about Korean, and the approach adopted here to explain

Korean grammar is indebted to Ross King and Jaehoon Yeon's *Elementary Korean* (Tuttle, 2000) and *Continuing Korean* (Tuttle, 2002). We would like to hear of any comments or suggestions for the improvement of this book, and can be contacted through the publishers.

Korean is an exciting language to learn and to speak, and we have enjoyed writing this book. Mark Vincent would like to dedicate his share of its production to Peter Dickinson and Steve Rees from Pindar School, Scarborough – two brilliant foreign language teachers from whom he learnt a great deal, not least a deep love of language, languages and all things foreign. Jaehoon Yeon would like to express heartfelt thanks to his former students at SOAS whose struggle with the Korean language has contributed unwittingly but enormously to making this book.

Mark Vincent
Jaehoon Yeon

About the authors

Mark Vincent graduated from the School of Oriental and African Studies, University of London in Korean and Linguistics. He went on to obtain both an MA and a PhD from the University of Durham, specializing in Hebrew and Biblical Studies. He has spent over a year living and studying in Seoul and has conducted research and published in several areas of Korean studies and the Hebrew Bible. He currently works in asset management for a major investment company.

Jaehoon Yeon received his BA and MA in Linguistics at Seoul National University, and his PhD in Linguistics at SOAS, University of London. He is the co-author of *Elementary Korean* and *Continuing Korean* (Tuttle Publishing Co.) and has published many articles on Korean linguistics. He is currently lecturing in Korean language and literature at SOAS, University of London.

introduction

Korean is a fascinating language to study. For a start, it has a completely different alphabet to ours, a writing system which is unique among the languages of the world. Its grammar is entirely different to English – so much so that at first everything seems to be expressed backwards in Korean! On top of this, it has sounds which are alien to any that we have in European languages. That's quite a lot to cope with already, and we haven't even mentioned the different cultural assumptions which underlie the different languages!

Korean is not an easy language to learn. But, as we hope you'll come to experience for yourself very soon, the challenges that the language presents are what make communicating in it so rewarding. When you begin to communicate in Korean, you will find it both entertaining and fulfilling.

Who speaks Korean, and why should you?

If you learn Korean, you will be speaking the language of 80 or 90 million other people, the language of the only nation on earth which remains divided, the language spoken by a country with one of the world's strongest economies, the language of a people of rich and diverse culture still largely unknown in the West. Koreans will appreciate it when you try to speak with them using their language, and they will be delighted to communicate with you. Korean is the eleventh largest language in the world in terms of the number of native speakers.

Being in Korea and speaking in Korean is both exciting and challenging. Although many Koreans are learning English, most do not speak it, and of those that do, many are not able to speak coherently, even though they know lots of English words. If you want to have a truly rewarding time when you visit Korea (whether for business or pleasure), learning Korean is the way forward.

And even in the West you can practise, too. There are now many Korean companies in Europe and the States, and there are growing communities of Koreans in Britain, on the West Coast of America, and elsewhere.

A potted history of Korean

Grammatically Korean is related to Japanese and Mongolian (the structure of the three languages is quite similar). Korean is thought to belong to the Altaic family of languages, meaning that it is also related to Tungusic and Turkish. This may all come as a surprise, since many people assume that Korean will be like Chinese. Grammatically Korean is totally different from Chinese. There is no connection between them.

However, many Korean words (as opposed to grammar) come from Chinese, since China has been the major influence in Korea's literature and culture. Probably 50 per cent of Korean words are originally of Chinese origin. This is a bit similar to the way in which English has many words which are borrowed from Latin.

Some tips for learning Korean

The first thing to remember is this: don't be put off by how different and difficult it all seems at first. It is different, and it is difficult. But, as long as you keep going, you will quickly begin to spot the patterns and come to understand the way that Korean sentences work. It is quite possible for a westerner to learn to speak Korean fluently – even a westerner with little previous experience of language learning. With a course like this one, you will find that although there are always new challenges along the way, you will progress rapidly and logically through the basics of the Korean language.

One of the exciting things about learning Korean is that there are so few westerners who can speak it. Despite Korea's rapid economic growth, and despite the constant American military presence in Seoul, there are still few westerners to be seen on the streets of even the largest cities. Very few of those can speak any Korean at all.

Koreans are absolutely delighted when you try to speak their language and they will bend over backwards to try to help and encourage you. They won't make you feel silly, and they won't take your efforts to speak Korean for granted, no matter how good you are.

Contrariwise, many Koreans are eager for opportunities to practise their English. If you go to Korea and are keen to improve your command of the language, it is best to be clear in your mind that you will try to speak in Korean, no matter how hard someone might try to persuade you to speak English! It is the best way to learn quickly.

The Korean alphabet

The Korean alphabet is unique among the writing systems of the world. This is because it is the only known alphabet in the world which was specifically commissioned or made to order. From ancient times literacy in Korea had existed only among the ruling classes, and consisted of classical Chinese, or sometimes of using Chinese characters and adapting some of them for use in a Korean context. Among the majority of the people, there was no literacy at all – not even Chinese.

However, in 1446 King Sejong, the most famous of all the Korean kings and queens, commanded extensive research to be conducted in order to produce a writing system especially designed for writing Korean. This was carried out by a team of scholars, and the accuracy and sophistication of their research and phonological analysis is still a source of amazement to scholars today. The Korean alphabet, *han'gul*, is perhaps the most outstanding scientific and cultural achievement of the Korean nation.

If you are to take seriously the task of learning Korean, there is no substitute for learning to read the Korean script. It is not especially difficult (certainly not as difficult as it looks), and you will soon come to appreciate both its uniqueness and its elegance.

All the dialogues in this book appear first in Korean script, followed by a romanized version. For the first few lessons you may well want to rely on the romanized version so that you can quickly begin to speak Korean words and sentences without being troubled by the initial difficulty of being slowed down by the writing system. But you must constantly practise reading the dialogues in the Korean script as well, without relying on the romanization. You should see romanization as a crutch to help you on your way as you learn Korean writing. By the time you have passed the first few lessons, you should be going first to the Korean texts, and looking at the romanization to test your pronunciation.

We're going to divide looking at the alphabet and pronunciation into three sections, first, to introduce you to the letters of the alphabet, then to look at the way that we have romanized those letters in this book, and finally to look at important rules of sound changes in pronunciation. First, then, the letters of the alphabet and principles of Korean writing.

The Korean script (*han'gul*) is indeed an alphabet, but it has one special feature which sets it apart from most others. In English we start writing at the beginning of a word and write a sequence of letters, each one following the next, until we reach the end. Usually (apart from the case of silent letters and other peculiarities) we pronounce each letter in turn in the sequence running from left to right.

Korean, however, instead of writing a string of letters in sequence, writes its letters in syllable blocks. Thus, take the Korean word which is pronounced as **komapsumnida**. It means *thank you*. In English we write the letters left to right, k-o-m-a-p-s-u-m-n-i-d-a, but Korean breaks the word into syllables: **ko-map-sum-ni-da**. Don't worry about the form of the letters, but simply have a look at the way this works in Fig. 1.

고맙습니다

Fig. 1

What we will be learning about first, then, is how to write Korean syllables. These syllables are then placed next to each other to make up words and sentences.

Writing Korean

Every Korean syllable begins with a consonant letter (if the syllable begins with a vowel then a special null consonant symbol is inserted in place of the consonant letter; this looks like a zero, and is the last consonant letter in Fig. 2). This consonant letter has a vowel letter either on its right or underneath it (some vowels go both to the right and underneath; we will deal with those later). Every syllable must have the consonant letter plus a vowel letter. Some syllables have another consonant letter written underneath the first consonant and the vowel, and occasionally you will meet syllables that have two consonants next to each other in this final, underneath position.

For now we will just concentrate on syllables that have one consonant letter and one vowel letter. Here are some consonant letters:

ㄱ ㄷ ㅂ ㅈ ㅁ ㄴ ㅇ

Fig. 2

These are pronounced as follows: **k** as in *kitchen*; **t** as in *toad*; **p** as in *potty*; **ch** as in *chamber*; **m** as in *miser*; **n** as in *nanny*; the last letter is the zero or null consonant, which means the syllable begins with a vowel sound – you must always write this null consonant whenever the syllable begins with a vowel sound.

Remember that we can add a vowel letter either to the right or underneath these. First, the vowels that go to the right-hand side. In Fig. 3 you will see the vowels **a** as in *bat*, **ŏ** as in *hot*, **ya** as in *yap*, **yŏ** as in *yonder*, **i** as in *hit* or *ea* in *heat* (this is why you need the recording to tell which one is to be used where!). On the next line we have made up syllables with the consonants you have learned. These are, respectively: **ka, kŏ, kya, kyŏ, ki, tya, ti, pa, pŏ, chi, chŏ, ma, mŏ, nyŏ, nŏ, i, ya.**

ㅏ ㅓ ㅑ ㅕ ㅣ

가 거 갸 겨 기 댜 디
바 버 지 저 마 머 녀
너 이 야

Fig. 3

There are also other vowels which have to be written under the consonant letter. Some of these are in Fig. 4, and underneath are some syllables for you to practise. The vowels are pronounced **o** as in *boat* (note that this is different to the vowel **ŏ** which you have learnt above); **u** as **oo** in *pool*; **yo** as in *yokel*; **yu** as in *yuletide*; **ŭ** as **u** in *curd* or **e** in *berk*. The syllables we have given you are: **to, tu, tyo, tyu, tŭ, ko, kŭ, pu, pyo, cho, chŭ, mu, myu, nyu, no, o, yo.**

ㅗ　ㅜ　ㅛ　ㅠ　ㅡ

도　두　됴　듀　드　고　그
부　뵤　조　즈　무　뮤　뉴
노　오　요

Fig. 4

You are now in a position to do Exercises 1 and 2 and you should do these at this point.

▶ Exercise 1
Read the following Korean words written in Korean script and listen to the recording.

1	바보	2	바나나
3	마마	4	가도
5	자주	6	아이
7	고교	8	묘기
9	드무오	10	머기

▶ Exercise 2
Read the following Korean words written in Korean script and listen to the recording.

1	아버지	2	어머니
3	너야	4	가구
5	두부	6	모유
7	거지	8	모기
9	모자	10	나가자

Now, as we remarked earlier, you can add another consonant underneath the first consonant and the vowel letter, to give three-lettered syllables. We need at this point to tell you that the null consonant symbol (the little circle) has two functions. At the beginning of the syllable it tells you that the syllable begins with a vowel sound. However, in last place in a syllable it represents the sound ng as in *bring*. Some combinations are illustrated in Fig. 5. The syllables we have given are: kim, pak, min, chŏm, kŏn, pyŏng, kom, chun, yop, tŭm, pang and ŭng.

김　박　민　점　건　병
곰　준　욥　듬　방　응

Fig. 5

It is now time to learn some more consonants. These are given in Fig. 6, and they are, respectively: l as in *ladle*, h as in *hope*, s as in *sat*.

ㄹ ㅎ ㅅ ㅋ ㅌ ㅍ ㅊ

Fig. 6

The final four consonants on the list are aspirated versions (made with a puff of air) of the four consonants you have met already: k, t, p and ch. We romanize the aspirated versions as k', t', p' and ch'. To make these aspirated sounds shape your mouth as you would to make the normal k, t, p or ch sound, and then make the sound by forcing air out of your mouth in a rush. If you put your hand to your lips as you make them (or hold up a sheet of paper) you should feel the puff of air as you make the sound (or should see the paper move). Imagine the difference between saying the c in *of course* if you were saying it calmly and naturally, and saying it again when you were irritated with someone 'don't be ridiculous, of *course* it's not, stupid!'. The first would be the Korean letter k, and the second would be k'. The difference can be important; as an example, the word pa means *concern, business* (as in 'it's not your concern'), but the word p'a means a *spring onion*!

In addition, the four consonants k, t, p and ch, along with s can also be doubled (that is, one written immediately after the other). This is a bit more difficult to explain than aspiration. Here you make your mouth (lips and tongue) very tense and make the sound lightly, without a puff of air. Once again the difference is important, and the best way to pick it up is to listen to the recording or a Korean speaker, and try to imitate the sounds. We romanize these by kk, tt, pp, cch. The consonant s can also be doubled to give ss. Fig. 7 has examples of syllables containing the double and aspirated consonants.

김 킴 낌 돈 톤 똔 분 푼 뿐
잔 찬 짠 산 싼

Fig. 7

There are also a few more vowels to learn. Fig. 8 contains the vowels ae as *a* in *care*; e as in *hen*; yae as in *yesterday*; ye also as in *yesterday* (there is no significant difference in sound between yae and ye). These sounds are illustrated in the syllables maen, p'en, yae, kye.

ㅐ ㅔ ㅒ ㅖ
맨 펜 얘 계

Fig. 8

Finally, certain vowels are made up of combinations of others (you read the one underneath first, then the one on the right-hand side). You can probably work out the pronunciations of these for yourself, but we give you them in any case. They are as in Fig. 9: **wa** (o + a) as in *wag*; **wo** (u + ŏ) as *wa* in *wanted*; **wae** (o + ae) as the word *where*; **we** (wu + e) as *we* in *wet*; **oe** (o + i) as in German *Goethe*; **wi** (u + i) as in French *oui*; **ŭy** (ŭ + i, say them together, fast), sometimes pronounced as e.

ㅘ ㅝ ㅙ ㅖ ㅚ ㅟ ㅢ

Fig. 9

Occasionally you will meet syllables that have two consonants in the final place. Unless we tell you otherwise (by missing one of them out in the romanization) both of these should be pronounced. You will find a couple of examples, along with some examples of the vowels in the last paragraph, in Fig. 10. The syllables we have given you are: **ilk, wae, kwon, hwan, palk, kwi, mwo, oen** and **ŏps**.

읽 왜 권 환 밝 귀 뭐 왼 없

Fig. 10

You have now learned the entire Korean alphabet, and are ready to tackle all the exercises.

You can also now look up in a dictionary any word you find written in the Korean script. The order of the Korean alphabet is given in Fig. 11. Notice that all the words beginning with vowels are grouped together under the null consonant symbol. This means that all the vowels (the last 21 symbols on the list), occur in the dictionary at the place marked by the asterisk.

ㄱ ㄲ ㄴ ㄷ ㄸ ㄹ ㅁ ㅂ ㅃ ㅅ
ㅆ ㅇ* ㅈ ㅉ ㅊ ㅋ ㅌ ㅍ ㅎ
ㅏ ㅐ ㅑ ㅒ ㅓ ㅔ ㅕ ㅖ ㅗ ㅘ
ㅙ ㅚ ㅛ ㅜ ㅝ ㅞ ㅟ ㅠ ㅡ ㅢ
ㅣ

Fig. 11

Exercise 3
The following Korean words written in Korean script are the names of countries which you should be able to recognize. Read the names and write down what the English equivalent is.

1 파키스탄   2 멕시코
3 뉴질랜드   4 네델란드
5 스웨덴   6 덴마크
7 인도네시아   8 폴란드
9 캐나다   10 아메리카

Exercise 4
The following Korean words written in Korean script are loan words from English which you should be able to recognize. Read the names and write down what the English equivalent is.

1 호텔   2 피아노
3 컴퓨터   4 텔레비젼
5 라디오   6 택시
7 레몬   8 아이스크림
9 햄버거   10 샌드위치
11 오렌지 쥬스   12 테니스
13 카메라   14 토마토

▶ **Exercise 5**
Read the following Korean words and listen to the recording.

1 빵   2 시내
3 오징어   4 과일
5 안녕하세요   6 선생님
7 사업   8 말씀
9 일본   10 영국

Romanization of Korean

This book gives you a romanized version of all the Korean dialogues and the lesson notes it contains (that is, written in English letters). In addition, Korean scripts are given for all the dialogues and the new vocabularies.

This is not because we believe the Korean alphabet to be unimportant. On the contrary, as we have already stressed, it is very important that you learn it. However, there are two reasons why we have consistently used romanization, in addition to printing the dialogues and the vocabularies in the Korean script. The first is that we want you to move quickly through the course, and become competent at handling Korean as a spoken language as soon as possible.

The second reason is that often Korean letters are not pronounced exactly as they are written, or rather, certain letters are pronounced in a different way under certain circumstances. We could explain all the rules for this and let you work out the pronunciation for yourself. However, by using the romanization guidelines, most of this is done for you.

There are several different methods of romanizing Korean, and the one we have used is a modified version of what is known as the McCune-Reischauer system.

You have already seen the way we romanize most of the letters from the previous explanation of the Korean alphabet, but there are a number of points to notice:

* k, t, p and ch are all written as such at the beginning of a word; however, in actual pronunciation, they can be pronounced g, d, b and j if they are preceded and followed by vowel sounds. We do not indicate this in the romanization, so that you can be sure where you should be looking up words in dictionaries or glossaries. If you listen to the recording (as you should), you will be reminded when these letters should be pronounced in the different way.

  However, in the middle of a word, these letters k, t, p, ch are written as g, d, b and j when they occur between vowels. Therefore, the word which is written in Korean letters as ha-ko (the dash marking the syllable break) will be romanized here as hago.

* The consonants m and n are romanized as such; double consonants are written as kk, tt, pp, cch; aspirated consonants are written as k', t', p', ch'; the zero or null consonant is not romanized since it has no sound – remember to write it in the Korean script when a syllable begins with a vowel however. As the last consonant in a syllable, we romanize it as ng, which is the way it is pronounced (as in *bring*).

* The letter h is sometimes not pronounced; in those cases we do not romanize it, although we indicate its presence in the vocabularies by writing it in brackets as in the word man(h)i, pronounced mani. When the letter h occurs as the last consonant in a syllable and the following syllable begins with k, t, p or ch, then those sounds become aspirated. Instead of

writing **hk** in romanization, therefore, we write **k'**, which is the way in which the Korean is actually pronounced.

- The consonant **s** is pronounced **sh** (as in *shall*) when it is followed by the vowel **i**, and we romanize it as **sh** in such instances. Note that **ss + i** is pronounced **sshi**, but we romanize it as **ssi**.

- Finally, the consonant **l** is a little tricky. Sometimes it is pronounced **l** (when one of the letters to the side of it is a consonant), but between vowels it is pronounced **r**. We romanize it as **l** or **r** according to the pronunciation. Take the word **il** for example, which means *day*. When the word is followed by the subject particle **-i**, the **l** is pronounced as an **r**, so we romanize it as **ir-i**. What you have to remember is that in the vocabulary this will be listed under **il**, and not **ir**. It sounds a bit puzzling at first, but you will soon get used to it, and there is no real difficulty.

The vowels are straightforward, and are romanized in the way we described when going through the letters of the Korean alphabet. Be careful to watch the two os, **o** and **ŏ** (as in over and other); also remember that **ŭ** is pronounced as the u in *burn*; **u** is pronounced as the u in *lute*. You should look over the description of the vowels again at this point to ensure that you are happy with them.

In conclusion, a word about double consonants. By this we mean two syllables in which the first ends with the same consonant as the initial consonant of the second (**om-ma; man-na; hal-la**). In these cases, hold on to the consonant sound a little longer than you would if there was just one, for example, with **omma**, say 'om', then, keeping your mouth closed and still making the humming sound of the m, make a little pause before you say 'ma'. Listen to this on the recording; don't get anxious about it, just remember to try to make the consonant sound a little longer than you would if there were only one of them.

You are now in a position to do the exercises on romanization.

Exercise 1
Write the following in Korean script.

1	Jaemin	2	kayo
3	chigŭm	4	yangju
5	marŭn anju	6	chungguk
7	mashida	8	pap
9	chinccha	10	uri

Exercise 2

Put the following Korean words in romanization form.

1 어때요?   2 사람
3 선생님   4 아니요
5 사무실   6 만나다
7 미국   8 학교
9 대사관   10 점심

▶ Pronunciation

Although Korean writing is consistent (that is, a word is always spelt in the same way), some syllables are pronounced in different ways in certain contexts (if surrounded by certain other syllables or sounds). For example, an n can, given certain conditions, be pronounced like an l. In Korean script the letter would still be written as an n, but Korean speakers would know to pronounce it as an l. You will know, not only because we are now going to tell you the most important of the pronunciation rules, but also because our romanization will tell you.

Rule 1

When the letters **k**, **t** and **p** precede **m** or **n** or **l**, they are pronounced (and romanized) as **ng**, **n** and **m** respectively. If the letter they precede is an **l**, then the **l** also changes to an **n** sound. The following examples show in the left column how they would be spelt in *han'gul*, and in the right-hand column, the way they are pronounced and romanized. We have put dashes in to indicate the syllable breaks.

hak-nyŏn	hang-nyŏn
tat-nun-da	tan-nun-da
hap-ni-da	ham-ni-da
tok-lip	tong-nip

Rule 2

l is pronounced as an **n** when immediately preceded by any consonant except **l** or **n**. Thus we have **tong-nip** as above (from **tok-lip**), **shimni** (from **shim-li**).

Whenever an **l** appears next to an **n**, either as **nl** or **ln**, the resulting pronunciation is **ll**: **chilli** from **chin-li**, **illyŏn** from **il-nyŏn**.

Rule 3

If a word ends in a consonant and it is not followed by a particle (a little word that attaches to nouns), or the verb -ieyo (to be learned in Unit 1), then the last consonant is pronounced in a special way. The last consonant is not released. That means that you say the word as you would in English, moving your mouth into position to make a final consonant sound (see below) and beginning to say it, but stopping short of releasing any air. It would sound to an English speaker almost as if the consonant had been swallowed.

If the last consonant is a **ch, ch', s, ss** or **h**, then the sound that you begin to make at the end of the word is the sound **t** (again, you don't release it).

We felt it was important to include these rules, because they make the book accurate and enable you to understand what is going on when it seems that the Korean text does not match up to the romanization or to what Korean speakers actually say. But we don't want you to become overly worried about it. If you listen to the recording regularly, and look carefully at the Korean script and the romanization, then you will soon pick up the rules, and the explanations we have given in this section will help you as you go.

There is a practice exercise, however, to enable you to practise the rules of this section. If you prefer, you can skip it and get straight on with the lessons themselves.

▶ Exercise 1

The following examples show in the left column how they would be spelt in *han'gul*, and in the right-hand column, the way they are pronounced and romanized. Listen to the recording and practise them.

1 먹는다   mong-nŭn-da
2 한국말   hang-gung-mal
3 숙녀   sung-nyŏ
4 갑니다   kam-ni-ta
5 닫는다   tan-nŭn-da
6 작문   chang-mun
7 국민   kung-min
8 심리   sim-ni
9 앞문   am-mun
10 십만   sim-man

▶ Exercise 2

A Korean never releases a consonant at the end of a syllable except when the word is followed a particle or ending that begins with a vowel. The following examples show in the left column when the last consonant is not released, and in the right column when the last consonant is released before vowels. Listen to the tape and practise them.

1	집	chip	집에	chib-e
2	앞	ap	앞에	ap'-e
3	옷	ot	옷이에요	osh-ieyo
4	낟	nat	낟은	nach-ŭn
5	낮	nat	낮이	nach'-i
6	낫	nat	낫이	nash'-i
7	국	kuk	국이에요	kug-ieyo
8	밖	pak	밖에	pakk-e
9	밭	pak	밭에	pat'-e
10	꽃	kkot	꽃이에요	kkoch'-ieyo

How to use the course

Most of the 14 units of this course follow the same pattern.

Introduction An introduction in English that explains what you will learn in the unit.

Dialogue In each unit there are two dialogues, followed by a list of new vocabulary and some simple comprehension questions in English or Korean. Each dialogue is followed by grammar notes which explain how to use the language patterns that have come up.

Phrases and expressions This section gives you expressions that are commonly used as set phrases, and also gives you translations of snippets of dialogue which contain difficult grammar patterns which you are not yet ready to analyse and which you must learn simply as set expressions for the time being.

Vocabulary New words from the dialogues will go into the vocabulary section. The list of words in the vocabulary follows the order in which they appear in the dialogue. Sometimes we also give you additional words which are closely related to the ones that occur in the dialogues.

The units are meant to teach you how to use Korean practically in everyday situations – how to order in a restaurant, how to complain when your hotel room isn't quite what it should be, how to express opinions and disagreements, and so on.

Grammar To be able to do these things, however, you need to have a good understanding of grammar. This is the purpose of the commentary sections. Do not be put off by the quantity of grammar explanations, therefore. You do need these in order to speak Korean properly. We have done our best to keep unnecessary details and minor exceptions to rules out of the text. Do not worry if you don't understand every single bit of grammatical structure in the Korean dialogues. The important thing is that you learn the dialogues thoroughly, and that you understand the main grammar points of each unit.

Practice Please do the exercises! Don't be tempted to skip to the next unit until you've done them, checked them in the key at the back of the book, understood your mistakes and learned the correct answers.

Take time to learn the Korean alphabet properly, and make sure you write the exercises out in Korean script, even if you also do them in romanization.

▶ If you want to have a good command of spoken Korean, you will find the recording essential. Listen to it as often as you can – take it with you in the car or in your walkman for example. Listen back over units that you studied previously; listen to future units – to make yourself familiar with the sounds and intonations – picking out what you can, even though you won't understand everything.

Although the going will seem tough at times, Korean is a fun language, and studying it can be very rewarding. Remember to enjoy youself – the best way to do so is to follow the maxim 'a little and often'!

01

where are you off to?/
cheers!

In this unit you will learn
- how to talk about where you are going and why
- how to ask questions
- how to order drinks and snacks
- basic structure of Korean sentences
- how to make polite requests
- how to form what is known as the polite style of speech

▶ Where are you off to?

Sangmin meets his friend Jaemin in the street and asks him where he is off to.

상민	재민씨! 안녕하세요!
재민	네. 안녕하세요! 잘 지냈어요?
상민	네, 네. 어디 가요?
재민	지금 시내에 가요.
상민	뭐 하러 시내에 가요?
재민	빵 사러 가요.
상민	나도 빵 사러 시내에 가요.
재민	그럼 같이 가요.
상민	네. 같이 가요.

Sangmin	Jaemin-ssi! Annyŏng haseyo?
Jaemin	Ne. Annyŏng haseyo! Chal chinaessŏyo?
Sangmin	Ne, ne. Ŏdi kayo?
Jaemin	Chigŭm shinae-e kayo.
Sangmin	Mwo ha-rŏ shinae-e kayo?
Jaemin	Ppang sa-rŏ kayo.
Sangmin	Na-do ppang sa-rŏ shinae-e kayo.
Jaemin	Kŭrŏm kach'i kayo.
Sangmin	Ne. Kach'i kayo.

1 How is Sangmin getting on?
2 Where is Jaemin going?
3 Why?
4 Who else is going there?
5 What does Jaemin suggest?

Phrases and expressions

annyŏng haseyo?	*hello!/how are you?*
annyŏng haseyo!	*hello!/fine* (note: this phrase is both a question and a reply)
chal chinaessŏyo?	*how have you been doing (getting on)?*
chal chinaessŏyo.	*fine, thanks (I've been getting on well)* (question and reply)
ŏdi kayo?	*where are you going?*
mwo ha-rŏ . . . kayo?*	*what are you going to . . . to do?*

(name) -ssi 씨	(title used with people's names; see section 2)
ne 네	yes
chal 잘	good, well (adverb)
ǒdi 어디	where?
ka- 가–	go (verb stem)
kayo 가요	go (stem plus polite ending -yo)
chigǔm 지금	now
shinae 시내	town centre
-e –에	to (preposition, attaches to nouns)
mwo 뭐	what?
ha- 하–	do (verb stem)
haeyo 해요	do (stem plus polite ending -yo, irregular form)
(verb stem) -rǒ –러	in order to (verb)
ha-rǒ 하러	in order to do
ppang 빵	bread
sa- 사–	buy (verb stem)
sayo 사요	buy (stem plus polite ending -yo)
na 나	I/me
-do –도	too, also (particle, attaches to nouns)
kǔrǒm 그럼	then, in that case
kach'i 같이	together

Grammar

1 Korean names

Korean names usually consist of three syllables. The first syllable is the surname (the most common Korean surnames being Kim, Lee and Pak), and this is usually followed by a two-syllable first name. There are odd exceptions: sometimes the first name will only contain one syllable. The two names in this dialogue, Jaemin and Sangmin, are both first names.

In Korean, the surname (when it is used) always comes first, the opposite of the English order. Therefore, Mr Pak Jaemin's surname is Pak, and his first name Jaemin. In this book we shall always use the Korean order (Pak Jaemin) rather than the English (Jaemin Pak). When you are writing Korean names in the Korean script, remember also that Koreans put no space between the surname and the first name – they are treated almost like one word.

2 Talking to friends and talking about them

When referring to someone you know well in a friendly situation, either to address them directly or to talk about them, it is quite acceptable to use their first name, just like we do in English. Following the name you should use the polite title -ssi. You can refer to friends you know quite well and with whom you are on a similar social level as John-ssi, Deborah-ssi, Jaemin-ssi, Kyuthae-ssi, and so forth.

It is only when you are speaking to a very close friend that this -ssi can be dropped and you can just use their name (though if other people are present it is best to carry on using it). If you use -ssi you won't make any mistakes or offend anyone, whereas if you try dropping it, you could make a social mistake.

3 Korean verbs

All the sentences (except the first) in the dialogue end with a verb (a 'doing-word' like *walk*, *go*, *kick*, *steal*). Korean sentences always end with verbs in this way. In English, the position of the verb is quite different: we would say, for example, *I go to the shops*, whereas a Korean will say *I shops-to go*. Main verbs always come at the end of the sentence, and getting used to this major difference in sentence structure takes a little while, since it can seem as though you are having to say everything backwards!

The dialogue also contains other verbs which occur in the middle of a sentence. Even these are at the end in a sense, however, because they are used to end a clause. A clause is a part of a sentence which has its own verb and which could stand on its own as a sentence if it were changed a little bit. For example, the sentence *If you come then I'll go* is made up of two clauses, both of which could stand on their own as sentences (*you come* and *I'll go*). To summarize, Korean clauses and Korean sentences must always have a verb at the end. More about clauses and clause endings later.

You will notice that all the verbs have endings to them. The verbs at the end of the sentences all end in -yo. This is a polite way of ending a sentence. The mid-sentence verbs in this lesson all end with -rŏ. This is explained in note 7.

Korean verbs are made up of stems onto which endings can be added. Every verb has a stem; it is the most basic part of a

Korean verb. Sometimes you might want to add as many as seven different endings at once onto a verb stem! In the vocabulary sections of this book we shall usually list verbs by their stem forms, and this is the form in which you should learn them. By the rules we teach you, you will learn how to make the other forms of the verb from these stems. In the first few lessons we shall remind you when we are teaching you the stem form. If we don't tell you a stem, it is because there is something odd (irregular) about it, or because we only want you to learn one particular form of the verb in question for the time being.

Verbs are listed in a dictionary in what is known as the 'dictionary form'. This is simply the stem with the syllable -ta after it. You can use verbs that you learn from the dictionary simply by taking off this -ta and using the stem as normal with the endings described in this book. There are some verbs which behave a bit oddly, however, and we will not go systematically through all the different kinds of verb stems until Unit 7, so you should hold fire a bit with the dictionary until that point. Otherwise you could make some bad mistakes!

The verbs in this lesson, ka- (go), ha- (do), sa- (buy), all occur with quite simple endings, and we will look at these now.

4 Polite sentences with -yo

The verb stems of this dialogue all end in vowels (ka-, ha- and sa-), and to these you can add what is called the polite sentence ending, -yo, to form a sentence. This polite sentence ending -yo is also known as a particle, and it is sometimes called the 'polite particle'. Note that the verb ha- is irregular, and the polite sentence form is haeyo, not hayo as you would have expected.

Kayo is in itself a complete sentence (or clause) which means I go, he goes, she goes, we go, etc, depending on the context. There is no need to specify precisely who does the going in order to make a good Korean sentence. Thus, if you are talking about your mother, for example, and want to say that she goes somewhere, Korean only requires that you say kayo – you don't need to use a word for she.

We ought to explain the term 'polite sentence ending' (or 'polite particle'). Korean has various styles or levels of speech which are used according to the social situation in which you are speaking. For example, when you are having a drink with close friends, you will use a very different speech style to that which you would use if you were addressing a meeting, or talking to somebody for the first time. The speech style is shown in Korean principally by the verb endings. Although we have formal and informal language in English, we do not have anything as systematic and widespread as the Korean system of verb endings. These verb endings are crucial to every Korean sentence, since you cannot say a Korean sentence without selecting a speech style in which to say it. You have now begun to learn the most common, -yo, which marks the polite style of speech. This can be used in most social situations, particularly if it is neither especially formal nor intimate. It is, if you like, a middle-of-the-road style!

Verbs in the polite style may be statements, questions, suggestions or commands – this is expressed in the tone of voice that you use to say the sentence rather than being shown explicitly in the form of the verb. You have seen this several times already in the dialogue. The phrase **kach'i kayo** is first a suggestion, then when it is used a second time it is a statement. **Chal chinaessŏyo** can be both a question, asking how someone is, or a statement, saying that you are fine. **Annyŏng haseyo** can also be both a question and a statement, depending on the way in which you say it.

5 Who are you talking about?

As we've already mentioned, Korean does not need you to specify the subject of the sentence, i.e. precisely who is doing the action the sentence describes. You can specify it if you want to for special emphasis, but as long as it is clear from the context, Korean does not require it. **Ŏdi kayo?** therefore, means *where are you going* – but it is not necessary to say 'you', because the context makes it clear that the speaker is asking the hearer. If you look at the last seven sentences in the dialogue (from line 3), you'll see that only one uses a subject (**na-do ppang sa-rŏ kayo**). The subject of that sentence (**na-do**) is stated for emphasis.

6 Word order

We have seen that the word order of Korean sentences is very different from English. **Chal chinaessŏyo?** is a nice example, as it literally means 'well have you been getting on?', which is the opposite of what we would say in English. Usually the order is *subject – object – verb* (*SOV* for short). This gives, *Peter the ball kicked, Mary the shops-to went.*

7 To go to do

The other verb ending introduced in this dialogue is -rŏ which means *in order to*. You add this onto a verb stem at the end of a clause, just as you added -yo to verb stems at the end of sentences. Note that, with verb stems which end in consonants (you haven't learned any yet, but will soon), you add the form -urŏ (rather than just -rŏ) to the verb stem.

The most complicated part here is sorting out the word order. Let's look at the English sentence 'I'm going to the shops in order to buy bread'. Korean says this by putting the two clauses the other way round: *in order to buy bread I'm going to the shops*. However, that's not all! Remember that in addition, Korean puts its verbs at the end of clauses and sentences, and puts verb and clause endings after that. This gives us *I [bread buy-in order to] to the shops go*. Notice the way one clause is embedded inside the other. Usually the subject of the sentence comes first (in this case, *I*), then the in-order-to clause, then the place where you're going, then the main verb:

| I (subject) | go to the shops | in-order-to buy bread | (English) |
| I (optional) | bread buy – in-order-to | shops-to go | (Korean) |

Therefore, the Korean sentence order is **na-do ppang sa-rŏ kayo** (*I-to bread buy-in-order-to go*). In other words, the main verb of the sentence is the going, for example **kayo** or **shinae-e kayo**. The other part of the sentence, the *in order to . . .* bit comes first, as in **ppang sa-rŏ kayo**, or **ppang sa-rŏ shinae-e kayo**. This is the correct order. Don't be tempted to try other orders – they will probably be wrong!

Note: This construction is only used with verbs of 'going' and 'coming'. It cannot be used with other verbs at the end of the sentence.

▶ Cheers!

Sangmin goes to a bar with his friends and orders from the waiter.

상민	아저씨, 소주 있어요?
아저씨	네, 네. 있어요. 소주, 맥주, 양주 다 있어요.
상민	그럼, 맥주 하나하고 소주 하나 주세요.
아저씨	네. 알겠어요.
상민	그리고 안주도 주세요. 뭐 있어요?
아저씨	과일하고 오징어하고 마른안주하고 파전하고 ... 다 있어요.
상민	그럼 과일하고 오징어 주세요.

A little while later, the waiter brings the order . . .

아저씨	여기 있어요. 맛있게 드세요.
상민	감사합니다.
상민	*(to friends)* 건배!

Sangmin	Ajŏssi, soju issŏyo?
Ajŏssi	Ne, ne. Issŏyo. Soju, maekju, yangju – ta issŏyo.
Sangmin	Kŭrŏm, maekju hana-hago soju hana chuseyo.
Ajŏssi	Ne. Algessŏyo.
Sangmin	Kŭrigo anju-do chuseyo. Mwo issŏyo?
Ajŏssi	Kwail-hago ojingŏ-hago marŭn anju-hago p'ajŏn-hago . . . ta issŏyo.
Sangmin	Kŭrŏm, kwail-hago ojingŏ chuseyo.

A little while later, the waiter brings the order . . .

Ajŏssi	Yŏgi issŏyo. Mashikke tŭseyo.
Sangmin	Kamsa hamnida.
Sangmin	*(to friends)* Kŏnbae!

1 What drinks does the waiter have?
2 How many drinks does Sangmin order?
3 What else does he ask about?
4 What side dishes does he order?
5 What does the waiter wish his guests?

Phrases and expressions

. . . issŏyo?	*do you have . . . ?*
. . . chuseyo	*please give me . . .*
algessŏyo	*fine/understood/right away*
kamsa hamnida	*thank you*
yŏgi issŏyo	*here you are/here it is*
mashikke tŭseyo	*have a good meal/enjoy your food*
kŏnbae	*cheers!*

ajŏssi 아저씨	*waiter!*
soju 소주	soju, *Korean wine/vodka*
iss- 있–	*(1) exist, there is/are (stem) (2) have (stem)*
issŏyo 있어요	*(as above, polite style)*
maekju 맥주	*beer*
yangju 양주	*spirits, western liquor*
ta 다	*all, everything*
hana 하나	*one*
-hago –하고	*and*
chu- 주–	*give (stem)*
chuseyo 주세요	*please give (polite request form)*
kŭrigo 그리고	*and (also) (used to begin a sentence)*
anju 안주	*snacks or side dishes for drinks*
-do –도	*also*
kwail 과일	*fruit*
ojingŏ 오징어	*squid*
marŭn anju 마른 안주	*dried snacks*
p'ajŏn 파전	*Korean-style pancake*
yŏgi 여기	*here*

Grammar

1 There is/there are

The verb issŏyo means *there is* or *there are*, depending on what you are talking about (*there is a book, there are some sheep*). The stem of this verb is iss-, and before the polite particle -yo can be added, the vowel -ŏ has to be inserted. This is because iss- ends with a consonant, whereas the verbs from the first dialogue all ended with vowels. To repeat, stems ending in vowels usually make the polite form by adding -yo (an exception is the verb ha- (*do*), which, as you will remember, becomes haeyo not hayo). Stems ending in consonants add the ending -ŏyo to form the polite style, unless the last vowel in the stem is an -a or -o, in which case -ayo is added to make the polite style.

Polite style
vowel-stem	+ yo	
consonant-stem	+ ayo	*if last vowel is -a or -o*
consonant-stem	+ ŏyo	*otherwise*

The opposite of the verb iss- is ŏps- (*there isn't* or *there aren't*). From the rules given earlier, you can work out that its polite style form is ŏpsŏyo.

This pair of verbs, as well as expressing existence and location (as in chŏgi issŏyo, *it's over there, it exists over there*), have another meaning of *have*. Issŏyo can mean *I have/he has (one/some)*, and ŏpsŏyo can mean *I don't have*. You can tell by the context which is the relevant meaning.

You will notice again that you can make a complete sentence just with a verb (like issŏyo). You don't need to specify the subject (who has), and you don't even need to specify what it is that you are talking about, provided that the context makes it clear. In English we usually do need to specify this sort of thing, but Korean likes to be economical and to cut out any unnecessary information.

2 Waiters and shopkeepers

The word ajŏssi literally means *uncle*, but it is used as a general term to refer to a shopkeeper, waiter, or even a man in the street on occasions when formality is not called for. It can only be used for males. For females the term is ajumma which literally means *aunt*, but is used for any woman who is, say, over 35. The term agassi should be used to refer to and attract the attention of young women.

3 Korean particles

In the introduction we talked about the way Korean adds little words called particles to the ends of words. You can see this clearly in the dialogues. We have shown the particles by inserting a dash between the word and the particle, as in na-do (*me-too*), shinae-e (*town centre-to* = *to town*). Notice that the particle always comes after the noun that it relates to. English often does the opposite of this. We would say 'with me' or 'to school', but Korean says *me-with* and *school-to*.

4 Giving lists, and saying 'and'

The Korean word for *and* is the particle -hago. Imagine that you want to say one thing *and* another: *cigarettes and matches*. In Korean, the particle -hago attaches to the first noun of the pair, so that you would say: *cigarettes*-hago *matches*. The hago becomes a part of the word cigarettes, since as a particle it has to be attached to a noun. If you want to pause between the two words, you must pause after saying hago, not before, e.g. *cigarettes*-hago (pause) *matches*. You must not say *cigarettes* (pause) **hago** *matches*. Once again, this is because **-hago** belongs to the noun it is with; it is not a free word like the English 'and'.

If there are more than two items in a list, each word is followed by **hago**, with the exception of the last, e.g.:

cigarettes-hago *matches*-hago *ashtray*-hago *lighter*

However, you can also add **-hago** onto the last noun of the group if you want to. This gives the sequence a vaguer ring – as though there might be even more items in the list, but you are deciding to stop there (or can't think of any more for the time being).

The particle **-hago** can also mean 'with'. Thus you can say **Jaemin-hago shinae-e kayo** (*I'm going to town with Jaemin*). Once again, you can add more names to the list, e.g. **Jaemin-hago Sangmin-hago shinae-e kayo**. When you are using **-hago** to mean *with*, you can also use a slightly extended form of the particle, **-hago kach'i**, e.g.:

Jaemin-hago kach'i shinae-e kayo.

5 Asking for things

You have learned about Korean verb stems and the polite ending **-yo**. You will see that this dialogue contains the verb **chuseyo**. The stem here is **chu-**, and the usual polite style ending is **-yo**. The bit in the middle however, you will learn about later. It is a form used to make polite requests, and for now simply memorize the form **chuseyo** as a word meaning *please give me*. You have also seen the same ending in the phrase **mashikke tuseyo**. **Mashikke** means *tastily*, and **tŭseyo** comes from a verb stem which means *imbibe* or *take in*. Therefore the literal meaning is 'please eat tastily'.

6 Asking for 'one'

In the dialogue, an order is made for a beer and a **soju**. Notice how the number **hana** (*one*) comes after what is being ordered. To ask for one beer you say **maekju hana chuseyo**. To ask for one tea you can say **ch'a hana chuseyo**.

ⓘ Korean drinking habits

Koreans love to get together and drink and the most popular drink particularly among men is **soju**, Korean wine/vodka, which has about a 25% alcohol content. The normal form of **soju** does not have an especially strong taste, though recently it is being drunk more and more in fruit flavours like cherry (*cheri soju*) and lemon (*lemon soju*), and there is also even cucumber flavour (*oi soju*). Beer is becoming increasingly popular, with Korean beers being typically sweeter and lighter than their western counterparts. Another favourite is **makkŏlli**, which is also made from rice, and has a thick milky consistency. It is the kind of drink that you will probably either love or hate.

Soju is usually drunk in shots like vodka, and the phrase *one shot!*, spoken in a quasi-American accent, is very popular in Korean bars (the word for bar is **sulchip**, literally *booze house*!). If you go out to drink with Korean friends there will be toasts before each shot, and you will be expected to say one (English will be quite acceptable, at first!). Another popular habit is for each person to sing a song, so be ready with a few Elvis or Beatles numbers, no matter how bad your singing voice might be! Another alternative is the national anthem!

Practice

You will need the following words for the exercises.

chungguk	중국	*China*
ilbon	일본	*Japan*
sulchip	술집	*pub*
hakkyo	학교	*school*
pap	밥	*rice (cooked rice)*
kŭ-daŭm-e	그 다음에	*after that . . .*
kage	가게	*shop*
mashi-	마시-	*drink (verb stem)*
anj-	앉-	*sit (verb stem)*
mŏk-	먹-	*eat (verb stem)*

As you are doing these exercises, don't be tempted to try to use any words we haven't given you. You shouldn't need any!

1 Unjumble the following sentences: write them in the correct order first in romanization, then in Korean script for practice. Don't forget to work out the meaning!

a kayo ilbon-e chigŭm
b issŏyo maekchu ajŏssi
c sa-rŏ kage-e mwŏ kayo
d chuseyo ojingŏ yangju-hago
e kŭrigo chuseyo anju-do
f na-do kayo kage-e
g marŭn ta pap anju-hago issŏyo maekju-hago

2 Make up Korean sentences to say that there is or there are the following things.

What other meaning could these sentences have?

3 Imagine that the following Korean sentences were spoken to you. Make up an appropriate response in each case.

1 어디 가요?
2 여기 있어요.
3 안녕하세요!
4 잘 지냈어요?
5 뭐 마시러 술집에 가요?
6 소주, 맥주, 양주 다 있어요.

4 Give the polite style form of the following verbs. Try making a short sentence out of each one.

a ka-
b iss-
c sa-
d mŏk- (eat)

e ŏps-
f ha-
g anj- (sit)

5 Translate the following sentences into Korean.

a What are you going to buy at the shop?
b Hello Mr Kim! How are you?
c What are you doing after that?
d Are you going to the town centre now?
e Where are you going?
f We have beer, fruit and bread – all of them!
g Please also give me some rice.
h Here is your squid. Enjoy your meal!
i We don't have western spirits. Then give me a beer please.
j Some Korean pancake and a soju, please.

6 Get the attention of the following people and ask them to give you the following things.

7 Read the following notes made by a waiter for two orders. What is required at each table?

1 소주	오징어
1 맥주	과일
마른안주	양주 – 위스키
	1 맥주

8   Make up two dialogues, based on the following scenarios.

a   You meet a friend who is going to the shop. Greet him and ask where he is going. Suggest that you go together. He agrees and suggests that after that you go to the pub for a beer.

b   You are in a pub where you meet a friend. Ask how he's been and order a beer and a soju for the two of you. Ask the waiter what snacks he has, make up an appropriate response and order some fruit.

02
long time, no see!/ it's not me!

In this unit you will learn
- how to meet, greet and introduce people
- how to find where you want to be
- how to say that something is or isn't something else
- how to give your sentences subjects and topics

▶ Long time, no see!

Mr Kim meets an old friend Mr Pak and is introduced to Mr Pak's wife.

박선생	김선생님, 안녕하세요?
김선생	아! 박선생님! 안녕하세요!
박선생	오래간만이에요!
김선생	네. 그래요. 진짜 오래간만이에요.
박선생	잘 지냈어요?
김선생	네. 잘 지냈어요. 요즘 사업은 어때요?
박선생	그저 그래요.

(*pointing to his wife*) 우리 집사람이에요.

김선생	아! 그래요? 반갑습니다. 말씀 많이 들었어요.
박선생 부인	반갑습니다. 저는 장윤희에요.
김선생	저는 김진양이에요. 만나서 반갑습니다.

Mr Pak	Kim sŏnsaengnim, annyŏng haseyo?
Mr Kim	A! Pak sŏnsaengnim! Annyŏng haseyo!
Mr Pak	Oraeganman-ieyo!
Mr Kim	Ne. Kŭraeyo. Chinccha oraeganman-ieyo.
Mr Pak	Chal chinaessŏyo?
Mr Kim	Ne. Chal chinaessŏyo. Yojŭm saŏb-un ŏttaeyo?
Mr Pak	Kujŏ kuraeyo.

(*pointing to his wife*) Uri chipsaram-ieyo.

Mr Kim	A! Kuraeyo? Pangapsumnida. Malssŭm mani turŏssŏyo.
Mr Pak's wife	Pangapsumnida. Chŏ-nun Chang Yunhuy-eyo.
Mr Kim	Chŏ-nun Kim Jinyang-ieyo. Mannasŏ pangapsŭmnida.

1 How long is it since they met?
2 How is Mr Pak's business doing?
3 What does Mr Kim say about Mr Pak's wife?
4 What is Mr Pak's wife's name?

Phrases and expressions

oraeganman-ieyo	*long time, no see!*
yojŭm saŏb-un ŏttaeyo?	*how's business these days?*
kujŏ kŭraeyo	*so-so*
malssŭm mani tŭrŏssŏyo	*I've heard a lot about you*
(mannasŏ)pangapsŭmnida	*pleased to meet you!*

Kim sŏnsaengnim 김 선생님	Mr Kim (**sonsaengnim** 선생님 also means *teacher*)
a! 애	*ah!*
Pak 박	*Pak (Korean surname)*
kŭraeyo (?) 그래요?	*really (?), is it/it is so (?) (question and reply)*
chincccha 진짜	*really*
yojŭm 요즘	*nowadays*
saŏp 사업	*business*
-ŭn –은	*(topic particle: see note 4)*
ŏttaeyo? 어때요?	*how is it?*
uri 우리	*we/our*
chip 집	*house*
saram 사람	*person*
chipsaram 집사람	*wife*
(*noun*)-ieyo –이에요	*it is (equivalent to) (noun)*
malssŭm 말씀	*words, speech*
man(h)i 많이	*much, many, a lot*
chŏ 저	*me*
-nŭn –는	*(topic particle)*
Jang Yunhui 장 윤희	*woman's name (surname first)*
Kim Jinyang 김 진양	*man's name (surname first)*

Grammar

1 Korean surnames and titles

When you want to address Korean men politely, you can use the title sŏnsaengnim, which literally means *teacher*, but in practice means Mr, Sir. The title can be used on its own to speak to someone you don't know, with the surname (**Kim sŏnsaengnim, Pak sŏnsaengnim**), or with the full name (**Pak Jaemin sŏnsaengnim**). It is never used just with someone's first name, so you cannot say **Jinyang sŏnsaengnim** (nor, for that matter, can you say **Kim-ssi** or **Kim Jinyang-ssi**, both of which would be considered to be quite rude). Notice that, like the polite title -ssi used with first names, the title comes after the person's name, not before as in English.

The title sŏnsaengnim originally meant the one who was born first, and it therefore shows respect in addressing the person being spoken about as an elder. It is also the normal word for a teacher, and the context is the only way of telling whether it means that someone is a teacher, or whether they are simply being addressed as Mr.

Addressing women is a little more complex. Often women are addressed as being their husbands' wives. This means that Mrs Cho who is married to Mr Kim (Korean women keep their own surnames rather than taking their husbands) may be addressed as **Kim sŏnsaengnim-puin** (*Kim-Mr-wife*). You could even say the English Mrs Cho (**Misesu Cho**), and sometimes Miss is also used (**Misu Pak**).

2 The copula

When you want to say that something *is* something else (e.g. *Mr Kim is a Japanese teacher, this (thing) is a table, this office is the Korean department office*), you use a special verb form called the copula. Like other Korean verbs, it comes at the end of the sentence. However, it behaves a little differently to ordinary verbs. To say 'A is B' (as in, *this is a Chinese book*), you would say:

A   B-ieyo (or B-eyo)
this Chinese book-ieyo

The form -ieyo is used when 'B' ends in a consonant, and -eyo is used when 'B' ends in a vowel:

sŏnsaengnim-ieyo   *is a teacher*
maekju-eyo   *is beer*

Please note that 'is' in this sense means 'is equivalent to, is identical with'; it does not mean 'is located in' or 'is a certain way' (e.g. *is green, is angry*). English does not make this distinction. Look at the following sentences:

this is a book
the book is on the table
the book is green

All these use the English 'is', and yet only the first 'is' means 'is identical to'. The second 'is' expresses location, the third describes the book. It is only for the first, when you are saying that 'one thing is equivalent to' or 'the same as something else' that the copula (**ieyo**) is used in Korean. You must be very careful with this, as when you start to learn Korean it can be tempting to use the copula where you should not.

We have described the form *A-B*-ieyo, but the simple form *B*-ieyo is just as common. This occurs several times in this lesson, and in all cases there is an implied *A* which is unspoken.

Look at the following examples (we have put the implied *A* in brackets!):

oraeganman-ieyo   *(a matter of) long time no see – it is*
uri chipsaram-ieyo   *(this person) my wife – is*

This is the same thing which we saw in unit 1: the context tells you what the subject of the sentence is, therefore you don't have to say it explicitly as you do in English.

3 *Ŏttaeyo* and *kŭraeyo*

Korean has a group of words which mean 'is (a certain way)'. Ŏttaeyo means *is how?*, as in:

sŏnsaengnim ŏttaeyo?   *what is the teacher like?, how is teacher?*
saŏb-un ŏttaeyo?   *what's business like, how's business?*

Kŭraeyo means *is like that*. It can be used as a statement, e.g. kŭraeyo (*it is like that, that's right, it is (so)*). As a question, kŭraeyo? means *is it like that? is that so? really?*

4 Topics

Korean has a particle which can be attached to a noun or a phrase to emphasize that it is the topic of the sentence, that is to say, the thing which is being talked about. Sometimes we do this in English with an expression like *as for . . .*, for emphasis. We might say, for example, *As for my business, it's going pretty well at the moment*, or *As for me, I don't like cake*. Korean does this kind of thing very frequently with the topic particle -un/-nun. In the two sentences above, the nouns *my business* and *me* would both be followed by the topic particle in Korean to show that they are the topics of their sentences.

The particle has two forms, -nŭn when the noun you are making a topic ends in a vowel, and -ŭn when it ends in a consonant. Examples are soju-nun (*as for soju*), Jaemin ssi-nŭn (*as for Jaemin*), sŏnsaengnim-ŭn (*as for teacher*), saŏb-ŭn (*as for business*).

5 Wives and family

There are at least three words for wife, and they can be divided into two categories, honorific words and non-honorific words. Koreans are very concerned about politeness, and therefore when they are referring to someone else's wife they use an honorific term **puin**. This term is never used to refer to your own wife, however. In Korean culture you are meant to downplay yourself, your family and your possessions, therefore to speak about your own wife as **puin** would be inappropriate and possibly even arrogant. Instead, you use either the word **chipsaram** (literally *house person*), or **anae**. It would be very rude to speak about someone else's wife with these non-honorific words.

Furthermore, when referring to your relatives, and even your house, you are expected to say **uri** (*our*) rather than **nae** or **che**, both of which mean *my*. Thus, you would say **uri chipsaram** (*our wife*) when you want to talk about your wife, even though she is no one else's. Everybody is expected to do this when they talk about their family members.

▶ It's not me!

Mr O is looking for the Korean teacher, Mr Kim. However, first he meets Mr Lee.

오선생 실례합니다
이선생 네?
오선생 한국말 선생님이세요?
이선생 아니요. 저는 한국말 선생님이 아니에요.
저는 일본말 선생님이에요.
오선생 아, 죄송 합니다. 여기가 한국학과 사무실이
아니에요?
이선생 네. 한국학과가 아니에요. 여기는 일본학과에요.
오선생 그럼 한국학과 사무실이 어디에요?
이선생 저기 있어요.

Mr O goes over to the Korean department.

오선생 실례지만, 여기가 한국학과 사무실이에요?
김선생 네. 무슨 일이세요?
오선생 한국말 선생님 만나러 왔어요.

Mr O	Shillye hamnida.
Mr Lee	Ne?
Mr O	Hangungmal sŏnsaengnim-iseyo?
Mr Lee	Aniyo. Chŏ-nun hangungmal sŏnsaengnim-i anieyo. Chŏ-nun ilbonmal sŏnsaengnim-ieyo.
Mr O	A, choesong hamnida. Yŏgi-ga hanguk hakkwa samushir-i anieyo?
Mr Lee	Ne. Hanguk hakkwa-ga anieyo. Yŏgi-nun ilbon hakkwa-eyo.

honorific term **puin**. This term is never used to refer to your own wife, however. In Korean culture you are meant to downplay yourself, your family and your possessions, therefore to speak about your own wife as **puin** would be inappropriate and possibly even arrogant. Instead, you use either the word **chipsaram** (literally *house person*), or **anae**. It would be very rude to speak about someone else's wife with these non-honorific words.

Furthermore, when referring to your relatives, and even your house, you are expected to say **uri** (*our*) rather than **nae** or **che**, both of which mean *my*. Thus, you would say **uri chipsaram** (*our wife*) when you want to talk about your wife, even though she is no one else's. Everybody is expected to do this when they talk about their family members.

▶ It's not me!

Mr O is looking for the Korean teacher, Mr Kim. However, first he meets Mr Lee.

오선생 실례합니다
이선생 네?
오선생 한국말 선생님이세요?
이선생 아니요. 저는 한국말 선생님이 아니에요.
저는 일본말 선생님이에요.
오선생 아, 죄송 합니다. 여기가 한국학과 사무실이
아니에요?
이선생 네. 한국학과가 아니에요. 여기는 일본학과에요.
오선생 그럼 한국학과 사무실이 어디에요?
이선생 저기 있어요.

Mr O goes over to the Korean department.

오선생 실례지만, 여기가 한국학과 사무실이에요?
김선생 네. 무슨 일이세요?
오선생 한국말 선생님 만나러 왔어요.

Mr O	Shillye hamnida.
Mr Lee	Ne?
Mr O	Hangungmal sŏnsaengnim-iseyo?
Mr Lee	Aniyo. Chŏ-nun hangungmal sŏnsaengnim-i anieyo. Chŏ-nun ilbonmal sŏnsaengnim-ieyo.
Mr O	A, choesong hamnida. Yŏgi-ga hanguk hakkwa samushir-i anieyo?
Mr Lee	Ne. Hanguk hakkwa-ga anieyo. Yŏgi-nun ilbon hakkwa-eyo.

Mr O	Kǔrǒm, hanguk hakkwa samushir-i ǒdi-eyo?
Mr Lee	Chǒgi issǒyo.

Mr O goes over to the Korean department.

Mr O	Shillye-jiman, yǒgi-ga hanguk hakkwa samushir-ieyo?
Mr Kim	Ne. Musǔn ir-iseyo?
Mr O	Hangungmal sǒnsaengnim manna-rǒ wassǒyo.

1 What does Mr O ask Mr Lee?
2 Who is Mr Lee?
3 Where are Mr O and Mr Lee having their conversation?
4 Where does Mr O go next?
5 Why has he come?

Phrases and expressions

shillye hamnida	*excuse me, please*
. . . iseyo?	*are you . . . , please?* (i.e. the person I'm looking for)
choesong hamnida	*I'm sorry*
. . . ǒdi-eyo?	*where is . . . ?*
shillye-jiman . . .	*excuse me, but . . .*
musǔn ir-iseyo?	*what is it? how can I help you? what's the problem?*
. . . manna-rǒ wassǒyo	*I came to see . . .*

hanguk 한국	Korea(n) (pronounced **han-guk** 항국)
mal 말	language
hangungmal 한국말	Korean language
aniyo 아니요	no
-i –이	(subject particle: see notes)
anieyo 아니에요	is not (opposite of -(i)eyo, negative copula)
ilbon 일본	Japan
ilbonmal 일본말	Japanese language
-ga –가	(subject particle)
hakkwa 학과	department (of college/university)
samushil 사무실	office
ǒdi 어디	where?
chǒgi 저기	(over) there
musun 무슨	what, which
il 일	matter, business, work
manna- 만나–	meet (stem)
wassǒyo 왔어요	came (past tense form)

Grammar

1 More on verb endings

We have seen that Korean verbs take many different endings. This lesson contains the phrase **shillye hamnida** (*excuse me*), which is made from the verb stem **shillye ha-**. The polite style form of this, as you would expect from the last lesson, is **shillye haeyo**, since **ha-** is irregular. The **hamnida** form is what is known as the formal style, and usually when you are asking someone to excuse you, this is the form you will want to use. The formal and polite styles can be interchanged in many cases; but the formal is generally more suitable when speaking to someone older or higher in status than you. You will learn about how to make the formal style later.

This lesson also contains the form **shillye-jiman**. This is an abbreviation of **shillye ha-jiman**, the **-jiman** ending meaning *but*. The complete expression means *I'm sorry, but* . . . Don't worry about the **-jiman** ending for now; you will learn it thoroughly later. Simply remember **shillye-jiman** as a set expression.

2 Joining nouns together

As you know, Korean attaches all kinds of particles on the end of nouns to give particular meanings. We have indicated particles by putting a dash between the noun and its particle. However, Korean also allows many nouns to be strung together in a sequence. Examples are **hanguk + mal**, which gives **hangungmal** (*Korean language*) and **hanguk hakkwa** which means *Korean department*. We write some of these as one word (like **hangungmal**), and flag the individual words and the compound form in the vocabulary.

3 Finding the person you want

The copula is Korean's special verb form which allows you to ask if something is something else. You could use it, therefore, to ask a person if they are Mr Kim, say, or Mr Pak. However, when you do this, it is normal to use a special form of the copula **-iseyo?** This form is an honorific form – it shows politeness to the other person. For the moment simply learn it as a phrase: . . . **iseyo?** for example:

Pak sŏnsaengnim-iseyo?   *Are you Mr Pak?*
Hangungmal sŏnsaengnim-iseyo? *Are you the Korean teacher?*

4 Sentence subjects

In the previous dialogue you met the topic particle, and this dialogue introduces you to the subject particle, which is similar. The subject particle -i attaches to the end of nouns which end in a consonant, and the subject particle -ga attaches to nouns which end in a vowel. This gives: maekju-ga, hakkyo-ga (*school*); sŏnsaegnim-i, kwair-i (from kwail, *fruit*).

Naturally enough, the particle marks out the subject of the sentence. For example, in the sentence *The man kicked the dog*, 'the man' is the subject. In the sentence *The man is fat*, 'the man' is again the subject.

However, unfortunately, things are not quite so simple! In both of these sentences, the man could also be the topic, if the topic particle -nun were used instead of the subject particle. What is the difference between the subject and topic particles?

When something is mentioned for the first time, usually the subject particle is used. Later on, when the subject is repeated in the conversation, you can switch to use the topic particle instead.

The topic particle, you will recall, is particularly for an emphasis like the English 'as for'. It is particularly common when comparing two things, e.g. *as for me* (me-nun), *I hate shopping. As for Mum* (Mum-nun), *she just loves it.*

Do not worry too much about whether, in a given sentence, it is more correct to use the subject or the topic particle. Most sentences will be correct with either, although some will sound more natural to a Korean (and eventually to you) with one rather than the other. Gradually you will get the feel of which particle to use as your sense of the language develops. It is important that you do use one or the other in your sentences whenever you can, however. Do not just leave off particles, as it can tend to confuse Koreans when foreigners do so, even though they often leave them out themselves in casual speech.

5 Negative copula

You have learnt how to say 'A is B' (this thing-A is a book-B). Now you must learn the negative copula, 'A is not B', as in 'this thing is not a book', 'Mr Kim is not my teacher', 'this book is not a Chinese book'. The form is:

(A-subj/top) (B-subj) **anieyo**	(subj = *subject particle*; top = *topic particle*; *you can use either*)
chŏ-nun sŏnsaengnim-i anieyo	*I am not a teacher*
(B-subj) **anieyo**	
hanguk hakkwa-ga anieyo	*(this) is not the Korean department*

Look at the examples in the dialogue very carefully to be sure that you have understood this pattern.

6 When 'yes' means 'no'

Answering questions that require 'yes' and 'no' answers can be a bit tricky in Korean.

If the question is positive (*Do you like mushrooms?*, *Are you going out tonight?*), then you answer as you would in English (*Yes, I like them* or *No, I don't*).

However, if the question is negative (*Don't you like mushrooms?*, *Aren't you going out tonight?*), then the answer you give will be the opposite to what you would say in English, e.g.:

Don't you like mushrooms?

English	*Yes, I do like them*	*No, I don't*
Korean	*No, I do like them*	*Yes, I don't*

Aren't you going out tonight?

English	*Yes, I am going out*	*No, I'm not*
Korean	*No, I am going out*	*Yes, I'm not*

It goes without saying that you need to think very carefully when answering negative questions in Korean!

7 Where is it?

To ask where something is in Korean, you say: (B-subj) **ŏdieyo?**

However, confusingly, you can also say (B-subj) **ŏdi issŏyo?**

When you answer a *where is . . . ?* question, you must always use the verb issŏyo: e.g.

hakkyo-ga kŏgi issŏyo	*the school over there is/exists, the school is over there*

ℹ️ Being introduced

Koreans are very concerned about politeness, and this characteristic is especially noticeable when you meet people for the first time. It is wise to bow slightly when you shake hands with people, and be sure not to shake hands too hard. The Korean style is for the more senior person to do the shaking, while the other person allows their hand to be shaken. Phrases such as **mannasŏ pangapsŭmnida**, which literally means *I've met you, so I'm pleased* are very common. The form **ch'ŏum poepkessumnida** is even more polite, and literally means *I am seeing you for the first time.*

Practice

For the exercises you will need the following additional vocabulary:

kŏngang	건강	health
hoesa	회사	company (i.e., the company, business)
kajok	가족	family
Miguk	미국	America(n)
adul	아들	son
hakkyo	학교	school
taehakkyo	대학교	university
shinmun	신문	newspaper
chapji	잡지	magazine
chigŭm	지금	now

1 The following Korean sentences have gaps where particles and word endings should be. Insert the appropriate word endings into the gaps from the selection given. If there is a choice A/B, then make sure you use the correct form. Then work out the meanings of the sentences.

a Sangmin ____ ! Na ____ shinae ____ kayo. (e, do, ssi)
b Mwŏ ha ____ hakkyo ____ ka ____ ? (yo, e, -rŏ)

c Kim sŏnsaengnim ____ ŏttaeyo?   (un/nun)
d Yŏgi ____ samushir-ieyo?   (i/ga)
e Anieyo. Yŏgi ____ samushir ____ anieyo.   (i/ga, un/nun)

2 Say hello to the following people, and ask about how things
   are with them. For example, for the first one you would
   write the Korean equivalent of *Hello Mr O, how's the
   company?* (as for the company, how is it?).

   a Mr O   the company
   b Mrs Cho   business
   c Mr Pak's wife   the family
   d Taegyu   school
   e Miss Pak   her health

3 Fill in the missing bits of the following dialogue with
   appropriate Korean sentences. Remember to check what
   comes after as well as what comes before, so that the whole
   conversation makes sense.

   a Paek sŏnsaengnim, oraeganman-ieyo!
   b _____
   a Ne, ne. Yojŭm saŏb-un ŏttaeyo?
   b _____
   a Chigŭm ŏdi gayo?
   b _____
   a Samushir-i ŏdieyo?
   b _____ (*over there*)
   a Musŭn ir-i issŏyo?
   b _____

4 Look at the following drawings. Imagine that you are
   teaching a child the names of the objects and, pointing at
   each one in turn, you say *this thing* (i-gŏsh-i) *is....*

Now make up five more sentences, saying that this thing is *not* what you see in the picture.

5 Translate the following dialogue into English.

a 실례합니다. 박선생님이세요?
b 아니에요. 저는 박선생님이 아니에요. 박선생님은 중국
선생님이세요.
여기는 중국학과 사무실이에요.
a 아! 죄송합니다. 실례지만 한국학과는 어디에요?
b 저기 있어요. 나도 지금 선생님 만나러 한국학과에 가요.
a 그럼, 같이 가요.

6 Make up five questions for the following five people. For the first two, ask if they are so-and-so. For the last three, ask negative questions (*you aren't so-and-so are you?*). For all five of your questions make up positive and negative answers. Make sure that you get the words for 'yes' and 'no' the right way round with the last three!

a an American person
b Mr Lee
c a Chinese teacher
d Mr Paek's son
e a school teacher

▶ 7 Translate the following sentences into Korean. Remember that you should not be translating literally, but getting across the meaning with the words, phrases and constructions you have been learning.

a I'm Pak Sangmin. *Oh, really? Pleased to meet you.*
b How is school nowadays?
c Excuse me, are you the Japanese teacher?
d Waiter! Do you have any squid? *How is the squid?* It's not bad.
e Isn't this the Korean department office? *No, it isn't.*
f I'm not Mrs Woo. *Oh, really? I'm sorry.*
g This is our Chinese teacher? *Really? I've heard a lot about you.*
h Is this the Japanese shop?
i I'm going to see the Korean teacher too.
j I came to meet Mr Pak's wife.
k Where is the Korean department?
l Where is the school office?

8 Make up a short dialogue in which two old friends meet up and ask each other how they are getting on. One of them has his son with him and introduces the son to the other person.

9 Kim Dukhoon is looking for the Chinese teacher in the Chinese department, but finds himself talking to the wrong person in the wrong place.

Dukhoon approaches the teacher and says:

Shillye jiman yŏgi-ga chungguk hakkwa samushir-ieyo? Chunggung mal sŏnsaengnim manna-rŏ wassŏyo.

How might the teacher respond?

03

sorry, wrong number!/are you ready to order yet?

In this unit you will learn
- how to make phone calls
- how to make arrangements to meet people
- about dining out in Korea
- how to ask for what you want
- how to discuss what you like and dislike
- numbers and counting
- how to say 'but'
- honorifics
- how to make suggestions and say that you can't do something

▶ Sorry, wrong number!

Tony is trying to contact his old Korean friend, Mr Kim, but at first he dials the wrong number.

토니	여보세요? 죄송하지만 김선생님 좀 바꿔주세요.
박	여기 그런 사람 없어요.
토니	거기 삼팔구의(에) 이오공육 아니에요?
박	아니에요. 전화 잘못 거셨어요.
토니	죄송합니다.

At last Tony gets through, has a brief chat to Mr Kim, and arranges to meet him for lunch.

토니	여보세요? 죄송하지만, 김선생님 좀 바꿔주세요.
김선생 부인	잠깐 기다리세요.
김선생	네. 말씀 하세요.
토니	아, 안녕하세요? 저는 영국대사관의 토니에요.
김선생	아, 안녕하세요. 오래간만이에요.
토니	오늘 점심에 시간 있어요?
김선생	네, 있어요.
토니	그럼, 제가 점심을 사고 싶어요.
김선생	네, 좋아요. 열두시에 롯데 호텔 앞에서 만납시다.
토니	좋아요. 그럼, 이따가 봅시다.

Tony	Yŏboseyo? Choesong ha-jiman, Kim sŏnsaengnim chom pakkwo-juseyo.
Mrs Pak	Yŏgi kurŏn saram ŏpsŏyo.
Tony	Kŏgi sam-p'al-ku uy(e) i-o-kong-nyuk anieyo?
Mrs Pak	Anieyo. Chŏnhwa chalmot kŏshyŏssŏyo.
Tony	Choesong hamnida.

At last Tony gets through, has a brief chat to Mr Kim, and arranges to meet him for lunch.

Tony	Yŏboseyo? Choesong ha-jiman, Kim sŏnsaengnim chom pakkwo-juseyo.
Mr Kim's wife	Chamkkan kidariseyo.
Mr Kim	Ne. Malssŭm haseyo.
Tony	A, annyŏng haseyo? Chŏ-nun yongguk taesagwan-ŭy Tony-eyo.
Mr Kim	A, annyŏng haseyo. Oraeganman-ieyo.
Tony	Onŭl chŏmshim-e shigan-i issŏyo?

Mr Kim	Ne, issŏyo.
Tony	Kurŏm, che-ga chŏmshim-ul sa-go ship'ŏyo.
Mr Kim	Ne, choayo. Yŏldu shi-e Lotte Hot'el ap'-esŏ mannapshida.
Tony	Choayo. Kurŏm, ittaga popshida.

1 Who does Tony ask for?
2 What number did he mean to dial?
3 Who does Tony identify himself as?
4 What does Tony ask Mr Kim?
5 Why does he want to know this?
6 Where do they decide to meet?

Phrases and expressions

choesong ha-jiman	*I'm sorry, but; excuse me, but . . .*
choesong hamnida	*I'm sorry; I apologize; excuse me*
. . . chom pakkwo-juseyo	*can I have/speak to . . ., please?*
(chŏnhwa) chalmot kŏshyŏssŏyo	*you've got the wrong number (you've misdialled)*
(chŏnhwa) chalmot kŏrŏssŏyo	*I've got the wrong number*
chamkkan kidariseyo	*please wait a moment*
malssŭm haseyo	*please speak (I'm listening!)*
shigan-i issŏyo? (issŭseyo?)	*do you have (free) time? (polite form)*
. . . -ul sago ship'ŏyo	*I want to buy . . .*
. . . ap'esŏ mannapshida	*let's meet in front of . . .*
ittaga popshida	*we'll see each other later/ see you later/let's meet later*

---

yŏboseyo 여보세요	*hello* (on the telephone)
chom 좀	*a little; please* (see note 2)
kŭrŏn 그런	*such a, that* (particular)
sam 삼	*three*
p'al 팔	*eight*
ku 구	*nine*
I 이	*two*
o 오	*five*
kong/yŏng 공/영	*zero*
yuk 육	*six*
chŏnhwa 전화	*telephone*
chalmot 잘못	*wrongly, mis-*
chal 잘	*well* (adverb)

chamkkan 잠깐	*a little* (while)
kidari- 기다리–	*wait*
yǒngguk 영국	*England, British*
taesagwan 대사관	*embassy*
-ǔy –의	*belonging to*
chǒmshim 점심	*lunch*
-e –에	*at* (a certain time)
shigan 시간	*time, hour*
che-ga 제가	*I* (humble form) (subject)
choh- 좋–	*good* (stem)
choayo 좋아요	*good, fine, OK* (polite style, notice the **h** is not pronounced)
yǒl 열	*ten* (pure Korean number)
tu 두	*two* (pure Korean number)
yǒldu 열두	*twelve* (pure Korean number)
shi –시	*o'clock*
hot'el 호텔	*hotel*
ap'esǒ 앞에서	*in front of*
manna- 만나–	*meet* (stem)
ittaga 이따가	*in a little while*
po- 보–	*see, look* (sometimes: *meet*)
pwayo 봐요	*see, look* (polite style, irregular)

Grammar

1 Sentences with 'but'

In Unit 2 you learned **shillye hamnida**, and a similar form **shillye-jiman**, which meant *I'm sorry, but* . . . or *Excuse me, but* . . . This unit takes another verb, **choesong hamnida**, and puts it in the -jiman form: **choesong ha-jiman**, to mean *I'm sorry, but* . . . As you will have guessed, **-jiman** is a verb ending which means *but*, and it can be attached to any verb base.

Here are a few other verb stems you have learnt, each put into the -jiman form:

ka-	*go*	ka-jiman	*goes, but* . . .
ha-	*do*	ha-jiman	*does, but* . . .
sa-	*buy*	sa-jiman	*buys, but* . . .
iss-	*is/are, have*	it-jiman	*has, but* . . .
mashi-	*drink*	mashi-jiman	*drinks, but* . . .
mǒk-	*eat*	mǒk-jiman	*eats, but* . . .
anj-	*sit*	anj-jiman	*sits, but* . . .

(Notice the form with iss-, where the double ss becomes pronounced as a t when -jiman is added. In Korean *han'gul* you still write the double ss, but the word is pronounced itjiman.)

Can you work out the meanings of the following sentence?

Kim sŏnsaengnim maekju chal mashi-jiman, chŏ-nun yangju chal mashyŏyo.

2 Making requests more polite

The word chom is flagged in the vocabulary as meaning *please*. It is not, however, of itself the direct equivalent of our English word 'please', because some of its uses are quite different. However, if you insert the word chom in a request immediately before the verb at the end of the sentence, it does have a similar effect to 'please'. It is most frequently used when asking to be given something, that is, before the verb chu- (*give*). In this unit you meet it in the sentence: Kim sŏnsaengnim chom pakkwo-juseyo (*Can I speak to Mr Kim, please*). You might use it in a sentence such as Maekju chom chuseyo (*Please give me some beer*). It softens the request, and consequently makes it more polite.

▶ 3 Numbers and counting

Korean has two completely different sets of numbers which makes things very awkward for the language learner. There is a Korean set, often called pure Korean numerals, and another set which are of Chinese origin, usually called Sino-Korean numerals. Numbers are used for counting things, and which set you use in any situation all depends on what it is that you want to count! To count hours, for example, you use the pure Korean numbers, but to count minutes, the Sino-Korean numbers must be used. You just have to learn which set of numbers are used with which objects. Taking an example from the next dialogue, someone orders two portions of something and two dishes of something else. You simply have to know that the word *portion* takes the Sino-Korean numbers (so the word for *two* is i), and that *dishes* takes the pure Korean numbers (so the word for *two* is dwu)! There is no shortcut, and we will tell you more about this as the course progresses. In this unit you will meet the Sino-Korean numbers only. They are as follows:

kong/yǒng	0				
il	1	shibil	11	ishibil	21
i	2	shibi	12	ishibi	22
sam	3	shipsam	13	ishipsam	23
sa	4	shipsa	14	(etc.)	
o	5	shibo	15		
yuk	6	shimnyuk	16		
ch'il	7	shipch'il	17		
p'al	8	shipp'al	18		
ku	9	shipku	19	ishipku	29
ship	10	iship	20	samship	30

Once you have learnt 1 to 10, everything is straightforward. Twenty is just 'two-ten', 30 'three-ten', etc.:

i-ship	20
sam-ship	30
sa-ship	40 (etc.)
ku-ship	90
paek	100
ch'ǒn	1000
man	10000

Here are a few more complicated examples for you to pick up the pattern:

ku-ship-p'al	98
o-shim-nyuk	56
paek-shib-il	111
sam-paek-p'al-ship-sa	384
i-ch'ǒn-ku-baek-chi'l-ship	2,970
sam-man-o-ch'ǒn-nyuk-baek-i-shib-o	35,625

As you will have observed, there are a number of oddities in the pronunciation of numbers when they are put together, especially concerning the number 6. However, we will always indicate these in the romanization. Just remember that the number 6 can be pronounced in any of the following ways, depending on the surrounding syllables: **yuk, yung, nyuk, nyung, ryuk, ryung, lyuk, lyung!**

Phone numbers are given in Korean by listing the digits in their Sino-Korean form. Seoul numbers have seven digits, and speakers usually give the first three, then the sound -e, then the second four. In English, one might quote the STD, then say -e, then the telephone number:

352–0873   sam-o-i-e kong-p'al-ch'il-sam
966–3491   ku-ryung-nyug-e sam-sa-ku-il
01535 568326   kong-il-o-sam-o-e o-ryuk-p'al-sam-i-ryuk

4 Introducing honorifics

In this unit you meet several verbs that end with -seyo. The ones you have seen are: haseyo (from ha-), kidariseyo (from kidari-), and issuseyo (from iss-). These verbs are in what we call the polite honorific form which is shown by the ending -seyo. All you have to do is add -seyo to a verb stem which ends in a vowel, and -useyo to a verb stem which ends in a consonant, like this:

mashi-   mashiseyo   iss-   issuseyo
ha-   haseyo   anj-   anjuseyo
kidari-   kidariseyo

The most common use for this ending is as a polite request asking someone to do something, e.g. *please (do it)*, so that kidariseyo means *please wait*. Notice that we've called the ending the polite honorific. You've met the polite ending -yo before, and this ending also has it, hence the name polite honorific. But it also has an -s- in it, which is the honorific bit. This serves to honour the person you are talking to, that is, the person you are requesting to do whatever it is. It is a form of respect, and it is this honorific part that makes the ending -(u)seyo into a polite request.

Although for the next few units this is the most common use you will meet for the polite honorific, there is another way in which it can be used, either to ask a question of somebody you particularly esteem, respect or wish to honour, or simply to make a statement about them. Thus the sentence Kimsŏnsaengnim-i hakkyo-e kaseyo means *Mr Kim is going to school*, and shows special respect or honour to Mr Kim. You will meet this usage in the next dialogue.

For now you should make sure that you are completely happy with the polite request meaning, but also be aware of the other use in the back of your mind, since these honorifics are something that we shall return to later on.

5 Saying what you want to do

The form -ko ship'ŏyo (the form ship'ŏyo coming from the stem ship'-) can be added onto any verb stem which describes an action, to produce the meaning *want to* (verb). Thus na-nun mŏk-ko ship'ŏyo means *I want to eat*. The -ko attaches straight to the verb stem, whether it ends in a consonant or a vowel, and there are no irregularities other than that the k of the -ko becomes pronounced as a g after vowels, as you would expect. Note that you can't put any other words between the -ko and the ship'ŏyo parts. Treat them as if they are inseparable, even though there is a space between them. Here are a couple of examples:

mŏk-	*eat*	chŏ-nun chŏmshim mŏk-ko ship'ŏyo
		I want to eat lunch
manna-	*meet*	Jinyang manna-go ship'ŏyo
		I want to meet Jinyang

6 Making suggestions

A final verb ending pattern to learn from this dialogue is -(u)pshida. -pshida is added onto a verb stem ending in a vowel, and -upshida is added if the verb stem ends in a consonant. This pattern of using the vowel u to add to nouns or verb stems that end in consonants is one that you are becoming familiar with. The example you have seen is the ending (ŭ)seyo, but the topic particle (n)ŭn is similar. You will meet many, many examples as you work through this book.

The meaning of (ŭ)pshida is *let's do (such-and-such)*, and it is a relatively polite or formal form, as opposed to something you would say in a very informal or colloquial conversation. Note once again that you can only add this form onto a verb which describes an action, just as you saw with -ko ship'ŏyo. Thus you can say 'let's go for a walk', since that describes an action, but you can't say 'let's be pretty' using -(ŭ)pshida, since being pretty is a state and not an action. Here are a couple of examples of the form:

Yŏldu shi-e kach'i shinae-e kapshida	*Let's go to town together at 12*
Ŭmryosu mashipshida	*Let's have a drink*

i The first dialogue was all about arranging to meet up for lunch, and this is a common enough Korean habit, just as it is in the West. You will actually find that Koreans tend to eat out a little more often than westerners, and also that eating out can be done more cheaply in Korea. In the West we tend to eat out for special occasions or for a treat and, of course, Koreans do this too and are prepared to spend quite a bit of money to do so. But on more normal, everyday occasions they will also often take an ordinary meal out and this can be done quite cheaply.

When eating out with Koreans, it is very rare to 'go dutch' and split the bill as we might among friends in our culture. In Korea it is normally one person who pays the bill, either the person who has done the inviting, or the most senior figure (in age or status). It is generally regarded as the senior person's job to pay for everyone else, and you must not offend Koreans by insisting on breaking their cultural tradition. After all, everyone ends up being the senior party at some time or other, so everything works out fairly in the end!

▶ Are you ready to order yet?

Tony and Mr Kim meet up and go to a restaurant for lunch. They order drinks, and then have a discussion about their culinary likes and dislikes.

종업원	어서 오세요. 이 쪽으로 앉으세요.
김선생	고맙습니다.
종업원	음료수 하시겠어요?
김선생	우선 맥주 좀 주세요.
김선생	한국 음식 좋아 하세요?
토니	네, 아주 좋아 하지만, 매운 거 잘 못 먹어요.
김선생	그럼 불고기나 갈비를 먹읍시다.
토니	네, 좋아요. 그리고 저는 냉면도 먹고 싶어요.

The waitress arrives to take their food order.

종업원	주문 하시겠어요?
토니	불고기 이인분하고 냉면 두 그릇 주세요.
종업원	물냉면 드릴까요? 비빔냉면 드릴까요?
토니	물냉면 주세요.

A little while later the waitress arrives with the food.

종업원	맛있게 드세요!

During the meal, to the waitress:

토니	아가씨, 물하고 김치 좀 더 주세요.

Chongŏpwon	Ŏsŏ oseyo. I cchog-uro anjuseyo.
Mr Kim	Komapsumnida.
Chongŏpwon	Ŭmryosu hashigessŏyo?
Mr Kim	Usŏn maekju chom chuseyo.
Mr Kim	Hanguk ŭmshik choa haseyo?
Tony	Ne, aju choa ha-jiman, maeun kŏ chal mon mŏgŏyo.
Mr Kim	Kŭrŏm pulgogi-na kalbi-rul mŏgŭpshida.
Tony	Ne, choayo. Kŭrigo chŏ-nun naengmyŏn-do mŏk-ko ship'ŏyo.

The waitress arrives to take their food order.

Chongŏpwon	Chumun hashigessŏyo?
Tony	Pulgogi i-inbun-hago naengmyŏn tu kŭrŭt chuseyo.
Chongŏpwon	Mul naengmyŏn tŭrilkkayo? Pibim naengmyŏn tŭrilkkayo?
Tony	Mul naengmyŏn chuseyo.

A little while later the waitress arrives with the food.

| Chongŏpwon | Mashikke tŭseyo! |

During the meal, to the waitress:

| Tony | Agassi, mul-hago kimch'i chom tŏ chuseyo. |

1 Do they order wine?
2 What does Tony think about Korean food?
3 Tony is content with Kim's suggestion. True or false?
4 What does Tony ask the waitress for?

Phrases and expressions

ŏsŏ oseyo	*welcome!*
i cchog-uro anjŭseyo	*please sit over here (over this side)*
komapsŭmnida	*thank you*
ŭmryosu hashigessŏyo?	*would you like something to drink?*
chumun hashigessŏyo?	*would you like to order?*
. . . tŭrilkkayo?	*would you like . . . (lit.: shall I give you . . .)*

chongŏpwŏn 종업원	*waiter, assistant* (remember **ajossi** is the term to call him over)
cchok 쪽	*side*
-(u)ro –(으)로	*towards, in the direction of*
anj- 앉–	*sit* (stem)
ŭmryosu 음료수	*drink*
usŏn 우선	*first*
ŭmshik 음식	*food*
choa ha- 좋아하–	*like* (stem)
aju 아주	*very*
maeun 매운	*spicy* (adj)
kŏ 거	*thing, object, fact* (abbreviation of **kŏt**, spelt **kŏs**)
mot 못	*cannot* (nb **mot** + **m-** = **mon m-**)
pulgogi 불고기	*pulgogi, Korean spiced marinated beef*
-na –나	*or* (particle)
kalbi 갈비	*marinated and fried spare ribs* (usually pork, cheaper than *pulgogi*)
naengmyŏn 냉면	*thin noodles with vegetables*
chumun ha- 주문하–	*order* (stem)
i 이	*two*
-inbun –인분	*portion*
tu 두	*two* (pure Korean number)
kŭrŭt 그릇	*dish/bowl*
mul- 물–	*water*
mul naengmyŏn 물 냉면	*thin noodles in cold soup* (spicy and refreshing!)
pibim 비빔	*mixed*
tŭrilkkayo 드릴까요	*would you like?* (lit.: *shall I give you?*)
agassi 아가씨	*waitress!* (lit.: *girl, unmarried woman*)
kimch'i 김치	*classic Korean side dish, marinated cabbage, spiced strongly with chillies*
tŏ 더	*more*

Grammar

1 *Choayo* and *choa haeyo*

There is an important difference between these two verbs. **Choayo** is a kind of verbal adjective which means 'is good'. It may by implication mean that you like it, but the root meaning is that something is good. It is important to see the distinction, and here is an example to illustrate the difference. **Kimch'i choayo** means that the kimch'i is good. You might conceivably recognize it as being good kimch'i (as far as kimch'i goes . . .) without actually wanting to say that you like it. Even if you hate kimch'i, you might still be able to discern between good and bad examples.

Contrariwise, **choa haeyo** means 'like'. **Kimch'i choa haeyo** means that you, or whoever else is being spoken about, actually likes the stuff. It might be the case that you like kimch'i, even if it's not quite at its best. You can say you like something without commenting on its relative quality.

Can you explain the difference, therefore, between **Kimsŏnsaengnim choayo** and **Kimsŏnsaengnim choa haeyo**?

The first means that Mr Kim is a good man, a good guy. The second means that you (or whoever) actually likes him.

2 Or

-na can be added after a noun to mean 'or', just like **-hago** can be added after nouns to mean 'and'. (noun)-**na** (noun), therefore, means (noun) *or* (noun). **Kalbi-na pulgogi mŏgŭpshida** means 'let's eat kalbi or pulgogi'.

You can make this *either . . . or* idea sound even more vague by adding **-na** to both nouns. Then the translation would be something like 'let's eat kalbi or pulgogi or something'. In a similar way you can have just one noun plus **-na** to make the sentence more vague so that it means '(noun) or something'. Take the sentence **kalbi-na mŏgupshida**. This would mean that you are not all that bothered about what exactly you eat, you are just suggesting kalbi. Something else might be just as acceptable.

3 When you can't do it

The little word **mot** can be added to a sentence to give the meaning that something cannot be done: **shinae-e mot kayo** (*I can't go to the city centre*). Note that your inability to do something is being described – you can't do it, rather than that you aren't able to or you won't. If you simply choose not to go to the city, or if you aren't going, don't want to go or refuse to go, you can't use this construction. It expresses impossibility. Whether you want to go or not, you can't.

The word **mot** goes as close to the verb as possible, right near the end of the clause immediately before the verb.

Watch out for the sound change that occurs at the end of **mot** when the verb following begins with an m. **Mot** plus **manna-** gives **mon mannayo** (*I can't meet*).

4 Measuring and counting

We will have a detailed section on measuring and counting later on, but for now notice the two patterns in this lesson which will give you the key:

pulgogi	i	inbun
naengmyŏn	tu	kŭrŭt
(*noun*)	(*number*)	(*measure*)

This is important. First you state the substance you are measuring, then the number you want, then the unit that you are measuring it by (here portions and dishes).

i Lotte Hotel is one of the famous buildings in Seoul, and is situated right next to the Lotte Department Store (Korea's biggest) between Myŏngdong and Shich'ŏng (City Hall). Lotte is one of Korea's **chaebŏl** or large conglomerates.

A Korean department store is a little different from its western equivalent. It contains literally hundreds of sales assistants (mainly female), with at least one on every single counter throughout the store. At first it can seem as though you're under pressure to buy, but this isn't really the case any more so than in the West, and you soon get used to it!

This lesson also introduced two famous Korean foods. **Kimch'i** is the marinated pickled cabbage – very spicy with lots of chilli powder – eaten as a side dish with virtually every Korean meal. There are certain other varieties, like **mul kimch'i** or water kimch'i which is less spicy and consists of kimch'i in liquid, and **mu kimch'i** which is made of white radish (**mu**) instead of cabbage. You also met **naengmyŏn** which is a kind of clear, thin noodle, rather like vermicelli, usually eaten in a cold soup as **mul naengmyŏn**. It is spicy (and is one of the few Korean dishes to contain mustard or something similar to it), but is extremely refreshing in the hot summer as it is served with lots of ice. **Pibim naengmyŏn** is another form, without water this time, and mixed with other vegetables.

Practice

Additional vocabulary for these exercises is as follows.

shiktang 식당	*restaurant*
paekhwajŏm 백화점	*department store*
wain 와인	*wine*
mal ha- 말하-	*speak, say*

1 Make up a sentence for each of the following sets of information, saying that you want to do A and B. For example, for the first, your Korean sentence will say 'I want to meet Mr Pak and Mrs Kim'.

a	Mr Pak	Mrs Kim	meet
b	bread	fruit	buy
c	pulgogi	kalbi	eat
d	English teacher	Japanese teacher	wait for
e	beer	whisky	drink
f	octopus	naengmyŏn	order

Now repeat the exercise, saying that you want to do either A or B.

2 The following is an excerpt from a page in someone's telephone book. Write out the names of each person and their number, in Korean script and in romanization (*doctor*: **uysa**).

MR KIM 582-5920

Jae Min 291-6482

DOCTOR 666-0231

PETER 01623 2960

MR PAK 01516879102

3 The following sentences are jumbled up. Can you unscramble them?

a	haseyo?	ŭmshik	choa	hanguk
b	Hilton Hot'el	ieyo	chŏ-nun	-uy	Sangmin
c	ap'esŏ	hakkyo	mannapshida	yŏlshi-e
d	onŭl	shigan-i	chŏmshim	issuseyo? -e
e	mul	chuseyo	usŏn	chom
f	mŏgŏyo	maeun	chal	kŏ	mot
g	naengmyŏn	kalbi	tu-kŭrŭt	saminbun -hago	chuseyo

4 Change the following sentences to say that they can't be done. For example, for the first you will write a Korean sentence saying that you can't go to the Japanese embassy.

a I'm going to the Japanese embassy.
b Chigŭm chŏmshim mŏg-ŭro shiktang-e kayo.
c Jaemin-ssi, Sangmin-ssi kidariseyo?
d Sangmin eats spicy food.
e I am meeting Mrs Jang in front of the Chinese embassy.
f Paekhwajŏm-e kayo.

5 Put the following verbs into the polite honorific form (ending in -seyo), and also into the 'let's do' form. Then make up four sentences, two with each of the two verb forms (you can use any verbs you want to make the sentences).

a	가-	d	앉-	f	사-
b	주문하-	e	기다리-	g	만나-
c	보-				

6 What is the difference between the following two pairs of sentences?

  a I-kalbi-ga aju choayo.   I-kalbi-rul aju choa haeyo.

  b Pak sŏnsaengnim-ŭy   Pak sŏnsaengnim-ŭy adul
      adul choayo.   choa haeyo.

7 The following sentences should be translated into Korean. They are intended to practise suggestions and also how to say 'but'.

  a Let's speak in Chinese.

  b Let's go to the department store.

  c Let's drink some beer or wine.

  d I want to go to America, but I can't.

  e I like whisky but I can't drink it. (implication: it isn't good for me or it makes me too drunk!)

  f I want to telephone Mr Kim, but I misdialled.

8 What are the following numbers in English?

  a kuship-ch'il.   **d** p'albaeng-nyukship-il.

  b oship-sam.   **e** samman-sach'ŏn-sabaek-kushib-o.

  c ibaek-ch'il.

9 Translate the following sentences into English.

  a 매운 거 좋아하지만 한국음식 잘 못 먹어요.

  b 실례지만 영국 대사관이 어디 있어요?

  c 이쪽으로 앉으세요. 음료수 하시겠어요?

  d 시간이 있으세요? 그럼 이따가 만납시다.

  e 김선생님? 잠깐 기다리세요.
     죄송하지만 여기 그런 사람 없어요. 잘못 거셨어요.

  f 거기 (팔육삼의 공오사이에요?

10 You are arranging to meet your friend. She asks you where you should meet. Answer her, suggesting a place and a time.

04

how much is it altogether?/ finding the way

In this unit you will learn
- simple shopping
- finding your way around
- more about negation
- how to say 'if'
- use of the direct object particle
- how to say where something is and where some activity takes place
- more numbers and money in Korean
- basic use of classifiers when counting things

▶ How much is it all together?

Chris goes to a Korean bookstore to buy some dictionaries and unfortunately has a little trouble over the price.

점원	뭘 찾으세요?
크리스	사전 있어요?
점원	네. 한영 사전 드릴까요?
크리스	네, 한영 사전하고 영한사전 둘 다 주세요.
점원	여기 있어요.
크리스	얼마에요?
점원	한 권에 만원씩, 모두 이만 원이에요.
크리스	한자 사전도 있어요?
점원	한자 사전은 세 가지 종류가 있어요.
크리스	제일 싼 거 주세요.
점원	잠깐 기다리세요...여기 있어요.
크리스	고맙습니다. 모두 얼마에요?
점원	한자 사전 삼만 원...그러니까 모두 오만 원이에요.
크리스	제일 싼 게 삼만 원이에요? 그럼, 제일 비싼 건 얼마에요? 십만 원이에요?
점원	아! 죄송합니다. 착각했어요. 모두 삼만 원이에요. 영수증도 드릴까요?
크리스	네, 주세요.
점원	알겠습니다. 여기 있어요. 안녕히 가세요!
크리스	안녕히 계세요.

Chŏmwon	Mwol ch'ajŭseyo?
Chris	Sajŏn issŏyo?
Chŏmwon	Ne. Han-yŏng sajŏn tŭrilkkayo?
Chris	Ne han-yŏng sajŏn-hago yŏng-han sajŏn tul ta chuseyo.
Chŏmwon	Yŏgi issŏyo.
Chris	Ŏlma-eyo?
Chŏmwon	Han kwon-e man won-ssik, modu i-man won-ieyo.
Chris	Hanja sajŏn-do issŏyo?
Chŏmwon	Hanja sajŏn-un se kaji chongnyu-ga issŏyo.
Chris	Cheil ssan kŏ chuseyo.
Chŏmwon	Chamkkan kidariseyo . . . yŏgi issŏyo.
Chris	Komapsumnida. Modu ŏlmaeyo?
Chŏmwon	Hanja sajŏn sam-man won . . . kurŏnikka modu o-man won-ieyo.

Chris	Cheil ssan ke sam-man won-ieyo? Kŭrŏm, cheil pissan kŏn ŏlma-eyo? Shim-man won-ieyo?!
Chŏmwon	A! Choesong hamnida. Ch'akkak haessŏyo. Modu sam-man won-ieyo. Yŏngsujŭng-do tŭrilkkayo?
Chris	Ne, chuseyo.
Chŏmwon	Algesssŭmnida. Yŏgi issŏyo. Annyŏnghi kaseyo!
Chris	Annyŏnghi kyeseyo.

1 How many dictionaries does Chris want to buy?
2 How much are the first two volumes?
3 What choice is he later offered?
4 What kind of Chinese character dictionary does he require?
5 Whose fault is the confusion over cost?
6 What sarcastic remark does Chris make?

Phrases and expressions

mwol ch'ajŭseyo?	*what are you looking for? can I help you?*
(modu) ŏlmaeyo?	*how much is it (all together)?*
algesssŭmnida	*I understand; okay, right, fine (formally)*
ch'akkak haessoyo	*I have made a mistake*
annyŏnghi kaseyo	*goodbye (to someone who is leaving)*
annyŏnghi kyeseyo	*goodbye (to someone who is staying)*

mwol 뭘	*what (object form)*
ch'aj- 찾–	*look for*
sajŏn 사전	*dictionary*
han-yŏng 한-영	*Korean–English*
yŏng-han 영-한	*English–Korean*
tul 둘	*two (when you mean 'the two of them', 'both')*
ŏlma 얼마	*how much*
han 한	*one (pure Korean, when used with a counter or measure word)*
kwon 권	*volume (measure word)*
man 만	*10,000*
won 원	*won (unit of Korean currency)*
-ssik –씩	*each, per (see note 3)*
modu 모두	*all together, everything, everyone*
hanja 한자	*Chinese characters*
se 세	*three (pure Korean)*
kaji 가지	*kind, example (counter for the noun **chongnyu**)*

chongnyu 종류	*type, sort, kind*
cheil 제일	*the most*
ssan 싼	*cheap* (adjective)
ssa- 싸-	*is cheap*
kǔrǒnikka 그러니까	*therefore, because of that*
pissan 비싼	*expensive* (adjective)
pissa- 비싸-	*is expensive*
kǒn 건	*thing, object* (abbrev of **kǒt** 것 + topic particle)
ch'akkak ha- 착각하-	*make a mistake*
yǒngsujǔng 영수증	*receipt*

Grammar

1 Counters

In English, we sometimes use counters (counting words) to count objects. We might say for example two *cups* of coffee, or three *packets* of soup. Cups and packets are counters or measures by which we count and measure things like coffee and soup. On other occasions we do not use counters, for example we say two books, three houses. However, in Korean, counters are frequently used when English does not use them. To say the two previous sentences, for example, a Korean might say:

| ch'aek tu kwon | *book two volumes* | *two books* |
| chip se ch'ae | *house three buildings* | *three houses* |

This is the usual pattern in Korean for counting things, or for talking about a certain number of something. Here are some common Korean counters which take the Sino-Korean numbers you have already learned:

pun	*minute*	sam pun	*three minutes*
ch'o	*second*	iship ch'o	*twenty seconds*
il	*day*	samshib il	*thirty days*
nyǒn	*year*	sa nyǒn	*four years*
ch'ǔng	*floors* (in building)	sam ch'ǔng	*three floors, third floor*
won	*won* (Korean money)	(*etc.*)	
myǒng	*person*		

Note that the word **myŏng** can also be used with pure Korean numbers.

You can ask how many of something there are with the word myŏt (spelt **myŏch'**), for example: myŏn-myŏng? myŏn-nyŏn? myŏt-pun?

This is not to say that Korean always uses counters. There are some words which do not take a special counter, that is to say, the word itself is the counter, as it is in English with books and houses. Thus, for counting days with il (*day*) you don't need to say il sam il. In fact, that would be wrong. You simply say **sam il.** If a counter is not used, therefore, the number comes before what it is that you are counting, instead of after it.

▶ 2 Pure Korean numbers

You now need to know the pure Korean numbers. We teach you up to 49. If you need more than that, you can simply use the Sino-Korean numbers instead. In fact, there are no pure Korean numbers above 99, and so Sino-Korean numbers have to be used for 100 and over. For smaller numbers, however (say, below 50), it is important to know the pure Korean numbers and to use them when they are required, since otherwise you will be easily misunderstood (or not understood at all!) by Koreans.

han(a)	1	yŏlhan(a)	11
tu(l)	2	yŏldu(l)	12
se(t)	3	yŏlse(t)	13
ne(t)	4		
tasot	5		
yŏsŏt	6		
ilgop	7		
yŏdŏl	8		
ahop	9		
yŏl	10	sŭmu(l)	20
		sŏrŭn	30
		mahŭn	40

The letters in brackets are only used when the number is not followed by a noun or a counter to which it refers.

Most counters are used with pure Korean numbers, so with the exception of those you have already learnt which take

Sino-Korean numbers, you are safe to use pure Korean numbers. Here are some examples of common counters which are used with pure Korean numbers:

shi	*o'clock*
shigan	*hours (duration)*
sal	*years of age*
saram	*person*
pun	*person* (honorific)
mari	*animal*
kwon	*volume* (for books)
chan	*cup(ful)*
sangja	*box*
pyŏng	*bottle*

3 Prices

This lesson introduces you to a construction for saying how much things cost, using the word ssik, which is difficult to translate, but gives the sentence the flavour of *so much each, so much apiece,* or *so much per* such and such a quantity. Study the following sentences to see how it is used:

han kwon-e man won-ssik	*10,000 won per book (volume)*
sagwa o-baek won-ssik	*apples 500 won each*
sagwa han sangja-e ch'ŏn won-ssik	*apples 1,000 won a box*

To make sentences out of these, all you have to do is add the copula:

Sagwa-ga o-baek won-ssig-ieyo	*Apples are 500 won each*

4 Introducing adjectives

You have now met several Korean words that function in the way that adjectives do in English. In Korean they are usually called modifiers, but they work rather like adjectives. Remember that they always come before the noun they describe. Here are the ones you have met so far, with a couple of extras thrown in:

pissan	*expensive*
ssan	*cheap*
kŭrŏn	*such a, that* (kind of)
maeun	*spicy*
choŭn	*good*
nappŭn	*bad*

You'll notice that they all end in **n**, and in a later lesson you will learn how they can be formed from their associated verbs.

One very common construction in Korean is to find these words before the noun **kŏt**, which means *thing* (and sometimes also *fact* or *object*). This noun **kŏt** itself needs a little explanation, as it commonly occurs in several different forms. On its own the word is pronounced **kŏt**, but written **kŏs** (remember your pronunciation rules!). It is sometimes abbreviated to **kŏ**. With the topic particle its form is **kŏs-un**, or, in casual speech, **kŏn**. With the subject particle its form is **kŏsh-i** (pronunciation rules!), but it is often shortened to **ke**.

An example of the noun **kŏt** with an adjective would be: **ssan ke** or **ssan kŏsh-i**, which mean *the cheap thing*, or, more commonly, *the cheap one*. You might put these into sentences as follows:

chŏ-nun pissan kŏ choa haeyo	*I like expensive things*
kŭrŏn kŏ mon mŏgŏyo	*I can't eat that (kind of) thing*

5 Superlatives

You can easily make superlatives in Korean (e.g. the most expensive, the most pretty, the best, the fastest) by putting the word **cheil** before the adjective/*modifier*:

cheil maeun ŭmshik	*the most spicy food, the spiciest food*
cheil pissan ke	*the most expensive (thing)* [subject]
cheil choŭn saram	*the best person*

6 Linking words

In continuous speech, Korean likes to show the way that sentences relate to each other by using linking words to begin consecutive sentences. In English we are encouraged not to begin sentences with 'but', 'and' and similar words, but Korean does this sort of thing a lot and it is good style. It makes your Korean sound natural. Here are the most common examples:

kŭrŏna	*but (whereas)*
kŭrŏch'iman	*but*
kŭrigo	*and*
kŭrŏnde	*however, but*
kŭrŏnikka	*therefore, that being so*
kŭrŏm	*so, therefore* (more colloquial)

7 Saying goodbye

You will see from the dialogue that Korean has two ways for saying goodbye. **Annyŏnghi kaseyo** is used to say goodbye to someone who is leaving (i.e. about to walk or go away) and **annyŏnghi kyeseyo** is used to say goodbye to someone who is staying there, while the person saying it is going. Sometimes both speakers will be going off of course, so in that case both would say **annyŏnghi kaseyo**. It sounds a bit tricky at first, admittedly, but once you get used to the idea it's really quite simple. All you have to think about is who is leaving and who is staying. **Annyŏnghi** means *in peace*, so **annyŏnghi kaseyo** means 'go in peace' (from **ka-**, *go*), and **annyŏnghi kyeseyo** means 'stay in peace' (made, surprisingly enough, from the honorific form of the verb **iss-**, *exist, stay*).

ⓘ Chinese characters

In the days before the Korean alphabet was invented, all writing in Korea was done in Chinese characters and then only by an elite that knew how. Even many years after King Sejong's great invention, Chinese characters still remained the most common way of writing for the educated, and it was not until the end of the 19th century that the Korean script began to grow in popularity.

Chinese characters are very complex and there are thousands of different ones, all of which have to be learnt. Fortunately you do not need to do this for your studies in Korean. However, many Korean newspapers use some Chinese characters interspersed within the Korean text and educated Koreans are expected to know around 1,800 characters which are recommended by the Korean education authorities. Unless you wish to be a scholar in Oriental studies, you can survive perfectly well with no knowledge of characters and should you wish to read a Korean newspaper you can buy one which does not use them. It is then only academic and technical books that will be off-limits to you.

Out of interest, the following shows an extract from an academic book which uses both the Korean script and Chinese characters.

그러나, 이러한 부정적인 경향의 평가만으로 廉想涉의 후기소설의 서술방법상의 두드러진 특징들을 다 설명했다고 할 수는 없다. 비록 후기소설에 대한 총체적 평가가 부정적인 쪽으로 쏠려버렸다 해도 그의 한 편의 소설 혹은 여러 편의 소설에 주목할 만하고 본뜰 만한 긍정적 서술방법이 숨어 있을 가능성을 외면할 수는 없기 때문이다.

우선, 앞서 인용한 바 있는 단문 〈나와 自然主義〉에서 廉想涉이 후진들에게 「말과 글을 배울 것」을 권고했던 것을 상기해둘 필요가 있다. 여기에다 「寫實主義를 硏究할 것」이라는 권고를 덧붙인 것을 보면, 그는 후진들에게 자신 있고 능력 있다고 생각하는 내용을 권장한 것임이 분명해진다. 우선, 廉想涉은 한 편의 소설을 만들어가는 과정에 있어서 최소한 「문장」에는 자신감을 가졌다. 廉想涉의 후기소설의 경우, 문제는 이렇듯 자신감에 넘친 문장력이 날카로우면서도 깊이 있는 주제의식과 잘 어울릴 기회를 갖지 못한 데 있다. 문장력은 작가로서의 관록과 비례되는 것이나, 사상이니 주제의식이니 하는 것은 그렇지 않다.

▶ Finding the way

Mr Pak needs to find a bank to get some money changed, but he has a few problems finding what he is looking for.

박선생   실례합니다. 이근처에 은행이 어디 있어요?
은행원 A   저 우체국에서 왼쪽으로 가면 상업 은행이 있어요.
박선생   고맙습니다.

At the counter in Sangŏp bank.

박선생   영국 돈을 한국 돈으로 좀 바꾸고 싶어요.
은행원 B   우리 은행은 외환 업무를 안 해요. 한국 외환 은행으로 가세요.
박선생   한국 외환 은행이 어디 있어요?
은행원 B   종로 쪽으로 가세요. 종로 사거리에서 오른 쪽으로 가면 한국 외환 은행 지점이 있어요.
박선생   여기서 멀어요?
은행원 B   아니요. 걸어서 오 분 정도 걸려요

Mr Pak   Shillye hamnida. I-kunch'ŏ-e ŭnhaeng-i ŏdi
issŏyo?

Unhaengwon A   Chŏ uch'egug-esŏ oencchog-uro ka-myŏn
sangŏp unhaeng-i issŏyo.

Mr Pak   Komapsumnida.

At the counter in Sangŏp bank.

Mr Pak   Yŏngguk ton-ul hanguk ton-uro chom
pakku-go ship'ŏyo.

Unhaengwon B   Uri ŭnhaeng-un oehwan ŏmmu-rul an haeyo.
Hanguk oehwan ŭnhaeng-uro kaseyo.

Mr Pak   Hanguk oehwan ŭnhaeng-i ŏdi issŏyo?

Unhaengwon B   Chongno cchog-uro kaseyo. Chongno
sagŏri-esŏ orun cchog-uro ka-myŏn Hanguk
oehwan ŭnhaeng chijŏm-i issŏyo.

Mr Pak   Yŏgi-sŏ mŏrŏyo?

Unhaengwon B   Aniyo. Kŏrŏsŏ o pun chŏngdo kŏllyŏyo.

1 Where is the Sangŏp bank?
2 What service is required?
3 What is the problem?
4 Where is the other bank located?

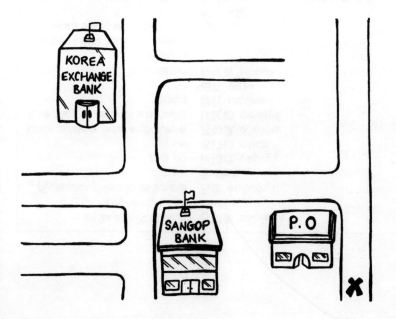

i- 이–	*this one* (+ noun), *this* (noun)
kŭnch'ŏ 근처	*district, area, vicinity*
ŭnhaeng 은행	*bank*
ŭnhaengwon 은행원	*bank clerk*
chŏ- 저–	*that one* (a long way away, old English 'yon')
kŭ- 그–	*that one* (nearer than **cho**)
uch'eguk 우체국	*post office*
-esŏ –에서	location particle (place in which something happens); *from*
oen 왼	*left*
(verb)-**myŏn** –면	*if* (verb) (clause ending)
sangŏp 상업	*trade*
Sangŏp Ŭnhaeng 상업은행	*Commercial Bank* (lit.: *trade bank*)
ch'anggu 창구	*window, cashier window*
ton 돈	*money*
-(r)ul –을/를	(direct object particle)
oehwan 외환	*exchange*
ŏmmu 업무	*business, service*
an 안	*not* (used to make verbs negative)
(Hangwuk) Oehwan Ŭnhaeng 외환은행	*Korea Exchange Bank*
Chongno 종로	*Chongno* (one of the main streets in Seoul, north of the Han river)
sagŏri 사거리	*crossroads*
orŭn 오른	*right*
chijŏm 지점	*branch*
yŏgi-sŏ 여기서	*from here* (abbrev of **yogi-eso**)
mŏrŏyo 멀어요	*is far* (polite style, irregular stem)
aniyo 아니요	*no*
kŏrŏsŏ 걸어서	*on foot*
pun 분	*minute*
chŏngdo 정도	*extent, about (approximately)*
kŏlli- 걸리–	*takes* (time duration)
kŏllyŏyo 걸려요	*it takes* (polite style)

Grammar

1 Directions

The particle -(u)ro is used to indicate direction towards. It won't surprise you to learn that the form -uro is added to nouns that end with consonants and -ro to nouns that end with a vowel. The meaning, then, is *towards, in the direction of*, and therefore it usually occurs with verbs of going and coming.

Another meaning is *into* (another shape or form), and the most important use for that is the one you meet in the dialogue, changing money from one currency *into* another one.

2 Saying 'from', and saying where something happens

The particle -esŏ on the end of nouns means *from* (a place). It could be used in the following circumstances, for example:

From the bank (-esŏ) to the post office (-kkaji) takes 10 minutes I've come from the embassy (esŏ): **taesagwan-esŏ wassŏyo**

There is another important (and slightly more complicated) use of -esŏ, in addition to this meaning. When you are describing where an activity is taking place, you mark the place noun with -esŏ. For example, if you want to say that you are doing your homework in the study, you put the particle -esŏ onto the word for study. -esŏ thus marks the place where an activity is happening. If you want to say that you are doing some drawing in your bedroom, you put the particle -esŏ onto the word bedroom, since that is where the activity of drawing is taking place.

Note that -esŏ is not used to say where something exists (that is, with issŏyo and ŏpsŏyo). In those cases, you simply mark the place noun with -e. Neither is it used to say where you are going to (motion towards is marked by -e, e.g. **hakkyo-e kayo**, as you have already learnt). Observe the following examples carefully:

Kage-e ch'aek issŏyo/manhayo
There are books in the shop/There are many books in the shop (existence once again)

Kage-esŏ ch'aek-ul sayo
I am buying a book in the shop (the activity of buying)

Shiktang-esŏ mannapshida
Let's meet in the restaurant (the activity of meeting)

Shiktang-e kayo
I'm going to the restaurant (motion towards the restaurant, going or coming)

Thus, -e is used with verbs of motion towards (coming and going), and to speak about the existence or non-existence of something in a particular place. -eso is used to say where an activity is taking place, or to mean *from*.

3 'If' clauses

The verb ending -(u)myŏn (-umyŏn after verb stems ending in consonants, otherwise -myŏn) can be added to the stem of any verb to make an if clause. The half of the sentence that comes before the -myŏn is the part that is governed by the 'if'. This is best illustrated by example:

Chongno cchog-uro ka-myŏn ŭnhaeng-i issŏyo
If you go in the direction of Chŏngno, there is a bank

Sŏnsaengnim maekju chumun ha-myŏn, na-do maekju chumun haeyo
If you (sir) order a beer, I'll order one too

Kim sŏnsaengnim ch'aj-ŭmyŏn chŏ-cchog-uro kaseyo
If you're looking for Mr Kim, go that way

4 The object particle

The direct object of a sentence is the bit of the sentence that gets something done to it by the subject or the actor in the sentence. This is best understood by examples. In the following sentences the objects are in bold type:

I want to drink **a beer** (what you, the subject, want to drink, the object, a beer)
He's playing **cricket** (what he, the subject, wants to play, the object, cricket)
Don't watch **television** all the time! (what you, the implied subject, want to watch, the object, TV)

Korean often marks the objects in its sentences by adding the object particle to the noun which is the object of the sentence. The object particle is -rul after a vowel, and -ul after a consonant. Here are examples:

Ch'aeg-ul sapshida
Let's buy a book

Ton-ul pakku-go ship'ŏyo
I want to change some money
(**NB** hangwuk ton-ul yŏngguk ton-uro pakkwu-go ship'ŏyo)

Maekju tu kaji jongnyu-rul sayo?
Are you going to buy two (different) kinds of beer?

Please note that the verbs **issŏyo** and **ŏpsŏyo** always take subjects, and not objects, so you will not find them in conjunction with nouns that have the object particle. This means that you will always see sentences of the form **na-nun ch'aeg-i issŏyo**; you would never see a sentence like **na-nun ch'aeg-ul issŏyo**, since **issŏyo** and **ŏpsŏyo** always take subjects. The same thing applies to verbs of quantity like **manh-**, since that verb and others like it are stating how much of something exists. They are thus similar to the verbs **issŏyo** and **ŏpsŏyo**.

5 Saying you're not doing something

In the last unit you learned the little word **mot** to say that you couldn't do something. Now it's time to learn how to say you do not, are not doing or are not going to do something (usually by choice). In other words, it is your decision, not circumstances beyond your control, which mean you are not doing whatever it is.

You use the little word **an** immediately before the verb, like this:

Na-nun maekju an mashyŏyo
I'm not drinking beer/I don't drink beer (it's your choice)

Jaemin-un shinae-e an kayo
Jaemin's not going into town (he doesn't want to, chooses not to etc.)
Compare: Jaemin-un shinae-e mot kayo (he can't, he has something else on, etc.) Sometimes, however, the word **an** simply means 'not'

Ŭmshik-i an choayo
The food is not good (it's the food's fault – **mot** would be inappropriate)

6 Verb stems ending in -*i*

You have now learnt several verb stems which end in -i. They include **mashi-**, **kolli-**, and **kidari-**. These verbs change slightly when you add the polite particle -yo. The last i changes to yǒ, to give you the polite style forms: **mashyǒyo**, **kollyǒyo** and **kidaryǒyo**.

ⓘ Banking and finance

Banking is simple enough in Korea and the use of credit cards is widespread. There are one or two peculiarities, however, including the fact that Korea does not use cheques. The online system is highly developed, and you can send money electronically very easily and at a much cheaper cost than is usually possible in the West.

Cash is still the most common method of payment, however, and in addition to the coins there are 1,000 won, 5,000 won and 10,000 won notes (**ch'ǒn won** and **man won**). There is also a 100,000 won note (**shimman won**), although it looks more like a western cheque than money.

Practice

Here is additional vocabulary for these exercises.

chan 잔	*cup*	
ilk- 읽–	*read*	
p'yo 표	*ticket*	
pyǒng 병	*bottle*	
tarǔn	*another, different* (modifier/adjective)	

1 Complete the following sentences with the words taken from the box at the bottom.

a 우리 은행은 ____ 업무를 안 해요. ____ 은행에 ____.
   Our bank does not do that (kind of business). Please go to another bank.

b 이쪽으로 ____ 식당이 있어요.
   If you go this way there is a restaurant.

c 실례 ____ 한영 ____ 있어요?
   Excuse me, but do you have a Korean–English dictionary?

d ____ 멀어요? 걸어서 ____ 걸려요.
   Is it far from here? On foot it takes 50 minutes.

e ____ 한국 외환은행 ____ ____ 이에요.
   I'm a bank clerk from the Korea Exchange Bank.

f 저 ＿＿＿ 에서 ＿＿＿ 쪽으로 가면 외환 ＿＿＿ 이 있어요.
If you go right at the post office there is an exchange bank.

g 맥주 두 가지 ＿＿＿ 있어요.
We have two kinds of beer.

h ＿＿＿ 팔만원이에요. 영수증 ＿＿＿?
All together it's 80,000 won. Would you like a receipt?

i 오래간만 ＿＿＿. 요즘 ＿＿＿ 은 어때요?
Long time no see! How's business nowadays?

j 제일 ＿＿＿ 술 마시고 ＿＿＿.
I want to drink the most expensive alcohol.

사전	은행원	여기서	종류가	다른
비싼	모두	지만	가면	이에요
우체국	그런	싫어요	드릴까요	오른
있어요	가세요	저는	오십분	사업
의	은행			

2 In the following English sentences, which nouns are direct objects and would thus be marked with -(r)ul if they were to be translated into Korean? Note that some sentences may have more than one object, and some may not have any.

a I want to watch a movie tonight.
b What are you going to do when you see him?
c How many cars does your family have?
d He just said a bad word.
e Can I eat some bread? No, but there are some crackers.

3 Think up appropriate Korean questions to go with the following answers.

a Choesong ha-jiman, yŏgi-nun kurŏn saram-i ŏpsŏyo.
b I'm sorry, I don't have time.
c Aniyo. Chal mot kŏshyŏssŏyo.
d Pleased to meet you. I've heard a lot about you!
e Chamkkan kidariseyo. Yŏgi issŏyo.
f No, I don't like Korean food.
g I don't particularly want to drink beer right now.

4 Here are a number of items, and the price per item. Make up a sentence which says in Korean what the cost per item is and then say what the total cost is. For example, if you see a picture of six glasses, and the cost per glass is 500 won, you would write something like **han-jan-e obaek won-ssig-ieyo. Kŭrŏnikka modu samch'ŏn won-ieyo.**

5 The following sentences have no particles in them. Put them in!

a 여기____ 왼쪽____ 가면 상업은행 지점____ 있어요.
b 시간____ 있으면 열시____ 호텔 앞____ 만납시다.
c 중국 돈____ 영국 돈____ 좀 바꾸고 싶어요.
d 우리 은행____ 외환 업무____ 안 해요.
e 저____ 매운 음식____ 못 먹어요. 갈비____ 먹고 싶어요.
f 여기____ 그런 사람____ 없어요.
g 그런 것____ 못 마시면, 물____ 마십시다.
h 영한사전 두 가지 종류____ 있어요.
i 한 권____ 이만원____, 그러니까 모두 삼만원이에요.

6 Practise counting the following things out loud.

a 3 books, 8 books, 22 books
b 1 day, 3 days, 67 days
c 1 person, 7 people, 34 people
d 3 octopus, 9 octopus, 14 octopus
e 2 bottles, 10 bottles
f 9 dogs, 1 dog (*dog* = kae)
g 1,000 won, 10,000 won

7 Make up five Korean sentences based around the following verbs. Each of your sentences should put the verb in the negative, with the word **an**.

a chumun ha-   d kidari-
b kŏlli-   e ilk-
c tŭseyo

Which of your sentences would still make sense if you replaced **an** with **mot**? What would be the difference in meaning?

8 Translate the following sentences into Korean.

a Excuse me, is there a restaurant in this area?
b I can't eat naengmyŏn. I can't eat kalbi either.
c How much is it? One plate is 2,000 won, so it's 6,000 won all together.
d Go left here. If you go five minutes, you'll see (= there is) Chongno crossroads. Go left. The bank is on your right.
e How much is the cheapest one?
f It takes about ten minutes on foot.
g There's no branch of the Korea Exchange Bank in this area.
h I want to change some money. I have about 50,000 won.
i In Korea there are ten kinds of kimch'i. In England there are none.
j Would you like a Korean language dictionary?
k What type would you like?
l Please give me the cheapest.
m Is Mr Kim a bad man?
n You're going to the post office? Okay, goodbye!

9 Make up a dialogue between a shopkeeper and a child going shopping. Here is the shopping list (**NB** *milk* = **uyu**; *bottle* = **pyŏng**).

SHOPPING LIST

2 bottles milk   Meat

Bread   10 beers

Kimch'i   Apples

05

is this the bus for Tongdaemun market?/this fruit doesn't look too good!

In this unit you will learn
- how to catch buses in Korea and make sure you have got to the right place
- how to shop for food at the market
- how to express surprise or exclamation
- comparisons
- how to join two sentences together to make one

▶ Is this the bus for Tongdaemun market?

65

is this the bus for
Tongdaemun market?/this
fruit doesn't look too good!

05

Mr Kim is a stranger in Seoul who wants to find his way to Tongdaemwun market. He ends up being persuaded to go to Namdaemwun market instead.

김선생 실례지만 여기 동대문 시장 가는 버스가 있어요?
이선생 저도 서울 사람이 아니라서 잘 모르겠어요.

To Mrs O, another passer-by.

김선생 이 정류장에 동대문 시장 가는 버스가 서요?
오선생 아니요. 이 정류장에는 동대문 시장 가는 버스가
        없어요.
        이십 번 버스를 타면 남대문 시장에 가요.
김선생 남대문 시장이요? 남대문 시장에는 뭐가 있어요?
오선생 뭐가 있느냐고요? 남대문 시장에는 안 파는 게
        없어요.
김선생 동대문 시장보다 물건이 더 많아요?
오선생 제 생각에는, 남대문 시장이 동대문 시장보다
        물건도 더 많고 재미 있어요. 그렇지만 남대문
        시장에서 원숭이는 안 팔아요.
        동대문 시장에서는 팔지만 . . . .
김선생 정말이에요? 그런데 저는 원숭이는 필요 없어요.
오선생 그럼 이십 번 버스를 타세요.
김선생 어디서 타요?
오선생 바로 길 건너편 정류장에서 타세요.
김선생 버스 요금이 얼마에요?
오선생 정말 촌사람이시군요! 사백 원이에요.
김선생 고맙습니다.
오선생 빨리 가세요. 저기 버스가 와요.

Mr Kim Shillye-jiman, yŏgi Tongdaemun shijang kanŭn bŏsu-ga issŏyo?

Mr Lee Chŏ-do Sŏul saram-i ani-rasŏ chal morŭgessŏyo.

To Mrs O, another passer-by.

Mr Kim I chŏngnyujang-e Tongdaemun shijang kanŭn bŏsu-ga sŏyo?

Mrs O Aniyo. I chŏngnyujang-e-nun Tongdaemun shijang ganun bŏsu-ga ŏpsŏyo. Iship pŏn bŏsu-rul t'a-myŏn Namdaemun shijang-e kayo.

Mr Kim Namdaemun shijang-iyo? Namdaemun shijang-e-nun mwo-ga issŏyo?

66

is this the bus for
Tongdaemun market?/this
fruit doesn't look too good!

05

Mrs O	Mwo-ga innŭnyagoyo? Namdaemun shijang-enun an p'anŭn ke ŏpsŏyo.
Mr Kim	Tongdaemun shijang-poda mulgŏn-i tŏ manayo?
Mrs O	Che saenggag-enun, Namdaemun shijang-i Tongdaemun shijang-poda mulgŏn-do tŏ man-k'o chaemi issŏyo. Kŭrŏch'iman Namdaemun shijang-esŏ wonsungi-nun an p'arayo. Tongdaemun shijang-esŏ-nun p'aljiman . . .
Mr Kim	Chŏngmal-ieyo? Kŭrŏnde, chŏ-nun wonsungi-nun p'iryo ŏpsŏyo.
Mrs O	Kŭrŏm iship pŏn bŏsu-rul t'aseyo.
Mr Kim	Ŏdi-sŏ t'ayo?
Mrs O	Paro kil kŏnnŏp'yŏn chŏngnyujang-esŏ t'aseyo.
Mr Kim	Bŏsu yogŭm-i ŏlma-eyo?
Mrs O	Chŏngmal ch'onsaram-ishigunyo! Sabaek won-ieyo.
Mr Kim	Komapsŭmnida.
Mrs O	Ppalli kaseyo. Chŏgi bŏsu-ga wayo.

1 Why can't the first person help?
2 What happens if you take bus number 20?
3 What is the choice like at Namdaemun?
4 Which market is preferred?
5 Is there anything you can't get at Namdaemun?
6 Where should you catch the bus?
7 Why is there surprise at the last question?
8 Why the hurry?

Phrases and expressions

(chal) morŭgessŏyo	*I don't know (at all)*
an p'anŭn ke ŏpsŏyo	*there's nothing which is not sold (you can buy everything)*
mwoga innŭnyagoyo?	*you're asking what there is? (you mean you don't know?) (based on iss-, there is, exists)*
che saenggag-enun	*in my opinion*

Tongdaemun 동대문		*Great East Gate (in Seoul), Tongdaemun*
shijang 시장		*market*
kanŭn 가는		*going to, bound for*
bŏsŭ 버스		*bus*
Sŏul 서울		*Seoul*
(noun)-ani-rasŏ –아니라서		*since it is not (noun) (here: since I am not . . .)*
tarŭn 다른		*another, different*

67

is this the bus for
Tongdaemun market?/this
fruit doesn't look too good!

05

-ege –에게		*to*
chŏngnyujang 정류장		*bus stop*
sŏ- 서–		*stop* (stem)
pŏn 번		*number*
t'a- 타–		*take* (transport), *travel on* (transport)
Namdaemun 남대문		*Great South Gate (in Seoul), Namdaemun*
-iyo –이요		(see note 3: used to check information, e.g. '*you mean*?')
p'anŭn ke 파는 게		*item for sale, items sold*
an p'anŭn ke 안 파는 게		*something which is not sold, not available*
-poda –보다		*more than*
mulgŏn 물건		*goods*
man(h)- 많–		*is many/is a lot* (**h** is not pronounced; polite style: **manayo**) (**NB** pronunc: **h** + **k** = **k'**; therefore **manh-** + **-ko** = **mank'o**)
che 제		*my* (humble form)
saenggak 생각		*thought*
-ko –고		*and* (to join clauses)
chaemi iss- 재미 있–		*is interesting, is fun*
wonsungi 원숭이		*monkey*
p'arayo 팔아요		*sell* (polite style form, stem is irregular)
p'aljiman 팔지만		*they sell, but . . .* (i.e. *they do sell . . . , however*)
chŏngmal 정말		*really*
p'iryo ŏps- 필요 없–		*is not necessary, is not needed, has no need of*
p'iryo iss- 필요 있–		*is necessary, is needed*
paro 바로		*directly*
kil 길		*road, route*
kŏnnŏp'yŏn 건너편		*opposite side*
yogum 요금		*fee, fare*
ch'onsaram 촌사람		country bumpkin, yokel
-ishigunyo –이시군요		(see note 7: based on copula)
ppalli 빨리		*quickly*
chŏgi 저기		*over there, over yonder*
kŏgi 거기		*over there* (nearer than **chogi**)
wayo 와요		*come* (polite style form)
o- 오–		*come* (stem)
pi-ga o- 비가오–		*rains, is raining* (polite style: pi-ga wayo)

68

is this the bus for
Tongdaemun market?/this
fruit doesn't look too good!

05

Grammar

1 -irasŏ, -anirasŏ

In the dialogue you will find the phrase sŏul saram-i ani-rasŏ. This is related to the negative copula anieyo and you will see that both forms include the part -ani-. ani-rasŏ is a different form of anieyo, and it means *since (it) is not a* (noun). The -rasŏ bit means *because* or *since*. The sentence in the dialogue therefore means *since I am not a Seoul person . . . , since I'm not from Seoul . . .*

To say the opposite of this, that is, *since something is something else*, you use the form -irasŏ instead of anirasŏ. Thus, you could say *since I'm a Korean* with the words: hanguk saram-irasŏ . . .

Here are examples of both constructions, and you should also study the example in the dialogue:

Hanguk saram-i anirasŏ hangungmal chal mot haeyo
Since I'm not a Korean I can't speak Korean very well

Yŏngguk saram-irasŏ sul chal mashyŏyo
Since I'm an English person I'm a good drinker

2 Particle order

You will have noticed that sometimes Korean allows you to put more than one particle onto the end of a word, as in the example **Namdaemun shijang-e-nun mwŏga issŏyo?** This makes a topic out of the phrase 'at Namdaemun market'. You have to be careful that the particles are put into the correct order, however. For example, you can say **hanguk-e-do issŏyo** (*they have it in Korea, too*), but **hanguk-do-e issoyo** is wrong. You can learn the correct orders by observing the example sentences in this course. There are some rules, however, which you will find useful.

69

is this the bus for Tongdaemun market?/this fruit doesn't look too good!

05

Many particles cannot occur together because their meanings would be contradictory (the same noun cannot be both subject and object, for example), so it is best to stick to only using combinations that you have seen.

However, the particles **-do** and **-ŭn/-nŭn** (*too, also* and topic) can be added after most other particles (but not the subject or object particles), both giving extra emphasis to the noun and particle to which they are added. Possible examples are **-esŏnun, esŏdo**, and so on. You might like to study the following two examples which illustrate the use of combined particles:

Kim sŏnsaengnim-un hanguk-edo ilbon-edo kayo
Mr Kim goes both to Korea and to Japan

Sŏul-enun shiktang manayo
In Seoul (topic) *there are many restaurants*

3 Checking on something

The particle **-yo** (or **-iyo** after consonants) can be added to any noun to check what has been said, to clarify something or to show surprise. In the dialogue one speaker asks which bus goes to Namdaemun market, and the other says **Namdaemun shijang-iyo?** This translates as *Namdaemun market? You said Namdaemun market, right? You want Namdaemun market?* or something similar. If a shopkeeper told you that an apple cost 10,000 won (a ridiculously high price), you might say **Manwon-iyo?** *10,000 won?* (*You must be joking!*). Depending on the intonation it can express surprise or incredulity or can simply be used to check whether what you heard was correct.

4 Comparing things

You can compare one thing with another quite simply in Korean. Let's take an example sentence. To say that English beer is better than Korean beer, the pattern is as follows (first

70

is this the bus for
Tongdaemun market?/this
fruit doesn't look too good!

05

with the English words to show how the construction works, then with Korean):

English beer (subject or topic) *Korean beer*-**poda** *is more good*
Yŏngguk maekju-nun Hanguk maekju-poda tŏ choayo

You can even omit the word **tŏ** if you want to. Here is another example in which something is claimed to be more tasty than something else:

Che saenggag-enun hanguk umshig-i chungguk umshik-poda
   (tŏ) mashi issŏyo.
In my opinion, Korean food is tastier than Chinese food.

How many other examples can you spot in the dialogue?

5 Many and few, big and small

Korean uses the word **manayo** to say that there are many of something. It uses another word **k'u-** to say that something is big (polite style **k'ŏyo**). The stem for the verb **manayo** is **manh-** (the **h** is still there in Korean writing in the polite form **manayo**, but is silent in pronunciation).

To say something is small you use the verb **chak-**, polite form **chagayo**; to say there is or are few of something use the verb **chŏk-**, polite form **chŏgŏyo**. Here are some examples:

Yŏnggug-enun yongguk saram-i manayo
In England there are many English people

Yongguk-enun hanguk saram-i chŏgŏyo
In England there are few Koreans

I-chaeg-un k'ŭ-go chŏ-chaeg-un chagayo
This book is big and that one is small

6 Joining sentences together

You have learnt the word **kurigo** which can be used to begin a second sentence with the meaning 'and . . .' Take the example sentences:

Hanguk ŭmshik choayo. Kŭrigo ilbon ŭmshik-do choayo
Korean food is good. And Japanese food is good too

These two sentences can be joined into one by taking the verb stem of the first (**choh-** from **choayo**), and adding the ending **-ko** to it:

Hanguk umshik choh-ko ilbon ŭmshik-do choayo

(**NB h + k = k'**, therefore **choh-ko** is pronounced **cho-k'o**.)

This verb ending -ko is common in Korean, and it can be used with all verbs. Here is another example:

Kim sŏnsaengnim-un ch'aeg-ul ilk-ko Chang sŏnsaengnim-un t'ellebi pwayo
Mr Kim reads books and Mr Chang watches TV

7 Exclamations

The verb ending -kunyo can be added to verb stems in order to express surprise. Look at the example in the dialogue, where you will find it with the copula. It is particularly common with the copula, often in the honorific form -ishi-gunyo, and it is this form that you have met:

Kim sŏnsaengnim-ishi-gunyo! Pangapsŭmnida
Ah, so you're Mr Kim (surprise, surprise!)! Pleased to meet you!

You do not need to use this form yourself, but you need to be able to recognize it if a Korean uses it. Here is an example of its use with the normal (non-honorific) copula:

Kim sŏnsaengnim adul-i-gunyo! Chigŭm ŏdi kayo?
So you're Mr Kim's son! Where are you going now?

ⓘ Markets

Seoul has several famous and fascinating markets, particularly Tongdaemun and Namdaemun which you have learnt something about in this lesson. Namdaemun is more compact, perhaps more pleasant to look round and has more tourists. Tongdaemun sprawls right on all the way down Ch'ŏngyech'ŏn (parallel to Chongno), and is cheaper for some goods. It depends a bit on what you want to buy as to which is best. Tongdaemun has a better selection of shoes and boots, for example, but both of them are well worth a visit.

Both Tongdaemun and Namdaemun are also night markets, and the best time to go is between one and six in the morning. The night markets can be good, but they can also sometimes be disappointing. If you're in Seoul for a while it's probably something which is worth trying once.

There are other markets too. Chegi shijang is much less well known (and therefore less touristy) and is great for food, Chinese herbs and medicines, and for ginseng products. Itaewon is well known for having hordes of foreigners and lots of Koreans who can speak English. But it's not the cheapest place to shop by any means. Cities out of Seoul also have good markets of course, and the fish market

71

is this the bus for Tongdaemun market?/this fruit doesn't look too good!

05

(much of it raw) at Pusan is a case in point. Korean markets are something you'll probably grow to love or hate!

▶ This fruit doesn't look too good!

In this dialogue a Korean girl, Minja, goes to the market looking to buy some boxes of apples. She has some trouble, but eventually manages to strike a good deal.

민자 여기 사과 얼마에요?
점원 A 한 상자에 삼만 원이에요.
민자 너무 비싸네요. 좀 깎아주세요.
점원 A 그럼 한 상자에 이만 팔천 원에 가져가세요.
민자 그래도 비싸요.
점원 A 그럼 다른 데 가보세요. (to himself) 오늘 아침부터 재수없네!

Minja goes to another grocers.

민자 이 사과가 싱싱해 보이지 않네요. 어떤 건 좀 썩었어요.
점원 B 그래요? 그럼 좀 깎아드릴께요.
민자 얼마나요?
점원 B 한 상자에 삼만 천 원만 주세요.
민자 뭐라고요?! 옆 가게보다 더 비싸네요.
점원 B 좋아요. 그럼 이만 칠천 원만 주세요.
민자 좀 더 깎아주세요.
점원 B 좋아요. 한 상자에 이만 오천 원 내세요.
민자 고맙습니다. 세 상자 주세요.

Minja	Yŏgi sagwa ŏlma-eyo?
Chŏmwon A	Han sangja-e samman won-ieyo.
Minja	Nŏmu pissa-neyo. Chom kkakka-juseyo.
Chŏmwon A	Kŭrŏm han sangja-e iman-p'alch'ŏn won-e kajyŏ-gaseyo.
Minja	Kŭraedo pissayo.
Chŏmwon A	Kŭrŏm tarŭn te ka-boseyo. (to himself) Onŭl ach'im-put'ŏ chaesu ŏmne!

Minja goes to another grocers.

Minja	I-sagwa-ga shingshing hae-poiji anneyo. Ŏttŏn gŏn chom ssŏgŏssŏyo.
Chŏmwon B	Kŭraeyo? Kurŏm chom kkakka-durilkkeyo.
Minja	Ŏlma-na-yo?
Chŏmwon B	Han sangja-e samman-ch'ŏn wŏn-man chuseyo.
Minja	Mworaguyo?! Yŏp kage-poda tŏ pissaneyo.

73

is this the bus for
Tongdaemun market?/this
fruit doesn't look too good!

05

Chŏmwon B	Choayo. Kurŏm iman-ch'ilch'ŏn wŏn-man chuseyo.
Minja	Chom tŏ kkakka-juseyo.
Chŏmwon B	Choayo. Han sangja-e iman-och'ŏn won naeseyo.
Minja	Komapsŭmnida. Se sangja chuseyo.

1 How much reduction does the first vendor give on a box?
2 What is the response?
3 What is the problem at the second stall?
4 What is the cause for surprise?
5 What is the final price?

Phrases and expressions

chom kkakka-juseyo	*please cut the price a bit for me*
(onul ach'im-put'ŏ)	*I've had no luck (all morning);*
chaesu ŏmne	*I'm unlucky*
shingshing haepoiji anhayo	*they don't look fresh*
mworaguyo?	*what did you say?*

sagwa 사과	*apple*	
sangja 상자	*box*	
-e –에	*each, per*	
nŏmu 너무	*too (much)*	
-neyo –네요	*mild surprise sentence ending*	
kkakka-ju- 깎아주–	*cut the price (for someone's benefit)*	
kajyŏga- 가져가–	*take*	
kŭraedo 그래도	*however, nevertheless, but still*	
te 데	*place*	
kabo- 가보–	*go and see, visit (a place)*	
ach'im 아침	*morning*	
-put'ŏ –부터	*from*	
chaesu 재수	*luck*	
shingshing ha- 싱싱하–	*is fresh*	
ŏttŏn 어떤	*certain, some (as a question word = which?)*	
ssŏgŏssŏyo 썩었어요	*has gone bad, has gone off (polite style, past tense)*	
kkakka-durilkkeyo 깎아드릴께요	*I'll cut the price for you (polite style)*	
-na –나	*approx, about (derived from the meaning 'or' you have learnt)*	
-man –만	*only*	
yŏp' 옆	*next door*	
nae- 내–	*pay*	

74

is this the bus for
Tongdaemun market?/this
fruit doesn't look too good!

05

Grammar

1 Only

The particle -man means *only*, so that samman won-man means *only 30,000 won*, and chaek-man chuseyo means *please give me the book only* or *please just give me the book*. Na-man wassŏyo means *only I have come*. -man can be added to any noun in this way.

2 More surprises

The verb ending -neyo can be added to any verb stem, and it indicates surprise, although usually of a milder form than -kunyo. This is perhaps a more useful pattern to learn to use for yourself. Look carefully at the examples from the dialogues:

Pi-ga o-neyo!	*Oh no, it's raining!*
Aegi-ga ch'aeg-ul ing-neyo! (*spelt* ilk-neyo)	*Wow, the baby is reading a book!*
Kurŏm, kŭ-saram-un hanguk saram-ineyo!	*So he's the Korean person, then! Or, so that person is a Korean, then!* (depending on the intonation)

▶ 3 Months of the year

The months of the year in Korean are as follows (note carefully June and October in which the number loses the last letter):

il-wol	*January*
i-wol	*February*
sam-wol	*March*
sa-wol	*April*
o-wol	*May*
yu-wol	*June*
ch'il-wol	*July*
p'al-wol	*August*
ku-wol	*September*
shi-wol	*October*
shibil-wol	*November*
shibi-wol	*December*

4 To and from (with people)

75

is this the bus for
Tongdaemun market?/this
fruit doesn't look too good!

05

When you want to say *to* a person (write *to* a person, speak *to* a person, give *to* a person), you use the particle -hant'e or the particle -ege (the particle -kke can be used when the person is honorific). For example:

Ŏmŏni-ege p'yŏnji ssŏyo	*I'm writing a letter to Mum*
Jaemin-hant'e chu-go ship'ŏyo	*I want to give it to Jaemin*
Abŏji-ege iyagi haeyo	*I'm speaking to Father*
Ŏmŏni-hant'e ponaeyo	*I'm sending it to Mother*

'From a person' is said with the particle -hant'esŏ or -egesŏ:

Ch'ingu-hant'esŏ ton padayo	*I receive money from my friend*
Wolyoil-lar-e ŏmŏni-egesŏ p'yŏnji padayo	*I receive a letter from my Mum on Mondays*
Abŏji-hant'esŏ chŏnhwa wassŏyo	*I got a phone call from Dad (a call came)*

ⓘ Cutting the price

There is plenty of bargaining to be done at Korean markets. The best advice is to go shopping with a Korean or someone who has been in Korea a long time and who knows how to get a good deal. Some shopkeepers already give the lowest price, and you must be aware that it is not fair to expect such dealers to cut. Others will give quite an inflated price when they see you are a foreigner. In general, however, Korea is a much safer place for not getting ripped off than somewhere like India or Thailand. In general, the places where there are fewer foreigners are more likely to offer the best deals (and less likely to speak English!).

76

is this the bus for
Tongdaemun market?/this
fruit doesn't look too good!

05

Practice

1 Answer the following questions in Korean, based on the dialogues in this lesson. Make sure to use full sentences in your answers.

   a 동대문 시장이 남대문 시장보다 더 재미있어요?
   b 동대문 시장에서 뭘 안 팔아요?
   c 이십 번 버스를 타면 어디 가요?
   d 남대문 시장에는 물건이 많아요?
   e 이십 번 버스를 어디서 타요?

2 Make up answers or appropriate responses to the following questions.

   a Tongdaemun shijang-e ka-go ship'ŏyo. Kach'i kayo?
   b Onul ach'im-e mwol haseyo?
   c I kwail-i an shingshing haeyo.
   d Bŏsu yogum-i ŏlma-eyo?
   e Hanguk choa haseyo? Hangungmal chaemi issŏyo?

3 Imagine that you suddenly recognize or are surprised by seeing the following people or things. This exercise is intended to practise the -kunyo form with the copula (don't forget to use the honorific form of the copula when appropriate).

   a Mr Kim's dog
   b Mr O's wife
   c a Japanese book
   d the Korea Exchange Bank
   e hyŏngjun
   f the Chinese teacher

4 Make up sentences comparing the following sets of information. For the first set you would make up a sentence to say that Korean food is more tasty than Japanese food.

   a Korean food   Japanese food   tasty
   b Here   there   more of them
   c Train   bus   faster (ppallayo)
   d Mr Kim   Mr Pak   more luck
   e Namdaemwun   Tongdaemun   more expensive

5 Write a dialogue between a Korean in Paris who wants to get a bus to the Louvre and a Japanese, who the Korean mistakenly thinks is a Korean. Fortunately, the Japanese can also speak Korean, and so, after explaining that he is Japanese not Korean, he tells him that the Louvre is nearby (not far). He doesn't need to take a bus and it only takes seven minutes to walk.

6 Translate the following sentences into English.

a Yogi pissaneyo. Yŏp kage-e ka-bopshida.
b Yŏgi-sŏ p'al-jiman tarun te-e ka-myŏn tŏ ssayo.
c Sŏul shinae-e kanun bosu-rul ŏdi-sŏ t'ayo?
d Onul ach'im-put'ŏ chaesu ŏmneyo!
e Ilbon-un Hanguk-poda tŏ pissayo. Kŭraedo Hanguk-do pissayo.
f Che saenggak-poda Hangug-e Yŏngguk saram-i manhayo.
g Kkakka-durilkkeyo. Han sangja-e mansamch'ŏnwon-e kajyŏ-gaseyo.
h Chumun hashigessŏyo?
i Yŏgi-ga Hanguk-anirasŏ Kimch'i-rul p'anun te chŏgŏyo.
j Wonsung-i innŭnyaguyo? Tongdaemun shijang-e ka-boseyo.

7 Which of the following particle sequences are acceptable and which are not?

a 시간에는 (shigan = time)
b 음식을은
c 어머니에게도
d 길에서는
e 버스에가
f 국이를 (kuk = soup)
g 아침부터를
h 밤부터는

8 Translate the following sentences and put them into the -neyo mild surprise form.

a My, these dictionaries are expensive!
b Taegyu is coming!
c What are you doing? (surprise!)
d This newspaper's really interesting.

9 Join the following pains of sentences, with the -ko clause ending.

a 이 사람이 박선생님이에요. 저 사람 강선생님이에요.
b 어머니 책 읽어요. 아버지 텔레비를 봐요.
c 고기 못 먹어요. 사과도 못 먹어요.
d 십일 번 버스가 남대문 시장에 가요. 이십 번 버스는 동대문 시장에 가요.
e 상준 버스 타요. 명택도 버스 타요.

Is this the bus for Tongdaemun market?/this fruit doesn't look too good!

10 Ŏnu bŏsu-ga hakkyo-e kanŭn bŏsu-eyo? Shipp'al pŏn bŏsu-ga ŏdi kayo?

06

off to the mountains/I've got a nasty headache!

In this unit you will learn
- how to talk about short-term plans
- how to suggest and discuss activities
- how to express your aches and pains, say that you are ill and get sympathy
- the probable future (what you expect to do or what is most probable)
- how to make suggestions and tell others what you are thinking of doing

▶ Off to the mountains

Mr Kim wants to take Tony mountain climbing, but with Tony's busy schedule they have some difficulty finding a convenient date.

김선생   요즘 날씨가 아주 좋아요.
토니   네. 한국은 영국보다 날씨가 좋아요.
김선생   내일 뭐 할 거에요? 별일 없으면 등산이나 갈까요?
토니   가고 싶지만 내일은 집사람하고 동대문 시장에서 쇼핑 하기로 했어요.
김선생   그럼 다음 일요일은 어때요?
토니   다음 일요일에는 대학 동창들하고 불국사에 갈까해요.
김선생   그럼 다음 일요일도 안 되겠네요. 언제가 좋을까요?
토니   그 다음 일요일은 아마 괜찮을거에요.
김선생   좋아요. 그럼 다음 일요일에 갑시다.
토니   저도 등산을 좋아 해요.
     그런데 영국에는 산이 많지 않아서 등산을 많이 못 했어요.
     그런데 어느 산에 갈까요?
김선생   도봉산이 편할거에요.
토니   그럼 도봉산 입구에서 만날까요?

Mr Kim	Yojŭm nalssi-ga aju choayo.
Tony	Ne. Hanguk-un yŏngguk-poda nalssi-ga choayo.
Mr Kim	Naeil mwo ha-lkŏeyo? Pyŏlil ŏps-umyŏn tungsan-ina ka-lkkayo?
Tony	Ka-go ship'-jiman naeil-un chipsaram-hago Tongdaemun shijang-esŏ shyop'ing ha-giro haessŏyo.
Mr Kim	Kŭrŏm taŭm ilyoir-un ŏttaeyo?
Tony	Taŭm ilyoil-enun taehak tongch'ang-hago pulguksa-e ka-lkka haeyo.
Mr Kim	Kŭrŏm taŭm ilyoil-do an toe-genneyo. Ŏnje-ga cho-ulkkayo?
Tony	Kŭ taŭm ilyoir-un ama kwaench'an-ulkŏeyo.
Mr Kim	Choayo. Kŭrŏm kŭ taŭm ilyoil-e kapshida.
Tony	Chŏ-do tŭngsan-ul choa haeyo. Kŭrŏnde yŏngguk-enun san-i manch'i anasŏ tŭngsan-ul mani mot haessŏyo. Kŭrŏnde ŏnu san-e ka-lkkayo?
Mr Kim	Tobongsan-i p'yŏn ha-lkŏeyo.
Tony	Kŭrŏm Tobongsan ipku-esŏ manna-lkkayo?

1 How does English weather compare with Korean?
2 What does Mr Kim suggest and under what circumstances?

3 What plans does Tony have for tomorrow?
4 With whom has he made plans for the following Sunday?
5 What is resolved?
6 What do you know about Tony's opinion regarding the
   experience of mountain climbing?

Phrases and expressions

naeil mwo halkŏeyo?	*what are you going to do tomorrow?*
pyŏlil ŏpsŭmyŏn . . .	*if you don't have anything special on . . .*
an twoegenneyo	*it won't be any good, then (unfortunately)*
ama kwoench'anulkŏeyo	*it will probably turn out (be) okay*

nalssi 날씨		*weather*
naeil 내일		*tomorrow*
-(ŭ)lkŏeyo -(으)ㄹ거예요		*(used to give verbs a future meaning, see note 3)*
pyŏlil 별일		*a special matter, something particular*
tungsan 등산		*mountain climbing*
-(ŭ)lkkayo -(으)ㄹ까요		*(verb ending meaning shall we?, see note 6)*
shyŏp'ing (ha-) 쇼핑(하-)		*shopping (do/go shopping)*
-kiro haessŏyo -기로 했어요		*decided to*
ilyoil 일요일		*Sunday*
ilyoillal 일요일날		*Sunday (longer form)*
taehak 대학		*university*
tongch'ang 동창		*colleague (fellow student in this case)*
pulguksa 불국사		*Pulguksa (Korean Buddhist temple, the largest in Korea, near Kyŏngju)*
-(ŭ)lkka haeyo -(으)ㄹ까 해요		*am thinking of doing*
ŏnje 언제		*when*
san 산		*mountain*
man-ch'i anasŏ 많지 않아서		*since there aren't many (written manh-ji anh-asŏ)*
haessŏyo 했어요		*did (past tense form of ha- do)*
ŏnŭ 어느		*which one*
Tobongsan 도봉산		*Tobongsan (mountain in Seoul)*
p'yŏn ha- 편하-		*is comfortable, is convenient*
ipku 입구		*entrance*

Grammar

1 Verb stems ending in *i*

This unit contains several verbs whose stems end in i, for example: **umjigi-** (*move*), **nolli-** (*tease*), and you have previously met **mashi-** (*drink*), **kidari-** (*wait*) and **kŏlli-** (*lasts, takes (time)*). All these verbs change the last i to yo and add yo in order to form the present polite style. This gives the polite style forms **umjigyŏyo, nollyŏyo, mashyŏyo, kidaryŏyo, kŏllyŏyo.**

▶ 2 Days of the week

The following are the days of the week in Korean:

wolyoil	*Monday*
hwayoil	*Tuesday*
suyoil	*Wednesday*
mokyoil	*Thursday*
kŭmyoil	*Friday*
t'oyoil	*Saturday*
ilyoil	*Sunday*

3 Probable future

The most common way to give a sentence a future meaning in Korean is to add -(u)lkŏeyo to the stem of the main verb. As you would expect, you add -lkŏeyo if the stem ends in a vowel, and -ulkŏeyo if the stem ends in a consonant. Thus **manna-** becomes **manna-lkŏeyo** (*I will meet*), and **anj-** becomes **anj-ŭlkŏeyo** (*I will sit*).

We have called the form the probable future, because there are other ways of expressing the future tense in Korean – there is a definite future, for example, which you might use if there is scarcely any doubt that you will do something, or if you want to stress your intention to do it. The probable future is the most common, and is used in most everyday situations when you want to say that you are going to do something:

Naeil chungguk taesagwan-e ka-lkŏeyo
I will (probably) go to the Chinese embassy tomorrow

Naenyŏn-e ch'a-rul sa-lkŏeyo
I'm going to buy a car next year (**naenyŏn**, *next year*)

The same form has another meaning, in addition to the future. It can also mean something like *is probably* (verb)*ing*.

Pi-ga o-lkŏeyo
It is probably raining

4 Making decisions

To say that you have decided to do something, simply add -kiro haessŏyo onto the verb stem of the verb you have decided to do. To say that you have decided to eat with Mr Kim, for example, you would say: Kim sonsaengnim-hago chomshim-ul mŏk-kiro haessŏyo:

Taehak tongch'ang-hago tŭngsan ha-giro haessŏyo
I've decided to go mountain climbing with my friend(s) from university

5 Thinking about it

Sometimes when you still haven't made definite plans, you want to say that you are thinking about doing something. You might say, for example, *I am thinking about going away for the weekend*. Korean provides an easy way of allowing you to do this. Simply add the ending -lkka haeyo to a verb stem ending in a vowel, or -ŭlkka haeyo to a verb stem ending in a consonant. That's all there is to it. To take one example, suppose you were thinking of going to Sŏraksan (Sŏrak mountain) on Sunday, you simply say, ilyoir-e sŏraksan-e ka-lkka haeyo. Can you work out the meaning of the following example? Chŏmshim-e pibimpab-ul mŏg-ŭlkka haeyo.

6 Shall we?

To say to someone 'shall we do something or other?', you add a verb ending very like the one you have just learned. Add -lkkayo? to a verb stem ending in a vowel, and -ŭlkkayo? to a verb stem ending in a consonant. To say to someone 'shall we sit here?' you would therefore say yŏgi anj-ŭlkkayo?, and to say 'shall we have a beer?' you would say maekjwu mashi-lkkayo?

i Koreans are very fond of mountain climbing and if you go to virtually any Korean mountain on a weekend or public holiday, you will be sure to find hordes of Koreans all dressed up in hiking gear, proceeding with great enthusiasm. For most Koreans mountain climbing means a strenuous hike rather than scaling rock faces, but that in no way diminishes the fun (or the steepness of the mountains!).

Sport is very popular, too, and nowadays the most popular sports are the American imports baseball (**yagu**, verb: **yagu ha-**) and basketball (**nonggu ha-**). Football (**ch'ukku**) is also popular and, for the wealthy, golf has great status (**golp'u**).

Other pastimes include the **noraebang** and *karaoke*; Koreans also love to drink, and sometimes break into song as they do so. Board and card games are also popular among some, the most common ones being **paduk** (*go* is the Japanese equivalent, and is somewhat known in the West), and **hwat'u.**

▶ I've got a nasty headache!

Yongtae is sick – everything seems to be hurting and his friend Jaehoon isn't very sympathetic. When he wants his friend Jaehoon to get him some medicine, Jaehoon has another suggestion. But Yongtae is not impressed.

재훈	저 시내에 가는데 같이 갈까요?
용태	글쎄요... 저는 몸이 좀 좋지않아요.
재훈	또 몸이 좋지않아요? 용태씨는 항상 꾀병을 부리지요!
용태	아니요. 그렇지 않아요. 오늘은 정말 아파요.
재훈	오늘은 어디가 아파요?
용태	두통이 있어요. 머리가 좀 아파요.
재훈	그게 다에요? 걱정 하지 마세요. 아마 날씨가 더워서 그럴거에요.
용태	아닌 것 같아요. 배도 아파요.
재훈	많이 아파요?
용태	그래요. 많이 아파요.
재훈	그럼 약을 사러 약국에 갑시다.
용태	저는 못 가요. 힘이 없어요. 게다가 다리도 좀 아파요.
재훈	다리도요? 전신이 다 아프군요. 안 아픈데가 있어요?
용태	시끄러워요! 놀리지 마세요. 약을 먹어야겠어요.
재훈	여기 만병통치약 술이 있어요! 사실 약보다 술이 더 좋아요.
용태	농담 하지 마세요. 술 못 마셔요. 정말 병원에 가야겠어요.

Jaehoon	Chŏ shinae-e ka-nunde, gach'i kalkkayo?
Yongtae	Kulsseyo . . . chŏ-nun mom-i chom choch'i anayo.
Jaehoon	Tto mom-i choch'i anayo? Yongtae-sshi-nun hangsang kkoebyŏng-ul purijiyo!
Yongtae	Aniyo. Kŭrŏch'i anayo. Onŭl-un chŏngmal ap'ayo.
Jaehoon	Onŭr-un ŏdi-ga ap'ayo?
Yongtae	Tut'ong-i issŏyo. Mŏri-ga chom ap'ayo.
Jaehoon	Kŭ-ge ta-eyo? Kŏkjŏng ha-ji maseyo. Ama nalssi-ga tŏwosŏ kurŏlkŏ-eyo.
Yongtae	Anin kŏt kat'ayo. Pae-do ap'ayo.
Jaehoon	Mani ap'ayo?
Yongtae	Kŭraeyo. Mani ap'ayo.
Jaehoon	Kŭrŏm yag-ul sa-rŏ yakkug-e kapshida.
Yongtae	Chŏ-nun mot kayo. Him-i ŏpsŏyo. Kedaga tari-do chom ap'ayo.
Jaehoon	Tari-doyo? Chŏnshin-i ta ap'ŭ-gunyo. An ap'ŭn de-ga issŏyo?
Yongtae	Shikkurŏwoyo! Nolli-ji maseyo. Yag-ul mŏgŏ-yagessŏyo.
Jaehoon	Yŏgi manbyŏngt'ongch'iyak, sul-i issŏyo! Sashil yak-poda sur-i tŏ choayo.
Yongtae	Nongdam ha-ji maseyo. Sul mot mashyŏyo. Chŏngmal pyŏngwon-e ka-yagessŏyo.

1 Why is there little sympathy at first?
2 What are the symptoms?
3 What is the suggested reason for the illness?
4 Why can't they both go for the medicine?
5 What cure-all is suggested?

Phrases and expressions

chŏ-nun mom-i chom choh-ch'i anhayo	*I don't feel very well*
kŭrŏhch'i anhayo	*of course not*
kkoebyŏng-ul purijiyo	*you're making it up! (feigning an illness)*
kŏkchŏng ha-ji maseyo	*don't worry! (colloquial form: kokjong maseyo)*
anin kŏt gat'ayo	*I don't think so; it doesn't seem like it*
chŏnshin-i ta ap'ŭgunyo!	*your whole body must be hurting!*
shikkŭrŏwoyo!	*shut up!, be quiet! (lit.: 'it's noisy')*
nolli-ji maseyo	*don't joke, don't kid me, don't tease*
yag-ul mŏgŏyagessŏyo	*I'll have to take some medicine*

-nŭnde –는데	(verb ending for clauses, see note 4)
kŭlsseyo 글쎄요	*I dunno, I'm not sure, who knows?*
mom 몸	*body*
cho-ch'i anh- 좋지 않–	*is not good* (from **choh-**)
tto 또	*again; moreover, also, furthermore*
hangsang 항상	*always*
kkwoebyŏng 꾀병	*a feigned illness*
ap'ŭ- 아프–	*hurts* (stem)
ap'ayo 아파요	*hurts* (polite style)
tut'ong 두통	*headache*
mŏri 머리	*head*
kŏkjŏng 걱정	*worry, concern*
kŏkjŏng ha- 걱정하–	*be worried*
-ji maseyo –지 마세요	*please don't*
ama 아마	*perhaps, probably*
tŏwosŏ 더워서	*because it is hot* (can also mean *because you're hot*, but here subject is weather)
kŭrŏlkŏeyo 그럴거에요	*it will probably be like that*
kat'- 같–	*seems like*
pae 배	*stomach*
yak 약	*medicine*
yakkuk 약국	*chemists, drugstore*
him 힘	*strength, energy*
kedaga 게다가	*on top of that*
tari 다리	*leg*
chŏnshin 전신	*the whole body*
ap'ŭn 아픈	*hurting, painful* (adjective)
nolli- 놀리–	*make fun of*
manbyŏngt'ongch'iyak 만병통치약	*cure-all medicine, miracle cure, panacea*
-yagessŏyo –야겠어요	*will have to*
sashil 사실	*fact (the fact is . . .)*
nongdam 농담	*joke* (noun)
nongdam ha- 농담하–	*jokes* (verb)
pyŏngwon 병원	*hospital*

Grammar

1 To hurt

The verb stem ap'ŭ- (*hurt*) belongs to another group of verbs all ending in -ŭ. These delete the u and add instead a or ŏ, followed by yo to form the polite style. Thus ap'ŭ- in the polite style is ap'ayo.

How do you know whether the last vowel before the yo will be an a or an ŏ? Simply remember this rule: if the preceding vowel is an a (as in ap'ŭ-) or o, then the ŭ becomes a, otherwise it is ŏ.

2 Don't do it!

When you want to tell someone not to do something, take the stem of the verb you want to tell them not to do and add -ji maseyo to it. Thus, maekju-rul mashi-ji maseyo means *please don't drink beer*. The two phrases in this dialogue, kŏkjŏng ha-ji maseyo and nolli-ji maseyo are quite common. The first means *don't worry!*, and the second means *don't tease me!*. What other useful examples can you think of? How would you say 'please don't wait here' and 'don't do the shopping'?

3 Long negatives

You have learnt how to make negative sentences in Korean with mot and an, by putting them immediately in front of the verb. There is another way also, which is known as the long negative. There is no particularly significant difference between the two, though there are some circumstances in which you are more likely to find the long form than the shorter one you have learnt already. To spell out these distinctions would be rather long winded and would also make the difference seem more important than it really is. The best advice is to look carefully at the dialogues in this book, and to imitate Korean speakers whenever you can. You will then pick up a feel for which to use. Generally, short negatives are better in short, simple sentences; long negatives should be used in more complex sentences.

Here is how to make the long negative. Instead of adding something before the verb you wish to negate, take the stem of that verb and add -ji an(h)ayo or -ji mot haeyo, depending on whether you want to give the sense of the Korean word an (*won't* or *isn't going to*) or mot (*can't*).

Therefore, **mot kayo** in the long negative form would be **kaji mot haeyo**, and **an mŏgŏyo** in the long negative form would be mŏk-ji an(h)ayo. Here is an example of each:

Abŏji-nun nongdam ha-ji anayo
Dad doesn't tell jokes

Yun sŏnsaengnim tŭngsan-ul choa ha-jiman Yun sŏnsaengnim
    puin tŭngsan ha-ji mot haeyo
Mr Yun likes mountain climbing, but his wife can't do it

4 Imminent elaboration

This sounds rather forbidding, but it isn't really all that difficult! Korean has a very common way of linking two clauses together to show that the first one is not all that you have got to say and that there is more coming in the second clause which relates to it. For example, look at the first sentence in the dialogue: **Na-nun shinae-e ka-nŭnde**. That is the end of the first clause. The meaning is straightforward enough, *I'm going into town*, but the -**nŭnde** added on to the end of **ka**- indicates that the speaker still has more to say which relates to what he has just said. It is a clue to the listener not to reply yet, but to wait until the rest has been said. The statement is not complete; there is more to come. In this case, the second clause is **kach'i kalkkayo?** (*shall we go together?*). Koreans use this pattern all the time to show that they have something more to say about what has just been said (in this case an invitation), and from now on you will meet the -**nŭnde** pattern frequently in the unit dialogues.

The formation of the pattern is easy: take any verb which expresses an action (that is, not an adjectival verb) and add -**nŭnde** to the stem. Note that you can also use -**nŭnde** with the verbs **iss**- and **ŏps**-, giving you the forms **innnŭnde** and **ŏmnŭnde**.

Verbs which describe things (e.g. is green, is hot, is foolish etc.) take the form -**(ŭ)nde** instead (**ŭnde** after consonant stems, **nde** after vowels). The copula also takes this form, -**nde**:

Cho-nun Pak Jaemin-i-nde Kim sŏnsaengnim manna-rŏ
    wassŏyo
*I'm Pak Jaemin (and I've got more to say): I've come to meet
    Mr Kim*

You have not learnt the past tense yet, but you might like to keep in the back of your mind the fact that -**nunde** is added to the past stem of all verbs, whether they describe an action or are adjectival. In other words, it doesn't make the distinction that the present tense does.

5 Descriptive verbs and processive verbs

Korean has two basic kinds of verbs – descriptive and processive. Processive verbs describe a process, the doing of something, an action. Thus, **mŏk-, anj-, ka-, ha-, manna-** are all processive verbs. Descriptive verbs describe something, so **choh-** is an example, because it describes something as good. **Cho(h)a ha-**, by contrast, is processive, because it describes the process or action of the speaker liking something. Descriptive verbs function like adjectives in English. They are adjectival verbs.

We tell you all this because some verb endings will only work with one of the two kinds of verbs. What we have just said about -**nŭnde**, for example, could have been said much more compactly by saying that -**nŭnde** can only be added to processive verbs, and that -(**ŭ**)**nde** is added to descriptive verbs and the copula. In the future we shall be making use of these two terms when we describe verb endings.

The two verbs **iss-** and **ŏps-** can be either processive or descriptive depending on their use, and we will tell you about whether or not they can be used with particular verb endings as we go along.

There is one other verb, the copula, which is in a class of its own. We will tell you about this also on a case-by-case basis, as we did with -**nunde**.

6 What you will have to do

This unit introduces you to one final pattern – how to say that you will have to do something.

To form the construction, take off the -**yo** of the polite style form of the verb and add -**yagessŏyo**. Take the verb **mŏk-** as an example. The polite style is **mŏgŏyo**, so taking off the -**yo** and adding the -**yagesŏyo** ending we have **mŏgŏ-yagessŏyo**. This can then be used in a sentence: **chigum mŏgŏ-yagessŏyo** (*I am going to have to eat now (I'm obliged to)*).

The dialogue had two examples of the pattern: **yag-ul mŏgŏ -yagessŏyo** and **pyŏngwon-e ka-yagessŏyo**. Can you remember what they mean?

ℹ️ Doctors and chemists

Most medicines can be bought over the counter without prescription at the **yakkuk** (*pharmacy*). Doctors are available at hospitals and generally speaking there is no equivalent of going to a doctor independent of the hospital. Koreans are enthusiastic takers of medicines for headache, tiredness, flu and so forth, and many frequently take tonics and health drinks in the interest of staying healthy.

Chinese medicine is also very popular in Korea and there are markets which concentrate on selling the herbs and potions which it prescribes.

Practice

1 Here is an exercise about putting verbs into different forms. We give you some sentences with the verb stem, you write out the sentences in full, putting the verb into the correct form.

Future
a Yangju mashi-myŏn naeil mŏri-ga ap'u-
b Ittaga chŏmshim-ul mŏk-
c Hanguk saram manna-myŏn hanja sajŏn p'iryo ŏps-
Decided
d Pyŏngwŏn-e ka-
e Wonsungi-rul sa-
f Onŭl-un ŭmshig-ul an mŏk-
Thinking of
g Chŏ-nun 'Star Wars'(!) po-
h Onŭl ach'im shyop'ing ha-
i Ilyoir-e pulguksa-e ka-
Shall we
j Ŏnje tŭngsan ka-?
k Kim sŏnsaengnim-ul ŏdi-sŏ manna-?
l Uch'eguk ap'-esŏ bŏsu-rul t'a-?

2 The following dialogue concerns a boy who wants to go mountain climbing with Mik'a, a reluctant girl who keeps making up reasons why she can't go with him. Can you fill in the missing parts, giving reasons why she can't go? (Note: **annyŏng** is a way of saying hello to a close friend, or someone younger than you.)

Boy	Mik'a, annyŏng! Naeil shigan-i issŏyo?
Girl	(*State another plan*)
Boy	Kurŏm ilyoil-e pyŏlil ŏps-umyŏn kach'i tungsan kalkkayo?
Girl	(*Too busy doing something else*)
Boy	Taum ilyoir-un ŏttaeyo?
Girl	(*Another plan*)
Boy	Ŏnje shigan-i issŏyo, kurŏm? Na-rul an choa haeyo?
Girl	(*Doesn't like mountain climbing*)
Boy	Kurŏm, an twoegennneyo.

3 Can you write a simple conversation between two friends, one who has a headache and the other who thinks she doesn't have any medicine and suddenly realizes that she does?

4 Here are some situations in which you might use one of the following idiomatic expressions. See if you can match them up. In some cases, more than one expression will fit, so be sure to find all the possibilities and then choose the most likely.

a Your friend is making fun of you.

b You want to go out tonight with your friend, but she can't make it.

c You're in awful pain, and every part of your body seems to hurt.

d Someone has just said something really stupid.

e You're trying to concentrate, but someone is making too much noise.

f You've made a mistake.
g Your junior colleague has just said something you disagree with.
h Your boss has just said something you disagree with.
i Your mother is panicking about your health.
j You didn't hear properly what your younger brother just said.

착각했어요   전신이 다 아프군요
놀리지 마세요   그렇지 않아요
시끄러워요   아닌 것 같아요
걱정하지 마세요   재수 없네요
뭐라구요?   안 되겠네요

5 This exercise is designed to help you practise the -nŭnde pattern. For each question we give you one of two clauses in which the first one always ends in -nŭnde. Your task is to make up an appropriate clause which fits with the one we have given you to make a complete sentence.

a Bŏsu-ga o-nŭnde _____
b _____ -(nŭ)nde an kayo.
c I-osh-i pissa-nde _____(os: *clothes*)
d Yŏngguk taesagwan-e ka-nŭnde _____
e Kŭ-saram cho(h)-ŭnde _____

6 Choose the best word from those given here to fit in the gaps in the sentences. More than one might be possible, so choose the best option.

kŭ'rŏch'iman   kedaga   kŭrŏnde
kŭ'rŏn   kŭlsseyo   kŭrigo

a Him-i hana-do ŏpsŏyo. ____ chŏnshin-i ta ap'ayo.
b Kach'i shyop'ing kalkkayo? ____. Tarun te-e ka-giro haennnundeyo.
c Sangmin-ssi-nŭ'n nongdam mani haeyo. ____ chaemi ŏpsŏyo.
d Pulguksa-e ka-giro haessŏyo. ____ mot kayo.
e Pak sŏnsaengnim hakkyo-e kaseyo. ____ Kim sŏnsaengnim-do kaseyo.

7 Put the following sentences into the long negative form.

a 고기를 좋아해요.   d 이 사과가 싱싱해요.
b 지금 못 가요.   e 버스 못 타요.
c 주문해요.

8 Ch'olho is in bed sick, with the following symptoms. Can you describe them?

review

Introduction

This unit is designed to give you the opportunity to soak up all the things you have learnt already and to give you more practice both with practical language use, and with the grammar patterns. In addition, the unit has another important section which you must work through carefully – it describes all the common types of Korean verb stems and the way in which the endings are put on them. It is very important to master this, as you need to be comfortable putting different verb endings onto the different types of verb stem in order to progress quickly with your Korean studies. You should use this section to work through the grammar points, as you normally would, but you will also probably want to keep coming back to it for reference.

The unit is a further opportunity for you to revise both the practical topics we've gone through so far (finding your way, ordering food, and so on), and to check you are happy with all the major grammar points. If you find there are some topics which you are not so comfortable with, make sure you go back to the relevant lesson and cover them again.

Topic revision

First of all, topic revision. Here is a list of the topics you have covered so far. Make sure that you know the basic words and phrases that you would need for each of them.

- meeting, identifying and introducing people
- finding out what other people are up to: where they are going and why
- buying drinks and going out for entertainment

- making simple phone calls and arranging to meet people
- discussing food and ordering food and drink in a restaurant
- shopping and money
- finding your way around
- catching the right bus
- planning your free time
- feeling ill

Korean verbs

You have been learning the stems of Korean verbs and you have learnt about the way in which endings are put onto these stems to give particular meanings. You have learnt about vowel stems to which the particle -yo is added to give the polite style; you have learnt about consonant stems to which you add either -ŏyo or -ayo to give the polite style. However, each of these two types of verb stem – consonant and vowel – can be broken down into further categories (one of these you have seen already – stems that end in -i). Each of these sub-categories has certain peculiarities which affect the way in which verb endings are added. We are now going to take you through each of the main types of verb stem in Korean, to show you how the endings are added. Some of this will be revision, but much will be new. Many of the verb stems we teach you are also new, and these may occur in the exercises from now on. They are all common verbs, and you should learn them.

Consonant stems

- Most stems which end in consonants take the polite style endings -ŏyo or -ayo, depending on whether or not the last vowel of the stem was an o or an a. Verb endings like -ko and -jiman attach straight to the consonant base. Endings like -(ŭ)lkkayo and -(ŭ)pshida attach the longer form (with the ŭ) to the verb stem. Here are some examples:

mŏk-	eat	mŏgŏyo	mŏk-jiman	mŏg-ŭlkkayo
anj-	sit	anjayo	ant-jiman	anj-ŭlkkayo
pat-	receive	padayo	pat-jiman	pad-ŭlkkayo
cho(h)-	is good	choayo	cho-ch'iman	cho-ŭlkkayo
ilk-	read	ilgŏyo	ilk-jiman	ilg-ŭlkkayo

- Certain Korean verb stems which end in l change the l to a t before endings that begin with a consonant (like -ko and -jiman). The only very common verb that does this is:

tul-   *listen,*   turoyo   *tut-jiman*   tur-ŭlkkayo
          hear

- Some verbs whose stem ends in p change the p to a w before adding the polite ending -oyo. The p remains in endings which begin with consonants (-ko and -jiman), but changes to the letter u before endings with two forms like -(u)lkkayo and -(u)pshida. The shorter form (without the -u-) is then added:

tŏp-	*is hot*	tŏwoyo	tŏp-ko	tŏu-lkkayo
ŏryŏp-	*is difficult*	ŏryŏwoyo	ŏryŏp-ko	ŏryŏu-lkkayo
ch'up-	*is cold*	ch'uwoyo	ch'wup-ko	ch'uu-lkkayo
kakkap-	*is near*	kakkawoyo	kakkap-ko	kakkau-lkkayo
maep-	*is spicy*	maewoyo	maep-ko	maeu-lkkayo

- Perhaps the most confusing category is the last, the l-irregular verbs. These all end in l, but the l disappears before all endings that have two forms (-(u)pshida, -(u)lkkayo and so on), that is, the last column of our table. The shorter endings (without the -u) are then added.

sal-	*live*	sarayo	sal-go	sa-lkkayo
nol-	*have fun, play*	norayo	nol-go	no-lkkayo
al-	*know*	arayo	al-go	a-lkkayo
p'al-	*sell*	p'arayo	p'al-go	p'a-lkkayo
mŏl-	*is far*	mŏrŏyo	mŏl-go	mŏ-lkkayo

Vowel stems

You will find that all the vowel bases are regular in the final two columns. The only difficulty is in the formation of the polite style.

- Most vowel bases add the ending -yo directly to the stem to form the polite style. Endings like -ko and -jiman are added straight to the stem; endings with two forms (-ulkkayo and -lkkayo; -upshida and -pshida) add the shorter form straight to the stem since the stem ends in a vowel (note ha- has an irregular polite style form):

ka-	*goes*	kayo	ka-go	ka-lkkayo
cha-	*sleep*	chayo	cha-go	cha-lkkayo
ttŏna-	*leave*	ttŏnayo	ttŏna-go	ttŏna-lkkayo
irŏna-	*get up*	irŏnayo	irŏna-go	irŏna-lkkayo
kugyŏng	*view,*	kugyŏng	kugyŏng	kwugyŏng
ha-	*sight-see*	haeyo	ha-go	ha-lkkayo
kongbu	*study*	kongbu	kongbu	kongbwu
ha-		haeyo	ha-go	ha-lkkayo

The verbs **o-** (*come*) and **po-** (*look or watch*) are regular apart from their polite forms **wayo** and **pwayo**. The stem **toe-** (*become, is all right*) also has an irregular polite style **twaeyo**.

- Stems that end in **-i** change the i to **yŏ** before the polite style yo is added. Everything else is as you would expect. Do remember, however, that some verb ending patterns are based on the polite style minus the -yo ending. For example, there is an ending -sŏ which attaches to the polite style minus the yo. In this case, the stem **mashi-** would be **mashyŏsŏ**, since it is based on the polite style (**mashyŏyo**) minus the yo, plus sŏ:

| mashi- | *drink* | mashyŏyo | mashi-go | mashi-lkkayo |
| karŭch'i- | *teach* | karŭch'yŏyo | karuch'i-go | karuch'i-lkkayo |

An exception is the verb stem **shwi-** (*rest*) which keeps the i in the polite style before adding **ŏyo**.

- Stems that end in the vowel **ŭ** delete this **ŭ** before adding the polite style ending as you would for a consonant base (either -**ŏyo** or -**ayo**):

ssŭ-	*use; write*	ssŏyo	ssŭ-go	ssŭ-lkkayo
ap'ŭ-	*hurts*	ap'ayo	ap'ŭ-go	ap'ŭ-lkkayo
pappŭ-	*is busy*	pappayo	pappŭ-go	pappŭ-lkkayo

Note, however, that verb stems which end in **lŭ** not only delete the **ŭ**, but add another **l** before the polite style ending -**ŏyo** or -**ayo**. Everything else is regular:

pparŭ-	*is fast*	ppallayo	pparŭ-go	pparŭ-lkkayo
morŭ-	*not know*	mollayo	morŭ-go	morŭ-lkkayo
purŭ-	*sing, call*	pullŏyo	purŭ-go	purŭ-lkkayo

- Bases that end in **u** change the **u** to **wo** before the polite
  style -yo is added. **Chu-** is generally not shortened like this,
  however, and has the polite form **chwoyo**:

paeu-	*study*	paewoyo	paeu-go	paeu-lkkayo
p'iu-	*smoke*	p'iwoyo	p'iu-go	p'iu-lkkayo
chu-	*give*	chuŏyo	chu-go	chu-lkkayo
		(or chwoyo)		

Practice

1 Translate the following sentences into English. Most of
  them should look familiar, as they are based closely on
  sentences you have met in the dialogues of units 1 to 6.

  a Kŭrŏm, kach'i kayo.
  b Onŭl chŏmshim-e shigan-i issŏyo?
  c Chinccha oraeganman-ieyo.
  d Chŏ-nun ilbon mal sŏnsaengnim-i anieyo.
  e Choesong hamnida. Chakkak haessŏyo.
  f Taŭm wolyoir-un ama koench'an-ulkŏeyo.
  g Chŏ-do Sŏwul saram-i ani-rasŏ chal morugessŏyo.
  h Chŏnshin-i ta ap'u-gunyo. An ap'un te-ga issŏyo?
  i Yŏngguk ton-ul chungguk ton-uro pakku-go ship'ŏyo.
  j Kŭrigo chŏ-nun naengmyŏn-do mŏk-ko ship'ŏyo.
  k Marŭn anju-hago p'ajŏn chuseyo.
  l Han sangja-e iman won-e kajyŏ-gaseyo.

2 Telling the time in Korean is easy. To ask what time it is,
  you say **myŏ-shi-eyo?** Literally this means *how many hours
  is it?* To ask at what time something happens you would say
  either **myŏ-shi-e hakkyo-e kayo?** or **ŏnje hakkyo-e kayo?**
  (Note the word **myŏ** is spelt **myŏch'**, but in normal speech
  the ch' is not pronounced).

  The hours are counted by the pure Korean numbers, and
  the minutes by Sino-Korean numbers. *9 o'clock* is **ahop-shi**;
  2 o'clock is **tu-shi**; *3.35* is **se-shi samshipo-bun**; *12.02* is
  yoldu-shi i-bun. You can say *at* a certain time with the
  particle -e. Thus, *at 2.40* is **tu-shi saship-pun-e** and so on.
  You can say half past with the word **pan**. *Half past one* is
  han-shi pan.

Answer the question **myŏ-shi-eyo** for each of the following.

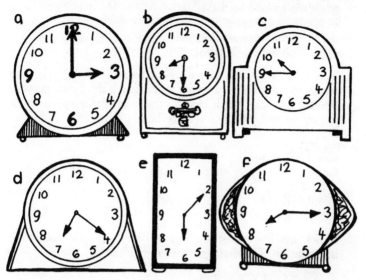

3 Give the polite style, the **-ko** form and the **-upshida** form of the following verbs.

   a ha-   d pappŭ-
   b tat- (*shut*) e umjigi- (*move*)
   c p'al-

   Check your answers carefully with the information about verbs that we have given you.

4 You are planning a trip away with your friend. Make up responses to his questions.

    a Ŏdi ka-lkkayo?
    b Mwo ha-rŏ kŏgi kayo?
    c Ŏnje ka-lkkayo?
    d Myŏ-shi-e manna-lkkayo?
    e Ŏdi-sŏ manna-lkkayo?

5 You go to a restaurant with your two friends. One of you
  wants to eat **pulgogi**, another **kalbi**, and a third **naengmyŏn**.
  Write a dialogue which includes the following questions from
  the waiter and your answers to them. (You decide to have a
  beer each).

  Can I help you?
  Can you eat spicy food? (literally, do you eat well spicy
    food?)
  Would you like anything to drink?
  Mul-do tŭrilkkayo?

6 Make up five short dialogues based on the following
  information. The dialogue pattern is like this:

    a Where are you going?
    b (*answer*)
    a What are you going to buy/do/drink/eat there?
    b (*answer*)

  Here is the information you need for the answers:

a	Kage	ojingŏ	d	Chip	cha-
b	Hakkyo	yagu	e	Shijang	kwail
c	Shiktang	pulgogi			

7 Here is a typical day for Mr Pak. Answer the questions that
  follow.

    7.30   *get up*
    9.00   *shopping*
   10.00   *meet Mr Lee's wife at Hilton Hotel*
    1.00   *lunch at Chinese restaurant*
    2.00   *doctor's appointment*
    6.00   *home for meal*
    7.30   *cinema*
  11.00   *bed*

    a 박선생님은 몇시에 일어나요?
    b 점심 때는 뭘 먹어요?
    c 밤에는 어디 가요?
    d 몇시에 자요?

8 Read the following questions and answer each one negatively with a full sentence (*no, I'm not* or *no, I don't*). Try to use the long negative pattern for one or two of the questions. Then make up another sentence saying what you do do instead.

a Ch'ukku choa haeyo?
b Maeun kŏ chal mŏgŏyo?
c Tellebijyŏn-ul mani pwayo?
d Norae-rul chal pullŏyo?
e Chunggung mal paewŏyo?

9 Look at the following street plan and answer the questions with full Korean sentences.

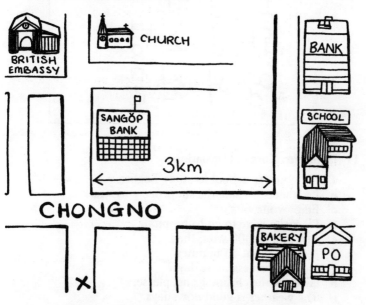

a Kyohoe-esŏ yŏngguk taesagwan-un mŏrŏyo?
b I-kunch'ŏ-e hanguk oehwan ŭnhaeng-i issŏyo?
c Hakkyo-ga ŏdi-eyo?
d Hakkyo-ga kakkawŏyo?
e Uchegug-un taesagwan-poda tŏ mŏrŏyo?
f Hakkyo-e ka-myŏn shigan mani kŏllyŏyo?
g Uchegug-i ŏdi-eyo?

kyohoe	*church*
hakkyo	*school*
chegwa	*bakery*

10 Jaemin has gone shopping. Have a look at his shopping list.
How would he ask the shopkeeper for the things on the list?
What might he say if the apples are too expensive? How
would he ask the total cost?

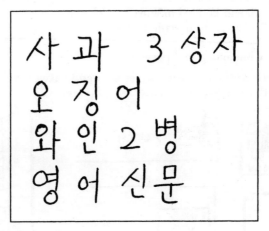

11 English to Korean translation.

  a I'm going to school to study English too.
  b Let's meet outside the shop. See you later!
  c Enjoy your meal.
  d I'll really have to go to hospital.
  e Just pay 15,000 won, then.
  f It takes about 15 minutes.
  g How's business these days?
  h Give me the cheapest one, please.
  i The weather is good nowadays.
  j I came to meet Mr Pak from the Korean embassy.
  k I can't eat spicy things.
  l Does the bus for the post office stop at this stop?

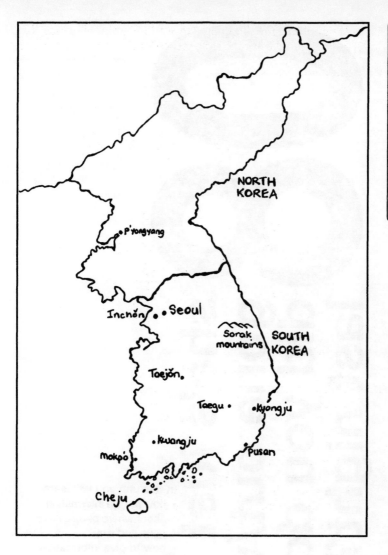

08

she's just gone out/what did you do last night?

In this unit you will learn
- how to give information about where people have gone and why
- how to give information about what happened in the past
- several important verb and clause endings
- one way of saying 'because'
- a way of asking for something to be done for your benefit

▶ She's just gone out

Jaemok rings up his girlfriend Chŏngmin to cancel a date with her, only to find that she'd already gone out for the evening with someone else!

윤선생	여보세요?
재목	여보세요. 정민씨 좀 바꿔주세요.
윤선생	네. 잠깐만 기다리세요.

A little while later.

	미안합니다. 조금 전까지 있었는데, 방금 나갔어요.
재목	혹시 어디 갔는지 아세요?
윤선생	잘 모르겠어요. 잠깐만 기다려 보세요. 우리 집사람이 아마 알고 있을거예요.
부인	정민씨 오늘 남자 친구랑 영화 보러 나갔어요.
재목	그래요? 이상하네. 오늘 저녁에 나하고 만나기로 했는데.
부인	저런, 정민씨는 다른 남자랑 데이트 하러 갔는데... 아마 밤 늦게까지 안 들어올거예요.
재목	그럼 잘 됐네요. 오늘 저녁 약속을 취소하려고 전화했거든요. 오늘 저한테 바쁜 일이 생겼어요.
부인	아, 그래요. 잘됐네요. 정민씨한테 전할 말이 있으세요?
재목	아니요, 없어요. 안녕히 계세요.

Mr Yun	Yŏboseyo?
Jaemok	Yŏboseyo. Chŏngmin-ssi chom pakkwo-juseyo.
Mr Yun	Ne. Chamkkan-man kidariseyo.

A little while later.

	Mian hamnida. chogŭm chŏn-kkaji issŏn-nŭnde, panggŭm nagassŏyo.
Jaemok	Hokshi ŏdi kannunji aseyo?
Mr Yun	Chal morŭgessŏyo. Chamkkan-man kidaryŏ-boseyo. Uri chipsaram-i ama al-go iss-ŭlkŏeyo.
Mrs Yun	Chŏngmin-ssi onul namja ch'ingu-rang yŏnghwa po-rŏ nagassŏyo.
Jaemok	Kŭraeyo? Isang ha-ne. Onŭl chŏnyŏg-e na-hago manna-giro haennŭnde ...

Mrs Yun	Chŏrŏn, Chŏngmin-ssi-nun tarun namja-rang deit'u ha-rŏ kannŭnde. . . .
	Ama pam nŭtke-kkaji an torao-lkŏeyo.
Jaemok	Kŭrŏm chal toenneyo. Onŭl chŏnyŏk yaksog-ul chwiso ha-ryŏgo chŏnhwa haet-kŏdunyo.
	Onŭl chŏ-hant'e pappun ir-i saenggyŏssŏyo.
Mrs Yun	A, kŭraeyo. Chal toenneyo.
	Chŏngmin-ssi-hant'e chŏn hal mar-i issuseyo?
Jaemok	Aniyo, ŏpsŏyo.
	Annyŏnghi kyeseyo.

Phrases and expressions

ŏdi kannŭnji aseyo?	*do you know where (she) has gone?*
ama al-go issŭ-lkŏeyo	*will perhaps know*
isang ha-ne	*(it is) strange!*
chŏrŏn	*oh dear!, Oh no!*
chal twoenneyo.	*it's turned out well, it's all for the better*
. . . hant'e chŏn hal	*do you have a message for . . . ?*
mar-i issuseyo?	

pakku- 바꾸–	*change*
chogŭm chŏn 조금 전	*a little while ago*
chogŭm 조금	*a little, a bit*
chŏn 전	*before*
chŏn-e 전에	*previously*
-kkaji –까지	*until*
-(ŏ)ss- –었	*(used to form the past tense, see note 4)*
panggŭm 방금	*just now*
naga- 나가–	*go out*
hokshi 혹시	*maybe, perhaps, possibly*
onŭl 오늘	*today*
namja ch'ingu 남자 친구	*boyfriend*
-(i)rang –(이)랑	*with (-irang after consonants)*
yŏnghwa 영화	*film, movie*
isang ha- 이상하–	*is strange, bizzare*
chŏnyŏk 저녁	*evening, supper*
deit'u ha- 데이트하–	*to date*
pam 밤	*night*
nŭtke 늦게	*late*
torao- 돌아오–	*come back, return*
yaksok 약속	*appointment*

chwiso ha- 취소하–	*cancel*	
-ryŏgo –려고	*with the intention of* (see note 5)	
chŏnhwa ha- 전화하–	*telephone* (verb stem)	
pappŭn 바쁜	*busy*	
-kŏdŭnyo –거든요	(see note 6)	
saenggi- 생기–	*to occur, happen, take place*	
chŏn ha- 전하–	*communicate*	

Grammar

1 Continuous states

In English we have a present continuous tense, used in sentences like *I am going, he is sitting.* This continuous tense is indicated by the ending *-ing.* In English we use the continuous tense fairly frequently, whereas in Korean the continuous form is used only for special emphasis, to stress that something is going on continuously. This means that when in English you meet a verb form that ends in *-ing,* you must not automatically assume that you should translate it by a Korean continuous form; in most cases you should probably not do so.

Let's take an example to illustrate this. In English it is quite common to say a sentence like *I'm going home.* This uses the continuous tense. It would be very unusual to translate this by the Korean continuous tense, and you would only do so if you particularly wanted to stress the process or the ongoing action of your going home. You would be far more likely to use the normal Korean present tense form **na-nun chib-e kayo.**

There are certain circumstances in which the Korean continuous form is used however, and you should note these. It is often used with the verb *to know.* The phrase **al-go issŏyo** literally means *I am knowing,* and the Korean emphasis is *I am in a state of knowing that,* and sometimes has the force *I already know that (you didn't need to tell me).* You meet that form in this unit.

Other common uses are to stress what you are in the process of doing right now. Thus, as answers to the question **mwol haeyo?** (*what are you doing?*), you might say:

chaek ilg-ŏyo
chaek ilk-ko issŏyo

They both mean *I'm reading a book*, but the second one stresses that you are in the process of reading the book even as you speak, that is what you are busy with and in the middle of doing.

Generally you should only use the present continuous tense when you are sure that you want to stress that particular meaning of continuous action.

To make the form, take the verb stem and add -ko iss-, for example, in the polite style, -ko issŏyo. You will not normally find negatives in the continuous pattern; you would simply use a normal verb form, for example **an ilgŏyo** (*I'm not reading*).

2 Probabilities

You will remember that we said in the last unit that the probable future form -ŭlkŏeyo can also be used simply to mean 'probably'. You have an example in this dialogue in the phrase **ama al-go issŭlkŏeyo** (*my wife will probably know, perhaps my wife will know*). Notice that this isn't a proper future tense; it is just a way of expressing probability.

3 Having a go at . . .

You have already learned the verb **kabo-**, which we told you meant 'go and see'. It is not really one verb at all, however, but a compound of the verb ka- (*go*) and the verb po- (*see*). You can make other compound verbs by adding the verb po- to another verb. You must take the other verb in the polite style -yo form, knock off the -yo, and then add on the verb po-. Here are some examples:

stem	polite	minus -yo	plus po-	meaning
ka-	kayo	ka-	ka-bo-	go and see
mŏk-	mŏgŏyo	mŏgŏ-	mŏgŏ-bo-	eat and see have a go at eating
kidari-	kidaryŏyo	kidaryŏ-	kidaryŏ-bo-	wait and see try waiting

The two most common uses for this pattern are as follows:

- It is often used in the polite honorific style to mean *please have a go at* (verb) *and see, please try out* (verb)*ing*. For example, **kidaryŏ-boseyo** in this lesson means *please wait and see, please try waiting, please have a go at waiting*.

- In the past tense it meas *have you tried* (verb)*ing?*, *have you had a go at* (verb)*ing?*, e.g. t'enisu-rul (*tennis*) hae-bwassŏyo? (*have you ever played tennis? have you ever tried playing tennis?*) (how to make the past tense is in the following point).

4 The past tense

The past tense in Korean is used very similarly to the past tense in English to say what someone did or was doing in the past. You just need to learn how to form it and, fortunately, that is fairly easy too. Take the verb you want in the polite style (e.g. mŏgŏyo, arayo, kidaryŏyo, anjayo), take the -yo off the end and add -ss. What you now have is the past stem (previously you have been learning the present stem of verbs). This past stem can then be made into a verb form in the normal way, by adding, for example, the polite style ending -ŏyo:

stem	polite	minus -yo	plus -ss	polite past
mŏk-	mŏgŏyo	mŏgŏ	mŏgŏss-	mŏgŏssŏyo
a-l-	arayo	ara	arass-	arassŏyo
kidari-	kidaryŏyo	kidaryŏ	kidaryŏss-	kidaryŏssŏyo
anj-	anjayo	anja	anjass-	anjassŏyo

Remember that you can put all sorts of endings on the past base, just as you can on the normal verb bases that you have learned previously. Sometimes the forms you make will look a bit odd because of the rules of sound change – the -ss- might disappear into another sound, but it will still be there in Korean writing. For example, with the past base mŏgŏss- you could made: mŏgŏssŏyo, mŏgŏt-kuna (mŏgŏss- +kuna), mŏgŏt-ko (mŏgŏss- +ko), mŏgŏn-neyo (mŏgŏss- +neyo), etc.

Remember that the forms haennŭnde and kannŭnde are also past tense forms in which the -ss- of the past tense has become n by the rules of sound change. These two forms are thus the past bases haess- and kass- with the imminent elaboration -nŭnde added to them. This past tense -nŭnde form is very common in Korean.

To make honorific past forms, take the present verb base, and add -shyŏss- to give you the honorific past base (if the stem ends in a vowel), or -ŭshyŏss- (if the stem ends in a consonant). This can then be made into, for example, anjŭshyŏssŏyo (*you (honorific) sat down*), from the honorific past base anjŭshyŏss-.

It looks difficult at first, but with the practice in the exercises, you should soon crack it. Everything is regular, you just have to remember the right rules and apply them.

5 With the intention of . . .

Very early in this course you learnt how to say sentences such as **ppang sa-rŏ shinae-e kayo** (*I'm going to the city centre to buy bread*). The constructions were made by adding -rŏ to the verb in the first clause, to mean *in order to*. That construction can only be used with the two verbs *go* and *come* at the end of the sentence, however. This lesson introduces you to a way to say a similar thing, *in order to, with the intention of*, which can be used with other verbs as well. You add -(ŭ)ryŏgo to the stem of the verb of the first clause (-uryŏgo if the stem ends in a consonant). Here is a reminder of the example of the construction which you saw in the dialogue: **Ch'wiso ha-ryŏgo chŏnhwa haessŏyo** (*I'm calling* (literally, *I have called*) *with the intention of cancelling (in order to cancel)*.

Here are some more examples:

Yŏngŏ paeu-ryŏgo yŏngŏ ch'aek sassŏyo
(I) bought an English language book with the intention of learning English

Ch'aek ilg-ŭryŏgo tosŏgwan-e kayo
(I) am going to the library in order to read books

Kyŏr(h)on ha-ryŏgo ton-ul pŏrŏssŏyo
I earned some money with the intention of getting married

yŏngŏ 영어	English language	
hangugŏ 한국어	Korean language	
-ŏ –어	language	
kyŏrhon ha- 결혼하–	get married	
pŏ-l- 벌–	earn	

6 -kŏdŭnyo

The verb ending -kŏdŭnyo is a common form in colloquial speech, although it is a bit difficult to pin down precisely what it means in English.

The pattern is used when you are adding an explanation to something that you have already said. Look carefully at the last sentence of Jaemok in the dialogue. He has just said 'it's turned out well then', and then he goes on to say another sentence which ends in -kŏdŭnyo. This sentence explains the reason why he has just said that it turned out well – because he was ringing to cancel the date in any case. In a way, therefore, -kŏdŭnyo means something like *it's because . . . , you see*, when you add an explanation to something. But you must have already said something else which the -kŏdŭnyo phrase is an explanation of! Work through the questions in the exercise carefully, thinking through why the -kŏdŭnyo form has been used in each case. If you can, try to mimic Koreans in the way they use this pattern. That's the best way to make sure you are using it properly.

The ending -kŏdŭnyo is added simply to the verb stem, either a present or a past stem, although the past is probably a bit more common.

If you are able to use it correctly, Koreans will be very impressed as it really does make your speech sound colloquial.

7 Saying 'and then' and 'because'

Along with the past tense, this grammar note is probably the most crucial part of this unit. It introduces you to a form which is used all the time in spoken and written Korean.

First, we will look at how to form it, and afterwards at what it means. It is used to end the first clause of a two clause construction, and you take off the -yo of the polite style present of the verb and add -sŏ. For example:

stem	*polite*	*minus* -yo	-sŏ *form*
mŏk-	mŏgŏyo	mŏgŏ	mŏgŏ-sŏ
mashi-	mashyŏyo	mashyŏ	mashyŏsŏ

The -sŏ pattern has two meanings. In both cases, imagine a sentence of the form (clause A)-sŏ (clause B).

• It can mean 'after having done A, then B', or 'A and then B', where there is a close sequential link between the two clauses (usually a link of time: *after A, then B*). An example would be: **hakkyo-e ka-sŏ kongbu halkŏeyo**, which could be translated as follows:

I'll go to school and then study
After going to school, I will study

Here are some more examples:

Ch'ingu-rul manna-sŏ sul chib-e kayo
I meet (my) friend and then (we) go to the pub

Hangug-e ka-sŏ hanguk ch'ingu-rul mannassŏyo
I went to Korea, and then I met a Korean friend

- It can mean 'because A, then B', and this is perhaps the meaning which you will use (and meet) most frequently. A good example would be:

Pi-ga wa-sŏ hakkyo-e mot kayo
It's raining, so I can't go to school
I can't go to school because it's raining

Here are some more examples:

Onŭl pappŭn ir-i saenggyŏ-sŏ yaksog-ul mot chik'yŏyo
Something has come up today, so I cannot keep the
appointment (lit. a busy matter has come up)

Mŏri-ga ap'a-sŏ sul-ul mot masyŏyo
My head hurts, so I cannot drink

▶ What did you do last night?

Yongt'ae has a new girlfriend, and his friend T'aegyu appears rather inquisitive – what's her name, where does she work, how did they meet, what do they do together?

용태 태규씨 안녕하세요?
태규 안녕하세요.
요즘 재미가 어떠세요?
용태 요즘 바빠요.
여자 친구가 생겨서 더 바빠요.
태규 그런 줄 알았어요.
여자 친구 이름이 뭐에요?
용태 김 정민이에요.
작년에 서울 대학교를 졸업하고 지금은 현대
자동차에서 일하고 있어요.
태규 어떻게 만났어요?
용태 친구가 소개해 주었어요.
처음에는 그렇게 마음에 들지 않았는데, 한 달
후에 파티에서 우연히 다시 만났어요.
그때부터 자주 만나기 시작했어요.
태규 지금은 거의 매일 만나서 데이트 하지요?
용태 그런 편이에요.

태규	어제 밤에도 내가 전화 했는데 없었어요.
	어제 밤에 어디 갔었어요?
용태	어제 밤이요?
	기억이 안나요. 아마 어딘가 갔을거예요.
태규	기억이 안나요? 그렇게 술을 많이 마셨어요?
용태	누가 술을 마셔요?
	태규씨가 오히려 매일 술만 마시잖아요?
태규	어쨌든 어제 어디 갔었어요?
용태	노래방에 갔었어요.
	내 여자 친구는 노래방을 아주 좋아해요.
태규	노래방에서 나와서 어디 갔었어요?
용태	탁구를 좀 쳤어요.
태규	그게 다에요? 솔직히 말해보세요.
용태	정말이에요. 아무 일도 없었어요.

Yongt'ae	Taegyu-ssi annyŏng haseyo?
T'aegyu	Annyŏng haseyo.
	Yojŭm chaemi-ga ŏttŏseyo?
Yongt'ae	Yojŭm pappayo. Yŏja ch'ingu-ga saenggyŏ-sŏ tŏ pappayo.
T'aegyu	Kurŏn-jul arassŏyo. Yŏja ch'ingu irum-i mwo-eyo?
Yongt'ae	Kim Chŏngmin-ieyo.
	Changnyŏn-e sŏul taehakkyo-rul chorŏpha-go chigŭm-un Hyŏndae chadongch'a-esŏ ilha-go issŏyo.
T'aegyu	Ŏttŏk'e mannassŏyo?
Yongt'ae	Ch'ingu-ga sogae hae-juŏssŏyo.
	Ch'ŏum-enun kurŏk'e maum-e tul-ji anannŭnde, han tal hu-e p'at'i-esŏ uyŏnhi tashi mannassŏyo.
	Ku-ttae-but'ŏ chaju manna-gi shijak haessŏyo.
T'aegyu	Chigŭm-un kŏuy maeil manna-sŏ deit'u hajiyo?
Yongt'ae	Kŭrŏn p'yŏn-ieyo.
T'aegyu	Ŏje pam-edo nae-ga chŏnhwa haennunde ŏpsŏssŏyo.
	Ŏje pam-e ŏdi kassŏssŏyo?
Yongt'ae	Ŏje pam-iyo?
	Kiŏg-i an nayo. Ama ŏdinga kassul kŏeyo.
T'aegyu	Kiŏg-i an nayo? Kurŏk'e sul-ul mani mashyŏssŏyo?
Yongt'ae	Nuga sul-ul mashyŏyo?
	Taegyu-ssi-ga ohiryŏ maeil sul-man mashijanayo?
T'aegyu	Ŏcchaettun ŏje ŏdi kassŏssyo?
Yongt'ae	Noraebang-e kassŏssŏyo.
	Nae yŏja ch'ingu-nun noraebang-ul aju choa haeyo.
T'aegyu	Noraebang-esŏ nawa-sŏ ŏdi kassŏssŏyo?
Yongt'ae	T'akku-rul chom ch'yŏssŏyo.
T'aegyu	Ku-ge ta-eyo? Solchikhi mal hae-boseyo.
Yongt'ae	Chŏngmal-ieyo. Amu il-do ŏpsŏssŏyo.

Phrases and expressions

yojŭm chaemi-ga ŏttŏseyo?	*how are you doing?*
	how are things these days?
kŭrŏn-jul arassŏyo	*I thought so*
maŭm-e tŭl-ji anayo	*I don't like (her)* (maum-e
	an turoyo)
. . . maŭm-e tŭ-l-	*(I) like . . .*
kŭrŏn p'yŏn-ieyo	*(we) tend to be so/do so (it's*
	usually like that, etc.)
kiŏg-i an nayo	*I don't remember*
ama ŏdinga kassŭl kŏeyo	*I expect (we) went somewhere*
	or other; maybe . . .
solchikhi mal hae-boseyo	*tell me the truth!*

yojŭm 요즘	*nowadays*
pappu- 바쁘–	*is busy*
yŏja ch'ingu 여자 친구	*girlfriend*
irŭm 이름	*name*
changnyŏn 작년	*last year*
taehakkyo 대학교	*university*
chorŏpha- 졸업하–	*graduate (verb stem)*
Hyŏndae chadongch'a	*Hyundai car (company)*
현대 자동차	
chadongch'a 자동차	*car*
ch'a 차	*car* (short form)
il ha- 일하–	*work (verb stem)*
sogaeha- 소개하–	*to introduce*
ŏttŏk'e 어떻게	*how?*
ch'ŏum 처음	*at first*
kŭrŏk'e 그렇게	*like that* (here: *particularly*)
irŏk'e 이렇게	*like this*
maŭm 마음	*mind, heart*
tal 달	*month*
hu 후	*after*
p'at'i 파티	*party*
uyŏnhi 우연히	*by chance, coincidentally*
tashi 다시	*again*
ttae 때	*time*
-put'ŏ –부터	*from*
chaju 자주	*often, frequently*
shijak ha- 시작하–	*begin, start*
kŏŭy 거의	*nearly, almost*

maeil 매일		*everyday*
kiŏk 기억		*memory*
ŏdinga 어딘가		*somewhere or other*
nuga 누가		*who? (subject form)*
ohiryŏ 오히려		*rather, on the contrary*
ŏcchaettŭn 어쨌든		*anyway*
noraebang 노래방		*'karaoke' singing room*
nae 내		*my*
che 제		*my (humble form)*
t'akku 탁구		*table tennis*
ch'i- 치–		*to play (tennis, table tennis etc.)*
solchikhi 솔직히		*frankly, honestly*

Grammar

1 For my benefit

You have learnt how to ask people to do things by using polite requests ending in -seyo. The construction you are about to learn enables you to make such requests even more polite, and to stress that they are for your benefit. Suppose you want to say 'please do it for me, please do it (for my benefit)'. Previously you would have said **haseyo**. Instead, take the polite style of the verb (**haeyo**), knock off the -yo (**hae-**), and add the verb stem **chu-** (*give*) and then add the verb ending you want. Usually you will still want to use the polite request ending, so you would make the form **hae + chu + seyo**, **hae-juseyo** (*please do it for me*). The literal meaning of the construction is *please do it and give* and you can see how the verbs make this meaning when they are put together, and imply that you are asking for something to be done for your benefit.

This is quite a common pattern. Here are a couple of examples:

Onŭl chŏmshim chom sa-juseyo?
Please will you buy my lunch for me today?

I-usan chom pillyŏ-juseyo
Please lend me your (this) umbrella

Hangung mal nŏmu ŏryŏwŏyo. Shwipke karŭch'yŏ-juseyo
Korean is so difficult (or too difficult). Please teach it simply for me

usan 우산	*umbrella*
pilli- 빌리–	*borrow*
pillyŏ-ju- 빌려주–	*lend*
shwipke 쉽게	*easily*

2 Beginning to do things

You can say that someone is beginning to do something in Korean by adding -ki shijak ha- to a processive verb stem (a verb of doing). Here are two good examples:

Hakkyo-esŏ ilbon mar-ul kongbu ha-gi shijak haeyo
(We) are beginning to study Japanese at school

Yojum ŏttŏn yŏngguk saram-i hangung mar-ul paeu-gi shijak
    haessŏyo
*Nowadays some English people have begun to learn the
    Korean language*

3 Sentence endings with -jiyo

You can end sentences with the form -jiyo added to any stem. As you can see, it is a bit like the polite style (since it ends in -yo). It means something like *I suppose, you know, I guess*, etc., and it gives your sentences a bit more flavour than the polite style. However, the exact meaning of -jiyo corresponds to a number of English meanings, depending on whether they occur in statements, yes–no questions, or suggestions. It is used when the speaker wants to draw the hearer in to what is being said. The following examples illustrate some of the ways it can be used:

Hangguk saram-ijiyo?	*I suppose you are Korean, aren't you?*
Chŏmshim pŏlssŏ mŏgŏt-jiyo?	*You've eaten lunch already, haven't you?*
Chigŭm chŏmshim mŏk-jiyo	*Let's have lunch now (I suggest we have lunch now)*
Sur-ul choaha-jiyo?	*I guess you like alchohol, don't you?*

4 The double past

Korean has what is known as a double past construction, which is a past tense of a verb formed in the normal way, with an additional -ŏss- added. Thus, **mŏgŏssŏss-** would be the double past base of **mŏk-**.

The precise meaning of the form is a bit more difficult to define and is beyond the scope of this book. It emphasizes the remoteness of a past event and shows that an event occurred and *was completed* in the distant past. What you do need to know about it, however, concerns its use with the two verbs **ka-** and **o-**, 'go' and 'come.' Compare the following two sentences:

Ŏje pam yŏgi wassŏyo	*I came here yesterday*
Ŏje pam yŏgi wassŏssŏyo	*I came here yesterday*

The implication of the first of these might well be that you are still here, you came and you remain. However, the implication of the second is that the action is over, that is, that you came, and that you went again and that it all took place in the past. The same would be true of **kassŏyo** and **kassŏssŏyo**.

This rule is something of a simplification, but it will explain most of the occurrences of the double past that you are likely to need to know about for the time being. Take a close look at the example in the dialogue to see that emphasis: *we came to this restaurant last night* (and, by implication, we left again afterwards). The act of our coming (and going) all took place last night.

Practice

1 Put the following sentences into the past tense.

  a 학교에 가요.
  b 맥주 많이 마셔요.
  c 약속을 못 지켜요.
  d 친구를 만나요.
  e 영화를 보고 싶어요.
  f 도봉산에 갈까 해요.

2 Make the following into polite requests (asking someone to do something for your benefit).

  a Haseyo.
  b *Please go shopping for me.*
  c Chŏmshim saseyo.
  d *Can you phone Mr Kim for me?*
  e *Please buy me some medicine.*
  f Shijak haseyo.

3 Complete the following by filling in the blanks.

오늘 ____ 친구를 만나 ____. ____ 바쁜 일이 ____ 못
만났어요. ____ 취소 ____ 전화 ____. 약속 못 ____.

했어요   그렇지만   하려고   아침에
지켰어요   기로 했어요   생겨서   그러니까

4 Write out the following sentences, and in each case add a
second sentence along the lines suggested in the brackets to
explain what has just been said in the first sentence. This is
practice for the -kŏdŭnyo pattern, and you might want to
look back at the lesson notes for that pattern before you do
the exercise.

a Onŭl hakkyo-e mot kayo   (*head aches*)
b Ilyoillar-e shinae-e mot kayo   (*another appointment*)
c Onŭl pam t'akku mot ch'yŏyo   (*arm (**pal**) has begun to
                                    hurt*)
d Noraebang-e kayo? Na-nun   (*don't like noraebangs*)
   kayo
e Jaemin-ssi mot kayo? Kurŏm   (*I can't go either*)
   chal toenneyo

5 Read the following page from someone's diary and then
answer the questions.

6월 (June)		6월 (June)	
월 6	토니와 점심 약속	월 13	不
화 7		화 14	대구 출장
수 8	회의	수 15	
목 9	회의	목 16	↓
금 10	김 선생 생일 파티	금 17	휴가 시작
토 11	대학 동창회	토 18	집 청소
일 12	집사람하고 쇼핑	일 19	도봉산 등산

	오늘은 6 월 7 일 화요일이에요.
a	이번 토요일에 무슨 약속이 있어요?
b	언제가 김선생의 생일이에요?
c	이번 일요일에 무엇을 하려고 해요?
d	다음 일요일에는 어디 가려고 해요?
e	언제부터 휴가에요?
f	어제는 누구하고 점심을 먹었어요?

6 Translate the following (using verb compounds with **po-** for the English to Korean examples).

  a T'ang mashyǒ-boseyo! (**t'ang**: *spicy soup*)
  b *You should visit Pulguksa one time* (literally, *Please visit . . . !*)
  c Pappǔ-jiman ka-boseyo.
  d T'akku-rul mot ch'yǒ-bwassǒyo? Kurǒm han bǒn hae-boseyo.
  e *Jaemin hasn't come yet? Please (try) waiting a little longer.*

7 Use the following pairs of information to make up Korean sentences, each with two clauses linked by **-sǒ**. The first three have the sense of 'because A, B', the last three are sequential, 'and then'.

  a busy matter has come up   can't go
  b no food in house   go to restaurant
  c business is not good   no money
  d let's go outside   and wait
  e go to Sangmin's   what shall we do?
  f go to city   buy some fruit

8 Translate the following into Korean.

  a I'm ringing to cancel my appointment. Something came up (you see).
  b Sangmin has just gone out to play table tennis.
  c At first I didn't particularly like kimch'i, but I got used to it. (*get used to*: iksuk haeji-)
  d When did you graduate?
  e We met by chance in a bar.
  f That's strange! Chris has come back already.
  g What did you do last night? Tell me the truth.

120
she's just gone out/what
did you do last night?
08

9 Ask your friend if they have tried doing the following things. Make up appropriate answers.

09

we bought him that last year!/ I'm sorry, I really didn't know!

In this unit you will learn
- how to disagree and to apologize
- about buying presents and traffic offences
- another way of saying that you can and can't do something
- more about honorifics
- modifier form of verbs

122

we bought him that last
year!/I'm sorry, I really
didn't know!

09

▶ We bought him that last year!

A husband and wife are deciding what to buy grandfather for his birthday. However, the task is not as easy as it sounds!

부인	내일이 할아버지 생신이에요.
남편	뭐? 벌써?
부인	그래요. 무엇을 사드릴까 결정해야겠어요.
남편	당신이 정할 수 없어요? 나는 바빠요.
부인	항상 내가 결정하잖아요. 이번에는 좀 도와주세요.
남편	좋아요. 잠바를 사 드릴까요?
부인	잠바는 벌써 열 벌이나 갖고 계세요.
	잠바는 더 이상 필요 없어요.
남편	그러면 셔츠는 어떨까요?
부인	셔츠도 더 이상 필요 없어요.
남편	그럼, 책은요?
부인	할아버지는 독서를 싫어하시잖아요?
남편	할머니는 독서를 좋아하시니까 대신 읽으시면 되잖아요.
부인	농담하지 마세요.
	좀 더 좋은 생각을 말해보세요.
남편	우산은 어떨까요?
부인	할아버지는 비 올때 나가지 않으시잖아요.
남편	그럼 양말은?
부인	작년에 사 드렸잖아요.
남편	그럼 새 전기 면도기는 어떨까요?
부인	그건 재작년에 사 드렸잖아요.
	그리고 할아버지는 면도를 잘 안 하세요.
남편	그것 보라구!
	당신은 내 의견을 좋아하지 않잖아요.
	내가 처음 말한대로 당신 혼자 결정하면 되잖아요.

Pwuin	Naeir-i harabŏji saengshin-ieyo.
Namp'yŏn	Mwo? Pŏlssŏ?
Pwuin	Kŭraeyo. Muŏs-ul sa-dŭrilkka kyŏlchŏng hae-yagessŏyo.
Namp'yŏn	Tangshin-i chŏng ha-l su ŏpsŏyo? Na-nun pappayo.
Pwuin	Hangsang nae-ga kyŏlchŏnghajanayo. I-bŏn-enun chom towa-juseyo.
Namp'yŏn	Choayo. Chamba-rul sa-dŭrilkkayo?
Pwuin	Chamba-nun pŏlssŏ yŏl pŏl-ina kat-ko kyeseyo.
	Chamba-nun tŏ isang p'iryo ŏpsŏyo.
Namp'yŏn	Kurŏmyŏn shyŏch'u-nun ŏttŏlkkayo?
Pwuin	Shyŏch'u-do tŏ isang p'iryo ŏpsŏyo.

123

we bought him that last
year/I'm sorry, I really
didn't know!

09

Namp'yŏn	Kurŏm, ch'aeg-ŭn-yo?
Pwuin	Halabŏji-nun toksŏ-rul shirŏ hashi-janayo?
Namp'yŏn	Halmŏni-nun toksŏ-rul choa hashi-nikka taeshin ilgushi-myŏn toe-janayo.
Pwuin	Nongdam ha-ji maseyo.
	Chom tŏ cho-un saenggag-ul mal hae-boseyo.
Namp'yŏn	Usan-un ŏttŏlkkayo?
Pwuin	Harabŏji-nun pi o-l ttae naga-ji anushi-janayo.
Namp'yŏn	Kurŏm yangmal-un?
Pwuin	Changnyŏn-e sa turyŏt-janayo.
Namp'yŏn	Kurŏm sae chŏnggi myŏndogi-nun ŏttŏlkkayo?
Pwuin	Ku-gŏn chaejangnyŏn-e sa turyŏt-janayo.
	Kurigo harabŏji-nun myŏndo-rul chal an haseyo.
Namp'yŏn	Ku-gŏt poragu!
	Tangshin-un nae uygyŏn-ul choaha-ji anch'anayo.
	Nae-ga ch'ŏum-e mal han-daero tangshin honja kyŏlchŏngha-myŏn toe-janayo!

Phrases and expressions

-nun ŏttŏlkkayo?	*how about . . . ?, what do you think about . . . ?*
kŭ-gŏt poragu!	*you see?!*
tangshin-un nae ŭygyŏn-ul choaha-ji anch'anayo	*you don't like my suggestions, you see!*
mal han daero	*as (I) said, like (I) said*

---

namp'yŏn	남편	*husband*
harabŏji	할아버지	*grandfather*
saengshin	생신	*birthday* (honorific form)
saengil	생일	*birthday* (normal form)
muŏs	무엇	*what* (full form of **mwo**)
kyŏljŏng ha-	결정하–	*decide*
tangshin	당신	*you* (often used between husband and wife)
chŏng ha-	정하–	*decide*
towa-ju-	도와주–	*to help*
-(l) su iss-/ŏps-	–(으)ㄹ 수 있/없–	(see note 4: *can/can't*)
pŏn	번	*time* (as in *first time, second time, many times*)
i-bŏn	이번	*this time*
chamba	잠바	*jacket* (*jumper*)
pŏl	벌	(counter for clothes)

124

we bought him that last year/I'm sorry, I really didn't know!

09

katko kyeshi- 갖고 계시–	*have, possess* (for honorific person; polite style: **katko kyeseyo**)
kyeshi- 계시–	*exist* (honorific of **iss-** in its existential *there is/are* meaning)
issŭshi- 있으시–	*have* (honorific of **iss-** in its meaning of possession)
tŏ isang 더 이상	*any more*
p'iryo ŏpsŏyo 필요 없어요	*is not needed*
p'iryo ha- 필요하–	*is needed* (**p'iryo iss-** also exists but is less common)
shyŏch'u 셔츠	*shirt*
toksŏ 독서	*reading*
shirŏ ha- 싫어하–	*to dislike*
halmŏni 할머니	*grandma*
-(ŭ)nikka –(으)니까	*because* (clause ending, added to verb stems)
taeshin 대신	*instead, on behalf of*
saenggak 생각	*idea*
usan 우산	*umbrella*
-(ŭ)l ttae –(으)ㄹ 때	*when*
yangmal 양말	*socks*
chŏnggi myŏndogi 전기 면도기	*electric shaver*
kŭ-gŏn 그건	*that thing* (topic)
chaejangnyŏn 재작년	*the year before last year*
myŏndo(-rul) ha- 면도(를) 하–	*shave*
ŭygyŏn 의견	*suggestion, opinion*
honja 혼자	*alone, on one's own*

Grammar

Note: The verb endings to some of the sentences in this unit (the ones with -sh- and -s- in them) are new, but we won't explain them until after the second dialogue.

1 Doing something for someone else

We learnt in the last unit how to ask someone to do something for your benefit by combining verbs with the verb chu- (*give*), as in sa-juseyo (*please buy it for me*). Now we are going to expand on this to look at how to talk about doing things for other people's benefit, for the benefit of someone else. The

125

we bought him that last year/I'm sorry, I really didn't know!

09

dialogue you have just looked at is all about buying presents for grandad, and there is an implied for 'grandad's benefit' in many of the sentences. Once more you can make a compound verb which means literally 'buy and give', but which in practice means 'buy for him', 'buy for his benefit'.

There are two ways of doing this, and it depends on whether the person for whose benefit you are doing something is esteemed (honorific) or not. Grandad is definitely honorific and this means that instead of making the compound with the verb **chwu-** as you would expect, Korean uses a special verb **turi-** which means *give (to someone honorific)*. Compare the following two sentences, the first one means that you will have to decide what to buy for someone honorific, the second means you will have to decide what to buy for someone of your own or lower status (for example, your child):

Muŏs-ul sa-dŭri-lkka kyŏljŏng hae-yagessŏyo
Muŏs-ul sa-ju-lkka kyŏljŏng hae-yagessŏyo

As you can see, Korean has two different verbs for *give*, depending on who you are giving to.

Here are some more examples using the two verbs for *give*:

Harabŏji-ege ch'aeg-ul ilgŏ-dŭryŏssŏyo
(I) read a book for my grandfather
Ch'ingu-ege ch'aeg-ul ilgŏ-juŏssŏyo
(I) read a book for my friend

Kim sŏnsaengnim-ul kidaryŏ-dŭryŏssŏyo
I waited for Mr Kim
Ch'ingu-rul kidaryŏ-juŏssŏyo
I waited for my friend

2 Wondering, worrying and deciding

In English we make quite a few constructions with the word 'whether', e.g. *I'm wondering whether, I'm worrying whether (or, that), I'm trying to decide whether* . . . Korean makes these kind of sentences by adding -lkka or -ŭlkka to the base of the verb (this is the same ending as -(ŭ)lkkayo? *(shall we?)* without the -yo; you met it also in -(ŭ)lkka haeyo *(I'm thinking of)*). The -(ŭ)lkka pattern is used in the following construction: **Kim sŏnsaengnim ka-lkka.** This would form part of a sentence and it means *whether Mr Kim will go*. It could be used with

126

we bought him that last
year/I'm sorry, I really
didn't know!

09

any of the following verbs: kŏkjŏng ha- (*worry*), kunggum ha-
(*wonder*), kyŏljŏng ha- (*decide*). Here are a couple of example
sentences:

Yŏja ch'ingu-ga yaksog-ul chik'i-lkka kunggumhaeyo
I wonder whether my girlfriend will keep the appointment
Unjŏnsu-ga sul-ul mani mashi-lkka kŏkjŏnghaessŏyo
I was worried that the driver had had a lot to drink

This basic -(ŭ)lkka pattern is also found in a few common
variations.

Sometimes -(ŭ)lkka is followed in colloquial speech by another
word, malkka, to mean *whether* or *not*, as in the following
example:

Kalkka malkka kŏkjŏng haeyo
I'm worrying whether to go or not

This form with malkka can only be used with verbs in which a
person is wondering whether or not they themselves will do
something. You could not use malkka in a sentence to mean *I'm
wondering whether it will rain or not*, since there is no decision
to be taken about whether or not to actually do something.

Often when Koreans are saying that they are worried that
something might happen, they use a slightly longer form of the
pattern: -ŭlkka bwa:

Pi-ga o-lkka-bwa kŏkjŏng haeyo
I'm worried that it might rain

Yŏja ch'ingu-ga na-rul pŏri-lkka-bwa kŏkjŏng haeyo
I am worried that my girlfriend might dump me

| pŏri- 버리- | *throw away* |

The other form is simply a contraction of this longer version.

3 Things you'll have to do

This unit should remind you of the way to say that you are
going to have to do something (often the context concerns
something that you'd really rather not have to do). The pattern
is -yagessŏyo, and it is added onto any processive verb base. The
form literally means something like 'only if I do such and such
will it do'; -ya is a particle which means 'only if'.

Naeil-kkaji I-il-ul kkŭnnae-yagessŏyo
I'll have to finish the work by tomorrow

Naenyŏn-enun kkok kyŏlhonhae-yagessŏyo
I'll have to marry next year

127

09

we bought him that last
year!/i'm sorry, I really
didn't know!

| kkŭnnae- 끝내– | finish (verb stem, to finish something) |
| kkok 꼭 | without fail, definitely |

4 You can and you can't

Korean has a very common way of saying that you can or can't do something (in the sense of being able to carry it out, rather than knowing how to). Take a processive verb stem (a verb of doing), add the ending -l su if the stem ends in a vowel and -ŭl su if it ends in a consonant, and then add either issŏyo, to say you can do the verb, or ŏpsŏyo, to say that you can't. For example:

mŏg-ul su issŏyo	*I can eat it*
mŏg-ul su ŏpsŏyo	*I can't eat it*
ka-l su issŏyo	*I can go*
ka-l su ŏpsŏyo	*I can't go*

It's as simple as that! But you must practise it until you can do it fast. The exercises should give you plenty of practice. Here are two examples:

Ilcchik torao-l su ŏpsŏyo
I won't be able to get home early

Chŏ-hanja-rul ilg-ŭl su issŏyo?
Can you read those Chinese characters over there?

| ilcchik 일찍 | early |

5 Retorting

Sometimes people say things which are really stupid and Korean provides a nice (and not too rude) way of pointing that out and implying (just gently) that the person should have known better. This dialogue has lots of examples. The man keeps suggesting what to buy for granddad for his birthday and the wife thinks his suggestions are a bit silly. For example, he suggests buying something they bought last year. The implication is that the

128

we bought him that last year!/I'm sorry, I really didn't know!

09

man should know what they bought for granddad last year, so he shouldn't have been so stupid as to suggest buying it again. Therefore the wife says:

Changnyŏn-e sat-janayo (from sa-ss-, past base of sa-)
We bought that last year!

Note the implication: you should know we bought him that last year, stupid! What did you go and suggest it again for?

One of the very common uses of the pattern is to give an answer when someone asks you something obvious, to which they should really know the answer. Suppose someone met you and you were dressed all in black and they asked you why. You could say 'because I'm going to a funeral!' and you would put -janayo onto the stem of the main verb of the sentence. Suppose you are going to get married and someone asked you why. You might respond:

Sarang ha-janayo!
It's because I love them, stupid!

---

sarang ha- 사랑하–   *love*

It's a very useful pattern, and one that makes your Korean sound natural and colourful.

The ending -janayo (spelt -janhayo) attaches to a present or a past base, and to honorific bases (note the sound change ss to t when -janayo is added to past bases).

6 Having one right there

You know how to say that someone has something by using the verb issŏyo. Korean has another verb form, which stresses a bit more the act of possessing: katko iss- and katko kyeshi- (the second one is the honorific form and is usually found in the polite honorific form katko kyeseyo).

Often it is has the force 'I have one right here', 'I have one with me now'. Imagine a situation in which someone wants a lighter. Someone else in the room has one and as he fumbles in his pockets, he might well say, na-nun katko issŏyo. This stresses that he has one with him right there.

This is a form you need to be able to recognize rather than to actually use frequently yourself.

▶ I'm sorry, I really didn't know!

A policeman catches a driver going the wrong way up a one-way street.

129

we bought him that last year/I'm sorry, I really didn't know!

09

경찰	실례합니다. 면허증 좀 보여주세요.
운전수	왜요? 무슨 문제가 있나요?
경찰	정말 몰라서 그러세요?
운전수	뭘 말이에요?
경찰	여기 주차한 차들을 한 번 보세요. 차를 다 똑같은 방향으로 주차했잖아요.
운전수	그래서요?
경찰	그러면 저 빨간 색 일방 통행 표지를 못 봤어요?
운전수	아! 일방통행로군요. 미안합니다. 정말로 몰랐어요.
경찰	큰 실수를 하셨어요. 일방통행로에 잘못 들어오면 아주 위험하고 벌금도 많아요.
운전수	정말 표지판을 못 봤어요. 한 번만 봐 주세요.
경찰	다음부터 조심하세요. 벌금은 오 만원입니다.
운전수	고맙습니다. 수고하세요.

Kyŏngch'al	Shillye hamnida. Myŏnhŏcchŭng chom poyŏ-juseyo.
Wunjŏnswu	Waeyo? Musŭn munje-ga innayo?
Kyŏngch'al	Chŏngmal mollasŏ kŭrŏseyo?
Wunjŏnswu	Mwol mar-ieyo?
Kyŏngch'al	Yŏgi chuch'ahan ch'a-dŭr-ul han pŏn poseyo. Ch'a-rul ta ttok kat'ŭn panghyang-uro chuch'a haet-janayo.
Wunjŏnswu	Kŭraesŏyo?
Kyŏngch'al	Kŭrŏmyŏn chŏ-ppalgan saek ilbang t'onghaeng p'yoji-rul mot pwassŏyo?
Wunjŏnswu	A! ilbang t'onghaengno-gunyo. Mianhamnida. Chŏngmallo mollassŏyo.
Kyŏngch'al	K'ŭn shilsu-rul hashyŏssŏyo. Ilbang t'onghaengno-e chalmot turŏ o-myŏn aju wihŏm ha-go pŏlgum-do manayo.
Wunjŏnswu	Chŏngmal p'yojip'an-ul mot pwassŏyo. Hanbŏn-man pwa-juseyo.
Kyŏngch'al	Taŭm-put'ŏ choshim haseyo. Pŏlgŭm-un oman won-imnida.
Wunjŏnswu	Komapsŭmnida. Sugo haseyo.

130

we bought him that last year!/I'm sorry, I really didn't know!

09

아 주 위험하고
벌금도 많아요!

ONE WAY

Phrases and expressions

mwol mar-ieyo?	*what are you talking about?*
chŏngmal molla-sŏ kŭrŏseyo?	*do you really not know (what you're doing)?*
kŭraesŏyo?	*so what?*
chŏngmal mollassŏyo	*I really didn't know/realize*
hanbŏn-man pwa chuseyo	*please let me off just this once!*
sugohaseyo!	*work hard!* (said to someone doing their job)

kyŏngch'al	경찰	*policeman*
unjŏnsu	운전수	*driver*
myŏnhŏcchŭng	면허증	*(driving) licence*
poyŏ-ju-	보여주–	*to show*
waeyo	왜요?	*why?*
musŭn	무슨	*what (kind of)*
munje	문제	*problem*
chuch'a han	주차한	*parked*
chuch'a ha-	주차하–	*to park*
ttok	똑	*exactly, precisely (often used with **kat'-**)*
kat'ŭn	같은	*same*
kat'-	같–	*be the same, be similar*
panghyang	방향	*direction*
ppalgan	빨간	*red*
saek	색	*colour*

ilbang t'onghaeng 일방 통행	one way	
ilbang t'onghaengno 일방 통행로	one-way street	
p'yoji 표지	sign, signpost	
k'ŭn 큰	big	
shilsu 실수	mistake	
shilsu ha- 실수하-	make a mistake	
turŏ o- 들어오-	to enter	
wihŏm ha- 위험하-	be dangerous	
pŏlgŭm 벌금	fine, penalty	
p'yojip'an 표지판	signpost	
choshim ha- 조심하-	be careful, be cautious	

131

we bought him that last year!/I'm sorry, I really didn't know!

09

Grammar

1 Questions with -nayo

The particle -na is often used as a way of asking questions and when you use it in the polite style, you should also add the polite particle -yo to give -nayo. (Without the -yo it is an informal question which you could only use between friends or to ask a question of someone younger or of lower status than you.)

It is added on to the stem of any verb (either the present stem or the past stem). Here are a couple of examples:

Chumun haen-nayo?	*Have you ordered?* (haess- past base of ha-)
Shinmun kŏgi innayo?	*Is the newspaper over there?* (from iss-)
Ŏdi ka-na?	*Where are you going?*
Chŏmshim mŏgŏn-na?	*Did you have lunch?* (mŏgŏss – past base of mŏk-)

2 Honorific forms

It's now time that we talked a bit more systematically about honorific verbs. You have already learnt that honorifics are used in Korean to show respect to the person you are talking about and in the present tense this is often done by using the form which you have learned as the 'polite request form' -(u)seyo. In actual fact this form is not only used to make requests, it is also used to make statements or to ask questions about anyone to whom you wish to show respect. It is very common in Korean, and you will use it whenever you meet and

132

we bought him that last year/I'm sorry, I really didn't know!

09

talk to new people of equivalent or senior status (to ask them questions, for example).

Actually, the form -(ǔ)seyo is an abbreviation of the honorific particle (ǔ)shi, plus the vowel -ǒ, plus the polite particle -yo. This contracts to give the form you know -(u)seyo.

Just as there are present and past stems, so also there are honorific stems. The honorific present stem is the usual stem plus the honorific particle -(ǔ)shi. The honorific past stem is the usual stem plus -(ǔ)shyǒss-:

stem	hon stem	hon past stem
anj-	anjǔshi-	anjushyǒss-
ilk-	ilgǔshi-	ilgushyǒss-
ka-	kashi-	kashyǒss-
o-	oshi-	oshyǒss-

You can add verb endings to the present honorific stem, as you would a normal verb with a stem ending in -i-. Everything about the honorific stems is regular apart from the present polite style which contracts to -(ǔ)seyo, as you have already learnt:

Harabǒji-nun unhaeng-e kashi-go halmǒni-nun uch'egug-e kaseyo
Granddad is going to the bank and grandma is going to the post office

Kim sǒnsaengnim unjǒn hashi-l su issǒyo?   *Can Mr Kim drive?*

Kim sǒnsaengnim unjǒn ha-l su issǔseyo?   *Can Mr Kim drive?* (identical)

Pǒlssǒ kashyǒt-kuna! (from kashyǒss-, past honorific base of ka-)   *He's already gone* (surprise, surprise!)

T'akku-rul ch'ishyǒss-ǒyo   *He played table tennis*

3 Introducing modifiers: making verbs into nouns

You now need to learn about something called modifiers, which are a kind of verb. First, we will show you how to make them, and then we will worry about what they mean. In this unit we shall just look at one of their uses and then in Unit 11 we shall look at the other uses.

How you make the modifier form of a verb depends on whether it is a processive or a descriptive verb.

133

we bought him that last year!/I'm sorry, I really didn't know!

09

Processive verbs

For processive verbs, add -nŭn- to the verb stem. Thus the modifier form of ka- is kanŭn, the modifier form of mŏk- is mŏngnŭn (written mŏknŭn), and so on. You will find that when you add -nŭn to verb stems that end in consonants, sound changes will take place. For mŏk-, therefore, the *hangul* letters will literally read mŏk-nŭn, but the pronunciation (according to the rules of sound change you learnt at the beginning of the book) will be mŏngnŭn.

To make a past tense modifier form for processive verbs you add -(ŭ)n to the stem, so that the past tense modifier forms of mŏk- and ka- are mŏgŭn and kan. You cannot do this with the verbs iss- and ŏps- (these verbs behave like processive verbs, so that the modifier forms are innnŭn and ŏmnnŭn in the present tense – they do not have past tense modifier forms).

Descriptive verbs

For descriptive verbs, simply add -n if the stem ends in a vowel, and -ŭn if it ends in a consonant. As you can see this is identical to the past tense modifier form for processive verbs. There is no past tense modifier form for the descriptive verbs.

Try to memorize these rules.

We will now look at just one meaning of the modifier form of verbs. Sometimes you want to talk about the act of doing things (doing verbs), as though they were nouns. In English, for example, we say things like *I like swimming* which means *I like the act of swimming*, and of course 'swimming' comes originally from the verb 'swim'.

Korean is able to express *the act of* (verb)*ing* by using a modifier form, plus the noun kŏt, often abbreviated to kŏ. Here are examples:

kanŭn kŏt	*the act of going*
yŏnghwa ponŭn kŏ	*the act of seeing a film*
yŏgi annŭn kŏ	*the act of sitting here* (from anj-)

You can then simply add verbs like choayo/choa haeyo/shirŏ haeyo/an choa haeyo afterwards to say what you think about those particular activities, e.g.:

Yŏnghwa ponŭn kŏ choa haseyo?
Do you like seeing films?

Yŏgi innŭn kŏ chom poseyo
Please look at what is here (literally, *the thing that is/exists here*)

134

we bought him that last
year!/I'm sorry, I really
didn't know!

09

P'yǒnji-rul ssunǔn kǒ shirǒ haeyo
I hate writing letters

Sul mashi-go unjǒn hanǔn ke wihom haeyo
It's dangerous to drink and drive

p'yǒnji 편지	*letter*	
ssǔ- 쓰–	*write*	

Practice

1 Say that you are worried about the following things.

  a That teacher will come (to a party).
  b That there won't be enough food.
  c That Mr Kim might not come.
  d That your girlfriend might not like you any more.
  e That it might rain.

2 Make the following passage honorific where appropriate. We have told you that normally you only need one honorific verb in a sentence, but for the purposes of this exercise use as many honorifics as you can. Look out for sentences that should not have them, however!

김선생님은 대학교 선생님이에요. 런던 대학교에서 한국말을 가르치고 일본말도 가르쳐요. 매일 아침 공원에 가서 산책해요. 개하고 같이 가요. 공원은 아주 좋아요. 김선생님의 개는 고기를 잘 먹어요. 작년부터 부인도 가끔 산책하기 시작했어요. 부인도 가면 둘이 식당에 가서 커피 한잔 마셔요.

3 Here are some situations. Make up Korean sentences to say what you will have to do because of them (using -yagessǒyo).

  a Your head hurts.
  b You can't meet your boyfriend tonight.
  c You need to use a dictionary, but you don't have one.
  d You go out and realize you've forgotten something. (You'll have to go back.)
  e You want to know what's going on at the theatre. (You'll have to look at the newspaper.)

4 You're trying to decide about the following things. Say so in Korean, using a similar pattern to the one you were using in question 1.

  a What to buy.
  b What to wear. (*wear*: **ip-**)

c   Where to sit.
d   What to order.
e   Where to go at the weekend.

5   Translate the following sentences into Korean, using the pattern -(u)l su issŏyo/ŏpsŏyo that you have learnt in this lesson.

a   Can I come too?
b   Is this edible?
c   Can you meet me tomorrow?
d   I can't speak Japanese.
e   I don't have any money, so I can't buy it.
f   I can't park here.

6   Make up retorts to the following Korean statements using the -janhayo pattern.

a   Wae an sassŏyo?   (*I bought it yesterday, didn't I!*)
b   I-saram-i namja(boy)   (*No, I'm already married,*
    -ch'ingu-eyo?   *stupid!*)
c   Myŏndo an haseyo?   (*I already did it!*)
d   I-chaeg-ul ilgŏ-boseyo. (*I hate reading, stupid!*)
e   I-saram-i nugu-seyo?   (*It's my wife! You only met her*
                             yesterday!)

7   Imagine you are talking to your sister and discussing with her what to buy your brother for a birthday present. You make the following suggestions of what to buy, but she manages to find a reason against it until the very last suggestion. Write out your suggestions and the answers she makes, trying to make the dialogue as interesting as you can. (Note: *jeans*, ch'ŏngpaji; *CD*, ssi-di)

135

we bought him that last year!/I'm sorry, I really didn't know!

09

10

what did you do with it?/nasty headaches

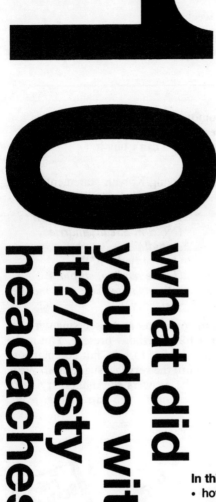

In this unit you will learn
- how to describe things that you have lost and say when and where you lost them
- how to buy medicine from a Korean *yakkuk* or chemist
- 'when' clauses
- how to say it seems as though something or other will happen

▶ What did you do with it?

손님	저 실례합니다. 저는 어제 친구들이랑 여기 왔었는데요, 가방을 놓고 갔어요.
종업원	제가 가서 한 번 찾아 보지요. 가방이 어떻게 생겼어요?
손님	네, 아주 크고, 검정색이고, 가죽으로 만들었어요.
종업원	저기 서류 가방이 있는데, 저거에요?
손님	아니요, 서류 가방이 아니에요.

A little while later.

종업원	없는 것 같은데요. 뭐 중요한 게 들어 있나요?
손님	예, 사실 아주 중요한 서류하고 책하고 은행카드가 들어있어요.
종업원	저런! 잠깐 기다려 보세요. 사장님한테 한 번 물어볼께요.

The manager comes.

사장	안녕하세요? 무슨일입니까?
손님	제 가방을 잃어버렸어요. 어제 여기서 식사하고 놓고 나왔어요.
사장	몇시에 저희 식당에서 나가셨나요?
손님	한 열 한 시 쯤이에요.
사장	영업 끝날 때 쯤... 아, 예, 생각나요. 오늘 아침 청소할 때 가방이 하나 있었어요.
손님	그걸 어떻게 하셨어요?
사장	경찰서에 보냈어요. 그 사람들이 보관하고 있을거예요.
손님	경찰서가 어디인지 좀 가르쳐주시겠어요?
사장	식당에서 나가서 좌회전 한 다음에 오른 쪽으로 세번째 골목에 있어요.
손님	정말 감사합니다. 안녕히 계세요.

Sonnim	Chŏ, Shillye hamnida. Chŏ-nun ŏje ch'ingu-dŭl-irang yŏgi wassŏnnŭndeyo, kabang-ul nok'o kassŏyo.
Chongŏpwon	Che-ga ka-sŏ han-pŏn ch'aja pojiyo. Kabang-i ŏttŏk'e saenggyŏssŏyo?
Sonnim	Ne, aju k'ŭgo, kŏmchŏng saeg-igo, kajug-uro mandŭrŏssŏyo.

| Chongŏpwon | Chŏgi sŏryu kabang-i innŭnde, chŏ-gŏ-eyo? |
| Sonnim | Aniyo, sŏryu kabang-i anieyo. |

A little while later.

Chongŏpwon	Ŏmnŭn kŏt kat'ŭndeyo.
	Mwo chungyo han ke turŏ innayo?
Sonnim	Ye, sashil aju chungyohan sŏryu-hago ch'aek-hago ŭnhaeng k'adu-ga turŏ issŏyo.
Chongŏpwon	Chŏrŏn! Chamkkan kidaryŏ-boseyo.
	Sajangnim-hant'e hanbŏn murŏ-bo-lkkeyo.

The manager comes.

Sajang	Annyŏng haseyo? Musŭn ir-imnikka?
Sonnim	Che kabang-ul irŏbŏryŏssŏyo.
	Ŏje yŏgi-sŏ shiksa ha-go no-k'o nawassŏyo.
Sajang	Myŏt shi-e chŏhuy shiktang-esŏ nagashyŏnnayo?
Sonnim	Han yŏlhan-shi cchŭm-ieyo.
Sajang	Yŏngŏp kkŭnna-l ttae cchŭm . . .
	A, ye, saenggang nayo. Onŭl ach'im ch'ŏngso ha-l ttae kabang-i hana issŏssŏyo.
Sonnim	Ku-gŏ-l ŏttŏk'e hashyŏssŏyo?
Sajang	Kyŏngch'alsŏ-e ponaessŏyo.
	Kŭ-saram-dur-i pogwan ha-go iss-ulkŏeyo.
Sonnim	Kyŏngch'alsŏ-ga ŏdi-inji chom karuch'yŏ-jushigessŏyo?
Sajang	Shiktang-esŏ naga-sŏ chwahoejŏn han taŭme orŭn cchog-uro se-bŏn-cchae kolmog-e issŏyo.
Sonnim	Chŏngmal kamsahamnida. Annyŏnghi kyeseyo.

Phrases and expressions

ŏmnŭn kŏt kat'ŭndeyo	it doesn't look as though there is anything/are any
musŭn ir-imnikka?	how can I help you?, what's the problem?
ŏttŏk'e saenggyŏssŏyo?	what does it look like?
(. . . -hant'e) han-bŏn murŏ-bo-lkkeyo	I'll just ask (such and such a person)
kŭ-gŏ-l ŏttŏk'e hashyŏssŏyo	what did you do with it?
. . . -i/ga ŏdi-inji chom karŭch'yŏ-juseyo	please tell me where (such and such) is
chwahoejŏn han taŭm-e	after doing a left turn
uhoejŏn han taŭm-e	after doing a right turn

sonnim 손님	*customer*
chŏ . . . 저...	*er . . . , hmm . . .*
kabang 가방	*a briefcase, a bag*
no(h)- 놓–	*put down, leave*
ch'aja po- 찾아보–	*have a look, look for*
ch'aj- 찾–	*search*
ŏttŏk'e 어떻게	*how?*
irŏk'e 이렇게	*like this*
kŭrŏk'e 그렇게	*like that*
saenggi- 생기–	*look (like)*
kŏmjŏng 검정	*black*
kajuk 가죽	*leather*
mandŭrŏssŏyo 만들었어요	*be made of* (past tense of **mandul-**, I irregular verb)
mandŭl- 만들–	*make* (I-irregular verb like **p'al-**, **nol-** etc)
sŏryu 서류	*document*
chungyo han 중요한	*important* (modifier form, like an adjective)
chungyo ha- 중요하–	*be important*
turŏ iss- 들어 있–	*be contained, be included*
ye 예	*yes* (politer form of **ne**)
sashil 사실	*in fact*
k'adu 카드	*a card* (e.g. credit card)
sajang(nim) 사장(님)	*manager* (honorific form)
murŏ-bo- 물어보–	*ask*
irŏbŏri- 잃어버리–	*lose*
shiksa ha- 식사하–	*have meal*
nao- 나오–	*come out*
chŏhŭy 저희	(humble form of **wuri**, *our*, *my*)
han (*number/time*) cchŭm 한...쯤	*about, around, approximately*
yŏngŏp 영업	*business*
kkŭnna- 끝나–	*finish* (as in *it finishes*)
-(u)l ttae -(으)ㄹ 때	*when* (see note 4)
ttae 때	*time (when)*
saenggang na- 생각나–	*remember, it comes to mind*
ch'ŏngso ha- 청소하–	*clean up*
kyŏngch'alsŏ 경찰서	*police station*
bonae- 보내–	*send*
bogwan ha- 보관하–	*keep*
chwahoejŏn 좌회전	*left turn*
uhoejŏn 우회전	*right turn*
cchae 째	*number* (time)
kolmog 골목	*alley, small road*

Grammar

1 Making plurals

You will have noticed that a Korean noun can be either singular or plural, depending on the context. In other words, Korean does not have one word for *dog* and another word for *dogs*; it has just one word **kae** which can mean either. It is very rare that there is any ambiguity or confusion because of this, however.

There is a plural particle which can be used to show explicitly that a word is plural – it is -**tŭl**. You can then add subject, object, topic (-i, -ŭl, -ŭn) or other particles (such as -do or -hago) onto the plural form. Thus you could have any of the following forms: -dŭl-do, -dŭr-un, -dŭr-i, -dŭr-ul, -dŭl-hago, -dŭl-hant'e, and so on.

2 Ending sentences with -*nŭndeyo*

We have already studied the clause ending -**nunde**, to indicate that you have something more to say, that you are going to elaborate on what you have just said. You can also end a sentence with -**nŭnde** by adding the polite particle -**yo** after it. The use is very like that for -**nŭnde**, except that saying -**nŭndeyo** allows you to make more of a pause than using -**nŭnde**. Often -**nŭndeyo** is used to explain who you are, where you have come from, or what you want to do. The following sentence would go on to give more specific information, either about what the person you are speaking to should do about it or what you would like to happen (on the basis of having explained who you are, for example!). This all sounds a bit confusing in writing, and it is perhaps best to explain by example. In the following sentences, the first could be ended in Korean with -**nŭndeyo**. Notice how the second sentence often makes an explicit request, or homes in to ask something:

I'm from the BBC (**nŭndeyo**)	I'd like to do an interview
I'd like to buy a bicycle (**nŭndeyo**)	Can you show me your range?
I'm the brother of your friend (**nŭndeyo**)	Pleased to meet you! May I have a seat?

Since -**nŭndeyo** is a colloquial expression, you will sometimes find it used in other ways which do not seem to fit exactly into the system we have described here. However, for using the form yourself, if you remember the rules we have given you, you won't go wrong.

Note also that -nŭndeyo and the related -nŭnde are added to the present stem of processive verbs, and on to the past stem of both processive and descriptive verbs. The form (ŭ)ndeyo and the related (ŭ)nde are only used for the present tense of descriptive verbs. Taking a processive verb and a descriptive verb in both past and present tenses, then, we would get the following forms:

	ha- (*processive*)	cho- (*descriptive*)
present	ha-nŭndeyo	cho-ŭndeyo
past	haen-nŭndeyo	choan-nŭndeyo

Remember that in the past examples the first of the two ns (before the hyphen) represents the double s of the past base which has become pronounced as an n through the pronunciation rules we described at the beginning of the course.

3 It seems like

You can say that 'it seems like something is happening' in Korean by using modifier forms of verbs plus kŏt kat'ayo. Kat'- is a verb which means *is like*, so pi-ga o-nun kŏt kat'ayo means literally 'the act of raining it is like', or, in effect, *it seems like it's raining*. Remember that the modifier forms are different depending on whether the main verb is processive or descriptive.

Here are some examples:

Sŏnsaengnim-i TV-rul po-nŭn kŏt kat'ayo	*It seems like the teacher is watching TV*
Minho-ga ppang-ul mŏng-nŭn kŏt kat'ayo	*It seems like Minho is eating bread*
Yŏnggug-un nalssi-ga nappŭ-n kŏt kat'ayo	*It seems like the weather is bad in England*
I chib-i choh-ŭn kŏt kat'ayo	*This house seems to be nice*

4 When something happens

You have met many times the form (ŭ)l added to the stem of verbs, for example in the endings: (ŭ)l kka(yo), (ŭ)l kka haeyo, (ŭ)l kŏeyo. In actual fact this (ŭ)l is the future modifier. It is a modifier just like -nǔn and -(ǔ)n, but it has a future meaning. This means that you can use the pattern you have just learnt (modifer + kǒt kat'ayo) to say *it seems like something will happen*:

Pi-ga o-l kǒt kat'ayo   *It seems like it will rain*
Ka-l kǒt kat'ayo   *It seems as though s/he will go*

An even more important use of -(ǔ)l is when it is followed by the noun ttae which means *time*. The whole construction (verb stem)-(ǔ)l ttae means *when* (verb) *happens*. Have a look at the examples:

hakkyo-e ka-l ttae   *when I go to school*
pi-ga o-l ttae   *when it rains*
ǒmǒni torao-l ttae   *when Mum gets back*

Here are some examples in sentences:

Pang-esǒ nao-l ttae pang-ul ch'ǒngsoha-seyo
When you come out of the room, please clean it up

Hanguk mar-ul karuch'i-l ttae haksaeng-dur-i manassǒyo?
Were there many students when you taught Korean?

▶ Nasty headaches

Mr Pak goes to the chemist to get some medicine for a nasty headache.

약사	어서 오세요.
	무슨 약을 드릴까요?
박선생	네, 두통이 아주 심한데, 두통약 좀 주시겠어요?
약사	네, 언제부터 아프기 시작했어요?
박선생	어제부터 아프기 시작했어요.
	회사에서 일을 너무 많이 하고 스트레스를 많이 받았어요.
	아마 과로하고 스트레스가 원인인것 같아요.
약사	그렇군요. 눈은 아프지 않으세요?
박선생	네, 조금 아파요.
약사	잠은 잘 주무세요?
박선생	아니요. 머리가 너무 아파서 잘 못 자요.
약사	알겠어요. 아마 스트레스하고 관련이 있는 것 같아요.
	이 약을 잡숴 보세요.
박선생	하루에 몇 번 씩 먹나요?

약사	두통이 심할 때는 네 시간마다 한 알 씩 드시고, 좀 나아지면 식후에 한 알 씩 하루 세 번 드세요.
박선생	부작용 같은 것은 없나요?
약사	이 약을 먹으면 졸음이 오니까 조심하세요. 그리고 쉽게 피로를 느껴도 놀라지 마세요.
박선생	네, 고맙습니다.

Yaksa	Ŏsŏ oseyo. Musŭn yag-ul tŭrilkkayo?
Mr Pak	Ne, tut'ong-i aju shim ha-nde, tut'ong yak chom chushigessŏyo?
Yaksa	Ne, ŏnje-but'ŏ ap'u-gi shijak haessŏyo?
Mr Pak	Ŏje-but'ŏ ap'u-gi shijak'aessŏyo. Hoesa-esŏ ir-ul nŏmu mani ha-go sut'uresu-rul mani padassŏyo. Ama kwaro-hago sut'uresu-ga wonin-i-n kŏt kat'ayo.
Yaksa	Kurŏk'unyo. Nun-un ap'u-ji anuseyo?
Mr Pak	Ne, chogum ap'ayo.
Yaksa	Cham-un chal chumuseyo?
Mr Pak	Aniyo. Mŏri-ga nŏmu ap'asŏ chal mot chayo.
Yaksa	Algessŏyo. Ama sut'uresu-hago kwallyŏn-i innun kŏt kat'ayo. I yag-ul chapswo-boseyo.
Mr Pak	Haru-e myŏt pŏn sshik mŏngnayo?
Yaksa	Tut'ong-i shim ha-l ttae-nun ne shigan-mada han al sshik tushi-go, chom naaji-myŏn, shikhu-e han al sshik haru sebŏn tuseyo.
Mr Pak	Pujagyong kat'un kŏs-un ŏmnayo?
Yaksa	I yag-ul mŏg-umyŏn chorum-i o-nikka, choshim haseyo. Kurigo shwipke p'iro-rul nukkyŏ-do nolla-ji maseyo.
Mr Pak	Ne, komapsumnida.

Phrases and expressions

ama sut'uresu-ga wonin-i-n kŏt kat'ayo	it seems as though it's because of stress
ne-shigan-mada han al sshik tŭseyo	take one tablet every four hours
shikhu-e han al sshik se-bŏn tŭseyo	take one tablet three times a day after meals
shwipke p'iro-rul nŭkkyŏ-do nolla-ji maseyo	don't be surprised if you feel tired very easily

yaksa 약사	*pharmacist, chemist*
shim ha- 심하–	*is serious*
ŏnje 언제	*when*
hoesa 회사	*company*
sut'uresu 스트레스	*stress*
pat- 받–	*receive*
kwaro 과로	*overwork*
wonin 원인	*reason, cause*
kŭrŏk'unyo 그렇군요	*ah, I see; it's like that, is it?!*
nun 눈	*an eye*
cham 잠	*sleep (noun)*
chumushi- 주무시–	*sleep (honorific equivalent of **cha-**)*
kwallyŏn 관련	*relation, link*
chapswo po- 잡숴보–	*try eating (honorific form)*
chapsushi- 잡수시–	*eat (honorific equivalent of **mok-**)*
han al 한 알	*one tablet*
naaji- 나아지–	*get better*
haru-e 하루에	*per day*
-mada –마다	*each, every*
shikhu 식후	*after meals, after the meal*
pujagyong 부작용	*a side-effect*
chorum 졸음	*sleepiness, drowsiness*
kat'ŭn kŏt 같은 것	*(a) similar thing, something similar*
shipke 쉽게	*easily*
p'iro 피로	*fatigue, weariness*
nŭkki- 느끼–	*to feel*
nolla- 놀라–	*to be surprised, be shocked*

Grammar

1 The future marker -*kess*

-kess can be added to verbs to make future forms. An explanation of this is given in Unit 12 and you do not need to be concerned about it until then.

2 Immediate future

You have previously learnt to put sentences in the future with the form -(ŭ)lkŏeyo. Korean has another future form -(ŭ)lkkeyo, added to the present stem of processive verbs which expresses a more definite (rather than probable) future, something you will certainly do, are promising to do or are just about to do. It is often used in circumstances where there is no doubt about whether or not you will be able to do the thing concerned. You can only use this form to say what you yourself will do, since you have control over your own actions. You cannot say what someone else will do, since you have no control over their actions and there is therefore always a certain element of doubt about them.

3 Asking polite questions

Korean often uses the ending -kessŏyo added to the honorific stem of verbs to ask polite questions. Examples are: **chigum kashiges-sŏyo?** (*are you going now?*), **chumun hashigessŏyo?** (*would you like to order?*). It can also be used to express requests: **hae-jushigessŏyo?** (*would you do it for me?*).

4 Honorific verbs

Korean has several verbs which are only used in the honorific form (the non-honorific form is a completely different verb). In this lesson you meet the verb **chumwushi-** which is the honorific stem of the verb **cha-** (*sleep*). Here is a list of the common honorific verbs and their non-honorific equivalents. Notice especially the verb **issŏyo**.

non-honorific	meaning	honorific	hon polite
cha-	sleep	chumushi-	chumwuseyo
mŏk-	eat	chapsushi-	chapsuseyo
iss-	exist, stay	kyeshi-	kyeseyo
iss-	have	issŭshi-	issuseyo
chuk-	die	tora-gashi-	tora-gaseyo
mŏk-/mashi-	eat/drink	tŭshi-	tuseyo

Practice

1 This exercise is designed to help you practise the -(nu)ndeyo form. If we give you a Korean sentence ending in -(nu)ndeyo, you must provide a second sentence that fits with it. If we give you the second sentence in Korean, then you are meant to make up a first sentence with -(nu)ndeyo along the lines of the English that we suggest.

a Yǒngguk taesagwan-uy Tony-indeyo. (*Create appropriate 2nd sentence*)

b (*I've come from England*) Kǒgi-sǒ hangungmar-ul chogum kongbu haessǒyo.

c (*I telephoned yesterday*) Kim sǒnsaengnim chom pakkwo-jushigessǒyo?

d Ǒje ch'ingu-hago yǒgi wan-nundeyo. (*Create appropriate 2nd sentence*)

e (*I want to buy a dictionary*) Hana poyǒ-jushigessǒyo?

f Chǒ-nun Kim sǒnsaengnim-uy puin-indeyo. (*Where has Mr Kim gone?*)

2 Make up a sentence for each of the following verbs. Put the verb into the 'it seems like' pattern with -(nǔ)n kǒt kat'ayo.

   a 비가 와요.
   b 박선생님이에요.
   c 독서를 싫어해요.
   d 동대문 시장에 갔어요.
   e 김선생님 오세요.
   f 가방을 여기 놓았어요.

3 You have lost your jacket and the man at the lost property office asks you to describe it. (*pocket*: **chumǒni**)

4 Join up the following sets of clauses, so that the meaning is 'when A, B.' Thus, the first one will be *When you eat your food, don't talk* or, in better English, *Don't talk when you're eating.*

   a When you eat food   don't talk
   b When you park your car   take care
   c When you are going into town call me
   d When the film's over   let's go to a restaurant
   e When I arrived home   I had a beer
      (**toch'ak ha-**, *arrive*)
   f When you go out   let's go together

5 Translate the following sentences into English.

  a ·어쨌든 지금 무엇을 하기로 했어요?
  b 우리 여자 친구 못 봤어요? 보면 저한테 전화하세요.
  c 좀 나아지면 약을 더 이상 먹지 마세요.
  d 언제 졸업할거에요? 그 다음에 무슨 계획이 있어요?
  e 이 서류가 중요해요? 중요하지요! 내 면허증이잖아요!
  f 데이트를 할 때 영화 보러 자주 가요.

6 Translate the following into Korean.

  a You've made a big mistake!
  b If you go into the city late at night it's dangerous.
  c Would you show me that dictionary? Where did you buy it?
  d Is there a problem? Yes, I seem to have lost my medicine.
  e I've had so much stress lately and I can't sleep at night.
  f You've lost your bag? What was inside?
  g You don't like my ideas!
  h So what did you do?

7 You have a headache and your friend, who has gone out while you were asleep, leaves you some tablets with a note about when to take them. What are his instructions?

심할 땐 네 시간마다
두 알 드세요.

좀 나아지면 ,
점심 때만 식전에 한 알씩
드세요

11

would you like to try it on?/ do you think it suits me?

In this unit you will learn
- how to shop for clothes
- commenting on prices, quality and style
- comparing one thing with another
- informal styles of speech (used between close friends)
- more about modifiers and honorifics

Minho and Pyŏngswu go to Namdaemun market to buy some clothes.

입어보시겠어요?

민호	저 셔츠 좀 봐라. 정말 좋다.
병수	그래? 내 생각에는 디자인이 좀 구식같다.
민호	아니야. 내 마음에 꼭 들어.
	아가씨, 저 셔츠 얼마예요?
점원 A	팔천 원이에요.
민호	와, 정말 싸다.
병수	에이, 그런데 이거 봐. 질이 별로 안 좋아.
민호	글쎄, 그럼 다른 곳에 가볼까?

Minho and Pyŏngsu decide to try out the department store instead.

점원 B	어서 오세요. 뭘 찾으세요?
민호	좀 활동적인 옷을 찾는데요, 좀 밝은 색으로요.
	청바지하고 같이 입을 수 있는 멋있고 질 좋은 옷이요.
점원 B	이거 어때요? 요즘 아주 유행하는 스타일이에요.
민호	재료가 뭐예요?
점원 B	백 퍼센트 면이에요. 한 번 입어보시겠어요?
민호	네, 고맙습니다...
	나한테 어울려요?

Minho	Chŏ shyŏch'u chom pwa-ra. Chongmal cho-t'a.
Pyŏngsu	Kŭrae? Nae saenggag-enun dijain-i chom kushik kat-ta.
Minho	Ani-ya. Nae maŭm-e kkok turŏ.
	Agassi, chŏ-shyŏch'u ŏlma-eyo?
Chŏmwon A	P'al ch'ŏn won-ieyo.
Minho	Wa, chŏngmal ssa-da.
Pyŏngsu	Ei, kurŏnde i-gŏ pwa. Chir-i pyŏllo an choa.
Minho	Kŭlsse, kŭrŏm tarŭn kos-e ka-bo-lkka?

Minho and Pyŏngsu decide to try out the department store instead.

Chŏmwon B	Ŏsŏ oseyo. Mwol ch'ajŭseyo?
Minho	Chom hwalttongjŏg-in os-ul ch'an-nŭndeyo, chom palgŭn saeg-uro-yo.
	Ch'ŏngbaji-hago kach'i ib-ul su in-nun mŏshit-ko chil choun osh-iyo.
Chŏmwon B	I-gŏ ŏttaeyo? Yojum aju yuhaeng ha-nŭn sut'ail-ieyo.
Pyŏngsu	Chaeryo-ga mwo-eyo?
Chŏmwon B	Paek p'ŏsentu myŏn-ieyo. Hanbŏn ibŏ-boshigessŏyo?
Minho	Ne, komapsŭmnida . . .
	Na-hant'e ŏullyŏyo?

Phrases and expressions

nae maŭm-e kkok tŭrŏ (yo)   *I like it very much*
hanbŏn ibŏ-boshigessŏyo?   *would you like to try it on?*
wa, chŏngmal ssada   *wow, that's really cheap*
. . . -hant'e ŏullyŏyo?   *does it suit . . . ?*

For any verb endings that you do not recognize, read the grammar section after reading the dialogue.

shyŏch'u 셔츠	*shirt*
dijain 디자인	*design*
kushik 구식	*old style, old fashioned*
kkok 꼭	*exactly, certainly, precisely*
wa! 와	*wow!*
ei! 에이	*hey!*
chil 질	*quality*
pyŏllo 별로	*(not) particularly (see note 2)*
kos 곳	*place*
hwalttongjŏk 활동적	*casual, active*
hwalttongjŏg-in 활동적인	*(modifier form of the above, like an adjective)*
palgŭn 밝은	*bright*
ch'ŏngbaji 청바지	*blue jeans*
mŏshiss- 멋있-	*be stylish, be handsome*
yuhaeng ha- 유행하-	*be popular, be in vogue*
sut'ail 스타일	*style*
chaeryo 재료	*stuff, (raw) material (also ingredients)*
p'ŏsent'u 퍼센트	*per cent*
myŏn 면	*cotton*
ŏulli- 어울리-	*suit (a person)*

Grammar

1 The plain style

The plain style is used between very close friends or when speaking to someone much younger than you. It can also be used when saying something to yourself out loud and it is used as a written form in notices and in books and newspapers.

Its form is very like that of the modifiers you met in Unit 9, but with some important differences. For processive verbs you add

-nŭn (after a consonant stem) or -n (after a vowel stem) onto the verb stem for the present tense, plus the verb ending -da. Hence: tun-nŭnda, kidari-nda, mŏng-nŭnda, ha-nda, mashi-nda etc. For the past tense you simply add -da onto the past stem of the verb: kidaryŏtta, mogŏtta, haetta, mashyotta.

For descriptive verbs, you add -da to the stem of the verb, either the past stem or the present stem according to whether you want a past or present meaning.

Here are some example sentences in the plain style.

Minho-ga shijang-e ka-nda	*Minho goes to the market*
Minho-ga shijang-e kat-ta	*Minho went to the market*
Minho-ga sagwa-rul mŏng-nŭnda	*Minho eats an apple*
Minho-ga sagwa-rul mŏg-otta	*Minho ate an apple*
Onŭl nalssi-ga cho-t'a	*Today, the weather is good*
Ŏje nalssi-ga choat-ta	*Yesterday, the weather was good*

In addition, there are two very common ways of asking questions in the plain style.

One of these you have learnt already: it is the question particle -na added to any verb stem (past, present, honorific) without the particle -yo on the end. Here are some examples: mwol mŏng-na? (*what are you eating?*), mwol ha-na? (*what are you doing?*).

Another common question pattern is to add -ni? to any verb stem: piga o-ni? ŏdi gan-ni? meaning *is it raining?* and *where did you go?* respectively.

Here are some examples of questions in the plain style:

Namdaemun shijang-i ŏdi-ni?	*Where is Namdaemun market?*
Onŭl ach'im musŭn yak-ul mŏgŏn-ni?	*What medicine did you take this morning?*

You can make commands in the plain style by adding -ra to the polite style of the present tense, minus the -yo. Thus, plain style commands would include: mŏgŏ-ra, hae-ra, ka-ji ma-ra *eat it!*, *do it!*, *don't go!* (from ha-ji maseyo)), and so on.

Plain style suggestions can be made by adding -ja to the present stem of any processive verb: mŏk-ja, ha-ja, iyagi ha-ja (*let's eat, let's do it, let's talk*) and so on.

2 The informal style

Korean also has another very important system of addressing those younger than you or very close to you, in addition to the plain style. In fact, it is perhaps even more common and it is very easy.

All you have to do is take the polite style of the verb (present, past or future) and take off the -yo particle! That's all there is to it:

Nae maŭm-e kkok tŭrŏ	*I like it very much*
Kŭrŏnde igŏ pwa	*But look at this*
Chil-i pyŏllo an choa	*The quality is not very good*

The one exception is the copula: instead of taking the -ieyo form and taking off the -yo, the informal style of the copula is -ya after a vowel, and -iya after a consonant:

Chŏ saram-un hanguk saram-iya	*That person is a Korean*
Kim sŏnsaengnim-un ŭysa-ya	*Mr Kim is a medical doctor*

3 Use of the particle -(ŭ)ro

The particle -(ŭ)ro has various functions, some of which you have learnt already. Here is a list of its different uses.

- instruments: *by, by means of*
kich'a-ro wayo	*come by train*
son-ŭro mandŭrŏyo	*make by hand*

- cause, reason: *because of*
Kyot'ong sago-ro chugŏssŏyo	*(He) died (because of/ in) a traffic accident*
Kaeinjŏgin iyu-ro kŏjŏl haessŏyo	*(I) refused for a private reason*

- stuff, raw material: *from, of*
I chib-un namu-ro madŭrŏssŏyo	*This house is made of wood*
Wain-un p'odo-ro madŭrŏyo	*Wine is made from grapes*

- unit, measure, degree: *by*
Yŏngug-esŏ-nun p'aundu/ k'iro-ro p'arayo	*They sell by the pound/kilo in Britain*

- direction: *towards*
London-uro kassŏyo	*(He) went to London*
Uri cib-uro oseyo	*Please come to my house*

4 More on modifiers

In Unit 9 you learnt how to make modifiers with -nŭn for processive verbs and -(ŭ)n for descriptive verbs. You learned how they could be used with the noun ke (kŏt) to mean *the act of* (verb)*ing*.

In fact, you can use modifiers in front of any noun and, as you would expect, their function is to modify the noun, to tell you something about the noun they modify. Here is a good example:

che-ga mŏng-nun sagwa

Here the noun is **sagwa** (*apple*), and **chega mŏngnŭn** (from the verb **mŏk-**) is modifying the noun 'apple'. The meaning of the phrase is *the apple I am eating*. In English, we put the noun first, and afterwards the modifying phrase ((which) I am eating), but in Korean it is the other way round. The noun and its modifying phrase can then be used as part of a sentence, as you would any other noun. For example, you might want to say *the apple I am eating has gone bad* or *where is the apple I am eating?* You could do this in Korean like this (the modifying phrases are in brackets and you can see that they are optional; the sentences would make perfect sense without them, but the modifying phrases show which particular apple you are talking about):

(che-ga mŏng-nŭn) sagwa-ga ssŏgŏssŏyo
(che-ga mŏng-nŭn) sagwa-ga ŏdi issŏyo?

▶ Do you think it suits me?

Minho tries the clothes on and they have another discussion.

점원   야, 아주 멋있는데요.
민호   (to Pyŏngsu) 나한테 어울리니?
병수   응, 잘 어울려. 그런데 좀 작은 것 같다.
점원   좀 큰 걸 입어보실래요?
민호   네.
점원   여기 있어요.

A little while later.

병수   그게 더 잘 맞는다.
점원   야, 아주 근사해요.
민호   그런데 얼마지요?

점원   삼만 이천 원이에요.
민호   뭐라고요?
점원   왜요? 싼 거예요. 겨우 삼만 이천 원인데요 뭐.
병수   제가 생각해도 좀 비싼 것 같은데요.
민호   남대문 시장에서는 비슷한 게 팔천 원이에요.
점원   아, 네, 남대문하고는 비슷해 보여도 질이 달라요.
       남대문 시장에서 옷을 사면 두 세 달 만에 못 쓰게
       돼서 새 옷을 사야 되거든요.
병수   그러면 이 옷이 남대문 시장 옷보다 네 배나 더
       오래가요?
점원   적어도요. 그리고 훨씬 더 잘 맞아요.
민호   음, 가서 생각 좀 다시 해봐야겠어요.

Chŏmwon	Ya, aju mŏshin-nŭndeyo.
Minho (to **Pyŏngsu**)	Na-hant'e ŏulli-ni?
Pyŏngsu	Ŭng, chal ŏullyŏ. Kŭrŏnde chom chagŭn kŏt kat-ta.
Chŏmwon	Chom k'ŭn gŏ-l ibŏ-boshi-llaeyo?
Minho	Ne.
Chŏmwon	Yŏgi issŏyo.

A little while later.

Pyŏngsu	Kŭ-ge tŏ chal man-nŭnda.
Chŏmwon	Ya, aju kŭnsa haeyo.
Minho	Kŭrŏnde, ŏlma-jiyo?
Chŏmwon	Samman ich'ŏn won-ieyo.
Minho	Mworaguyo?
Chŏmwon	Waeyo? Ssan kŏ-eyo. Kyŏu samman-ich'ŏn won-indeyo mwo.
Pyŏngsu	Che-ga saenggak hae-do, chom pissan kŏt kat'undeyo.
Minho	Namdaemun shijang-esŏ-nun pisut han ke p'alch'ŏn won-ieyo.
Chŏmwon	A, ne, Namdaemun-hago-nun pisŭt hae-poyŏ-do chir-i tallayo. Namdaemun shijang-esŏ os-ul sa-myŏn tu se tal man-e mot ssŭ-ge toe-sŏ sae os-ul sa-ya toe-gŏdunyo.
Pyŏngsu	Kurŏmyŏn i-osh-i Namdaemun shijang ot-poda ne-bae-na orae kayo?
Chŏmwon	Chŏgŏ-do-yo. Kŭrigo hwolsshin tŏ chal majayo.
Minho	Um, ka-sŏ saenggak chom tashi hae-bwa-yagessŏyo.

Phrases and expressions

che-ga saenggak hae-do	*it seems to me*
kyŏu samman-ich'ŏn won-indeyo mwo	*it's only 32,000 won (it's not much)*
chŏgŏ-do-yo	*at least*
ka-sŏ saenggak chom tashi hae-bwa-yagessŏyo	*I'll have to go away and think about it*

ŭng	응	*yes* (casual form)
maj-	맞–	*to fit well* (**maj + nunda = man-nunda**)
kŭnsa ha-	근사하–	*look super, look good*
kyŏu	겨우	*only*
pisŭt ha-	비슷하–	*look similar*
tarŭ-	다르–	*be different* (polite style: **tallayo**)
man-e	만에	*within, in only (2 or 3 months)*
ssŭ-ge	쓰게	*usable*
toe-	되–	*become*
bae	배	*double, (two) times*
orae	오래	*long*
ka-	가–	here: *last, endure*
hwolsshin	훨씬	*by far, far and away*

Grammar

1 Ending sentences with *mwo*

Sometimes Koreans will add **mwo** to the end of certain sentences as a kind of afterthought. It has no real translation (despite literally meaning *what!*), and you don't need to use it yourself. It means something like *you know*, *isn't it* or *I think*, but you should not try to translate it or think that it has any great significance when you come across it.

2 Even if it looks the same

This dialogue has a rather complex verb in it which is a good example of how Korean uses particles and compounds verbs in quite complicated ways to build up important meanings. The form is **pisŭt hae-poyŏ-do**. We will work through it slowly to see how it is formed.

The basic verb is **pisŭt ha-** which means *is similar*. To this the verb **poi-** (*to look like, to appear*) has been added to give the meaning *to look similar, to appear similar*. You have seen verbs compounded before with the verbs **chu-** and **po-** and you remember that these verbs are added on to the polite style of the main verb, with the -yo particle taken off (for example, **mŏgŏ-bo-seyo**, *please try eating it*). This example is just the same; the polite style of *is similar* is taken (**pisŭt haeyo**), the yo is removed (**pisŭt hae-**) and the next verb **poi-** is added (**pisut haepoi-**).

You have also learnt the form -(**ŏ**)**do** before, which means *even though*, and once again this is added to the polite style of the verb, minus the yo.

This means that the meaning of the entire verb set **pisuthae poyodo** is *even though it looks similar, even though it appears similar*.

3 Use of the verb *toe-*

The verb **toe-** means *is okay, (it) will do*, and it can be used after verbs with the particle -**do** (*even though*), to mean *it's okay if. . . .* Here are two examples:

naga-do toeyo	*it's okay to go out* (lit.: *even if/even though you go out, it's okay/it will do*)
mŏgŏ-do toeyo?	*is it okay to eat this?* (lit.: *even if/though I eat this, is it okay?*)

This is a very useful pattern and is often used by Koreans to ask for and to give permission.

Another meaning of the verb **toe-** is *becomes*. You saw it in the dialogue with the word **mot ssu-ge** (*unusable*), meaning *it becomes unusable*. You can add the ending -**ge** onto other verb stems, and follow it with **toe-** to say that something becomes or comes to a particular state. Here are some other examples:

Mon mŏk-ke toeŏssŏyo	*It has become inedible (it's gone off!)*
Hanguk yŏja-hago kyŏrhon ha-ge toeŏssŏyo	*I came to marry a Korean girl*

4 Speech styles and honorifics

We are taking this opportunity to remind you about the essential difference between speech styles and honorifics in Korean. It is absolutely essential that you are clear about the distinction, which is why we are going over it again and giving you a few more examples.

Remember, speech styles are decided according to the person you are talking to. Mostly you will use the polite style, but in formal situations you might use the formal style (which you will learn later), and to close friends and young people or children you might use the informal style or the plain style.

The person you are talking *about*, however, will govern whether or not you use an honorific. There is thus no incompatibility between honorifics and informal speech styles. Imagine you are talking to a child and asking the child where his granddad has gone. You would use the informal or plain style (because you are talking to a child) and you would use an honorific (because you are talking about grandad, who is an older, esteemed person).

When you are addressing someone as 'you' and talking about them, things will be much more straightforward. If you are asking a child what he is doing, you would use an informal style and, of course, no honorific since the person you are talking about (the child) is not an honorific person. In contrast, if you are talking to a professor and asking him what he is doing, you might use the polite or even the formal style and you would certainly use an honorific.

Here are a couple of examples of different combinations of speech styles and honorifics. Make sure you understand in each case the social level of the person being addressed and the social level of the person being spoken about:

Minho, harabŏji mwo ha-shi-ni?	*Minho, what does your granddad do?*
Minho, nŏ mwo ha-ni?	*Minho, what do you do?*
Sŏnsaengnim, harabŏji mwo ha-se-yo?	*Professor, what does your granddad do?*
Sŏnsaengnim, Minho mwo hae-yo?	*Professor, what does Minho do?*

5 Do you want to/do you feel like?

The pattern -(u)llaeyo can be added to the stems of processive verb bases (present tense) to ask in a casual way if someone wants to do or feels like doing something. You met it in the phrase **han-bŏn ibŏ-boshi-llaeyo**, where it is added to the honorific form of **ibŏ-po-** (*to try on*) to give the meaning *would you like to try it on?* Other examples would be:

| Kŏp'i mashi-llaeyo? | *Do you want to drink coffee, do you fancy some coffee?* |
| Noraebang-e ka-llaeyo? | *How about going to a noraebang?* |

Practice

1 Put the following sentences into the plain style.

a 이 옷이 정말 좋아요!
b 비가 와요.
c 뭘 하세요?
d 밥을 먹고 있어요.
e 걱정하고 있어요?
f 조금 더 기다리면 버스가 올 거에요.
g 밥 먹어요.
h 어제 밤 어디 갔어요?
i 조심했어요?

2 Translate the following phrases into Korean using the modifier forms you have learnt in this lesson.

a clothes made of cotton
b the beer we drank yesterday
c the book Mr Kim is reading
d the shirt he is wearing
e the film we saw last year
f the food I hate

3 Join the following two sets of information with -ǒ/a-do to give the meaning 'even if A, then B' (or, 'even though A, B'). For example, the first will be: *Even if it looks good, it isn't.*

a It looks good   it isn't
b It's expensive   it'll be tasty
c It's raining   I want to go out
d I don't like him   I'll have to meet him
e It's a bright colour   it doesn't suit you
f I've got a headache   thinking of going to a *noraebang*

4 Make up a dialogue between two people arguing about which film to see on TV tonight. One of them wants to see a film which the other one says they saw last year. He wants to see a different film, but the other thinks it's on too late and that it's boring anyway. To help you, here are three phrases that you might like to use:

Kǔ-gǒs-un uri-ga changnyǒn-e pon yǒnghwa-janayo!
Yǒldu shi-ga nǒmu nǔjǒssǒyo? Musǔn mar-ieyo?!
Chǒngmal chaemi ǒmnun kǒt kat'ayo.

Now say the dialogue aloud using the informal style for all the verb endings and taking out any honorific suffixes you might have used.

5 Translate the following sentences into Korean.

   a That person who speaks Korean well is coming.
   b I don't like those clothes you bought yesterday.
   c He's a stylish man.
   d Even though the quality is better, it's four times as expensive.
   e Can I try on those clothes you are wearing?
   f What did you say?
   g Please take care when you are driving at night, even though you haven't been drinking.
   h Do you have anything similar?

6 You are looking for a new bag and come across the following pair. Compare one with the other (price, quality, size, colour) and say which one you would like to buy.

REAL LEATHER   £50

100% COTTON   £1

12 do you have a spare room?/the towel is dirty and the food is cold

In this unit you will learn
- about booking hotels and inquiring about vacancies and facilities
- about making complaints when things don't go quite as they should
- more about the formal style of speech and the future tense
- quoted speech and reporting what other people said

▶ Do you have a spare room?

161

do you have a spare room?/
the towel is dirty and the
food is cold

12

Mr Lee is looking for a couple of rooms in a hotel.

손님	빈 방 있어요?
주인	네 있어요. 침대방을 드릴까요, 온돌방을 드릴까요?
손님	침대방 하나하고 온돌방 하나 주세요.
주인	네 알겠습니다.
	침대방은 하루에 오만원이고 온돌방은 하루에 사만원입니다.
	얼마동안 묵으시겠습니까?
손님	우선 삼일 동안요. 그리고 좀 더 묵을지도 몰라요.
주인	오일 이상 예약하시면 5% 할인해 드리는데요.
손님	아, 그럼 우리 집사람하고 좀 의논해 봐야겠어요.
	아침식사도 포함되어 있지요?
주인	네, 물론 아침식사도 포함되어 있습니다.
	7시부터 10시 사이에 지하식당에 가시면 됩니다.
	그리고 이천원만 더 내시면 손님 방까지 배달도 해 드립니다.
손님	아니오, 직접 식당에 가서 먹겠어요.
	이 호텔에 또 무슨 시설들이 있습니까?
주인	수영장, 사우나, 오락실, 노래방, 스텐드바, 그리고 한식당과 양식당이 있습니다.
손님	방에 텔레비젼과 전화도 있나요?
주인	물론입니다. 그리고 미니바도 있습니다.
손님	오, 아주 훌륭하군요. 오일 동안 예약하는 게 좋을 것 같아요.
	아마 우리 집사람도 좋아할 거에요.

Sonnim	Pin pang issŏyo?
Chuin	Ne, issŏyo. Ch'imdaebang-ul tŭrilkkayo, ondolpang-ul tŭrilkkayo?
Sonnim	Ch'imdaebang hana-hago ondolpang hana chuseyo.
Chuin	Ne, algessŭmnida.
	Ch'imdaebang-un haru-e oman won-i-go ondolpang-un haru-e saman won-i-mnida. Ŏlma-dongan mugushigessumnikka?
Sonnim	Usŏn sam-il-dongan-yo. Kurigo chom tŏ mug-uljido mollayo.
Chuin	O-il-isang yeyak ha-shimyŏn o-p'ŏsent'u harin hae-tŭrinŭndeyo.

162

do you have a spare room?/
the towel is dirty and the
food is cold

12

Sonnim	A, kǔrǒm uri chipsaram-hago chom ǔynon hae-bwayagessǒyo.
	Ach'im shiksa-do p'oham toeǒ-itjiyo?
Chuin	Ne, mullon ach'im shiksa-do p'oham toeǒ-issumnida.
	Ilgop-shi-but'ǒ yǒl-shi-sai-e chiha shiktang-e ka-shimyǒn toemnida.
	Kǔrigo ich'ǒn won-man tǒ nae-shimyǒn sonnim pang-kkaji paedal-do hae-durimnida.
Sonnim	Aniyo, chickchǒp shiktang-e ka-sǒ mǒkkessǒyo.
	I-hot'er-e tto musun shisǒl-dur-i issǔmnikka?
Chuin	Suyǒngjang, sauna, orakshil, noraebang, sut'enduba, kurigo hanshiktang-gwa yangshiktang-i issumnida.
Sonnim	Pang-e t'ellebijyǒn-gwa chǒnhwa-do innayo?
Chuin	Mullon-imnida. Kǔrigo miniba-do issǔmnida.
Sonnim	O, aju hullyung ha-gunyo! O-il-dongan yeyak hanun ke cho-ul kǒt kat'ayo. Ama uri chipsaram-do choa ha-lkǒeyo.

Phrases and expressions

ǒlma-dongan mug-ǔshigessǒyo?	*how long will you be staying for?*
chom tǒ muk-ǔljido mollayo	*we may stay longer (I don't know if we might . . .)*
chipsaram-hago chom ǔynon hae-bwayagessǒyo	*I'll have to discuss it with my wife*
chikchǒp shiktang-e ka-sǒ mǒkkessǒyo	*we'll go to the restaurant to eat*
o-il-dongan yeyak hanǔn ke cho-ǔl kǒt kat'ayo	*it seems like it would be a good idea to book for five nights*

pin 빈	*empty, vacant, free* (of seats and rooms)
pang 방	*room*
ch'imdaebang 침대방	*room with bed*
ch'imdae 침대	*bed*
ondolbang 온돌방	*room with bed on floor*
haru-e 하루에	*per day*
haru 하루	*one day* (duration)
ǒlma-dongan 얼마동안	*how long*
-dongan –동안	*during*
muk- 묵–	*stay, lodge, spend the night*
isang 이상	*more than*

163

do you have a spare room?/
the towel is dirty and the
food is cold

12

yeyak ha- 예약하-	*reserve, book*
harin ha- 할인하-	*give a discount*
harin 할인	*discount*
ŭynon ha- 의논하-	*discuss*
ŭynon 의논	*discussion*
ach'imshiksa 아침식사	*breakfast*
ach'im 아침	*morning; breakfast* (abbreviated form)
ach'im ha- 아침하-	*have breakfast*
p'oham doeŏ-iss- 포함되어 있-	*be included*
sai-e 사이에	*between*
chiha shiktang 지하 식당	*basement restaurant*
chiha 지하	*basement*
paedal ha- 배달하-	*deliver*
chikchŏp 직접	*direct(ly)*
shisŏl 시설	*facility*
suyŏngjang 수영장	*swimming pool*
suyŏng ha- 수영하-	*swim*
sauna 사우나	*sauna*
orakshil 오락실	*amusements* (electronic games, etc.)
sut'enduba 스텐드바	*bar* (standing bar)
hanshiktang 한식당	*Korean restaurant* (serving Korean food)
yangshiktang 양식당	*western restaurant*
miniba 미니바	*mini-bar*
hullyung ha- 훌륭하-	*is excellent, great*

Grammar

1 The formal style

The formal style is the last important speech style for you to learn. It is used in formal situations, often by officials or representatives (such as the hotel worker in the dialogue), but it can be used by anybody when some formality is called for. It is perhaps slightly more common among men than women and, if you are a man, it is a good idea to say some sentences in the formal style occasionally, as if you always use the polite style it can sound to Koreans as though your Korean is a bit effeminate. It is quite common to mix formal and polite speech styles in this way, with some sentences in the formal style and some in the polite style.

164

do you have a spare room?/
the towel is dirty and the
food is cold

12

To make statements in the formal style (that is, normal sentences which state facts, not questions, commands or suggestions), you add the ending -(sŭ)mnida to the stem of the verb (either the present stem, past stem, or honorific present or past stem). Note that the ending is spelt -(sŭ)pnida, but pronounced -(sŭ)mnida. To consonant stems you add the form -sŭmnida, and to vowel stems -mnida:

	wear	*buy*
stem	ip-	sa-
	ipsŭmnida	samnida
past	ibŏss-	sass-
	ibŏssŭmnida	sassŭmnida
honorific	ibŭshi-	sashi-
	ibŭshimnida	sashimnida
hon past	ibŭshyŏss-	sashyŏss-
	ibŭshyŏssŭmnida	sashyŏssŭmnida

Note that the past formal forms have a treble -s, and so are spelt for example, **sass-sŭmnida**. We just write two ss in romanization, however. You will recognize these formal statements from expressions like **mian hamnida**, **choesong hamnida** and **algessŭmnida**. All those expressions are almost always used in the formal style.

To make questions in the formal style, you add the ending -(sŭ)mnikka? as follows:

	wear	*buy*
stem	ip-	sa-
	ipsŭmnikka?	samnikka?
past	ibŏss-	sass-
	ibŏssŭmnikka?	sassŭmnikka?
honorific	ibŭshi-	sashi-
	ibŭshimnikka?	sashimnikka?
hon past	ibŭshyŏss-	sashyŏss-
	ibŭshyŏssŭmnikka?	sashyŏssŭmnikka?

Commands in the formal style always go on honorific present stems, and the ending is -pshio (pronounced rather as if it were -pshiyo):

stem	ip	sa-
honorific stem	ibŭshi-	sashi-
formal command	ibŭshipshio	sashipshio

You have already learnt how to make suggestions in the formal style, way back in the early lessons of the course: -(ŭ)pshida. Note that this form is never added to an honorific stem, as suggestions (e.g. *shall we . . .*) always include yourself, and Korean never allows you to refer to yourself in honorific terms.

165

do you have a spare room?/
the towel is dirty and the
food is cold

12

2 The future marker -*kess*

The future marker -kess can be added to any present stem (normal or honorific) to make a future stem. You can then add verb endings to this (such as the polite or formal styles, or a clause ending such as -jiman) in the normal way. You have two good examples in this unit:

Ŏlma-dongan mugŭshi-gess-ŏyo?	*How long will you be staying for?*
Chipsaram-hago ŭynon hae-bwaya-gess-ŏyo	*I will have to discuss with my wife . . .*

The -kess future marker is used in the ending -yagessŏyo (as in the second example) which you have already learnt. It is also used in certain idiomatic phrases like algessŭmnida and morugessŭmnida (*I understand* and *I don't understand*).

Although this form does express the future (it can also be used to express probability), the most common way to put a normal sentence into the future is with the -(ŭ)lkŏeyo form which you have already learnt. -(ŭ)lkŏeyo is a more useful form than -kess for most situations, and the precise difference between them is something that you do not really need to worry about for this course. It is sufficient to be able to recognize the -kess as the future marker, and to know that it can be used to make future stems which can then be used in other constructions.

3 I don't know whether

You can say that you don't know whether you will do something or other by adding -(u)lji-do moru- to a verb stem. The example from the dialogue was **chom tŏ mwug-ulji-do mollayo** (*I don't know whether we will stay a bit longer, it might be that we stay a bit longer*). Here are a couple of other examples:

chorŏp ha-lji-do mollayo	*I don't know whether I'll graduate (or not)*
ka-l su iss-ŭlji-do morŭmnida	*I don't even know if I'll be able to go or not*

166

do you have a spare room?/
the towel is dirty and the
food is cold

12

4 If you do, it will be OK

The sentence **ka-shimyŏn toemnida** means *if you go, it will be OK*, and this pattern, one clause ending in -myŏn, plus a form of the verb **toe-** is a common pattern. In the context of the dialogue it is used to say that breakfast is available between certain times, so that if they go to the restaurant between those times, *it will be OK*. It can be used to ask for permission to do something: **chigŭm ka-myŏn toeyo?** (*is it okay to go now?*).

A very similar pattern is used in the next dialogue, where there is a similar sentence to this: **chŏ-hant'e mal ha-myŏn an toeyo?** (*can't you tell me? if you tell me, won't it be okay?*). A similar use would be **pakk-e naga-myŏn an toemnikka?** (*can't I go outside? won't it be OK if I go outside?*).

The next dialogue is quite advanced in parts and you should be satisfied if you understand the gist of what is going on. If you can understand the details of the dialogue then you can be sure that your Korean is coming on very well indeed.

▶ The towel is dirty and the food is cold

Unfortunately, the hotel didn't turn out to be as good as it looked . . .

손님	지배인 좀 바꿔 주세요.
종업원	실례지만, 무슨 일이세요?
손님	이 호텔 서비스에 대해서 할 말이 있어요.
종업원	죄송하지만 저한테 말씀하시면 안될까요?
손님	지배인한테 직접 말하고 싶은데요.
종업원	좋습니다. 잠깐 기다리세요.

A little while later.

지배인	네, 지배인입니다. 말씀하시지요.
손님	이 호텔 서비스에 문제가 많은 것 같아요. 직원들이 불친절하고 무뚝뚝해요. 그리고 오늘 아침에 식당에 갔는데 음식이 다 식어 있었어요. 어제도 마찬가지였고요.
지배인	그래요? 정말 죄송합니다. 웨이터한테 말씀하셨습니까?

167

do you have a spare room?/
the towel is dirty and the
food is cold

12

손님	물론 종업원 아가씨한테 얘기했지요.
	그런데 아가씨가 불친절한데다가 제 한국말을 못
	알아듣겠다고 하면서 음식에 아무 문제가 없다고
	했어요.
	음식이 다 식었고 맛이 없는데도 말이에요.
지배인	아, 정말 죄송합니다.
	항상 최선의 봉사를 하려고 노력하는데도 가끔
	실수가 발생합니다.
	제가 즉시 식당 종업원들에게 얘기하겠습니다.
손님	그리고 또 있어요.
	오늘 아침 수건을 갈아달라고 했는데
	수건이 너무 더러웠어요.
	그리고 내 아들 방은 아직까지 청소도 안 했어요.
지배인	그것 참 이상하군요.
	손님처럼 불평하는 경우가 지금까지 없었는데요.
손님	그것 뿐이 아니에요. 내 방의 텔레비젼은 고장
	났고, 냉장고 문은 열리지도 않아요.
	솔직히 말해서 이 호텔 서비스하고 시설은 엉망이
	네요.
지배인	죄송합니다. 그렇지만 저희도 손님처럼 불평많은
	사람은 필요없으니까 오늘 당장 나가 주세요.
	요금은 다시 환불해 드리겠습니다.

Sonnim	Chibaein chom pakkwo-juseyo.
Chongŏpwon	Shillye-jiman, musŭn ir-iseyo?
Sonnim	I-hot'el sŏbisu-e taehaesŏ ha-l mar-i issŏyo.
Chongŏpwon	Choesong ha-jiman chŏ-hant'e malssum ha-shimyŏn an toe-lkkayo?
Sonnim	Chibaein-hant'e chikchŏp mal ha-go ship'undeyo.
Chongŏpwon	Chosŭmnida. Chamkkan kidariseyo.

A little while later.

Chibaein	Ne, chibaein-imnida. Malssŭm hashijiyo.
Sonnim	I-hot'el sŏbisu-e munje-ga man-un kŏt kat'ayo. Chigwon-dur-i pulch'inchŏl ha-go muttukttuk haeyo. Kurigo onŭl ach'im-e shiktang-e kannunde umshig-i ta shigŏ-issŏssŏyo. Ŏje-do mach' angaji-yŏt-goyo.
Chibaein	Kŭraeyo? Chŏngmal choesong hamnida. Weit'ŏ-hant'e malssum hashyŏssumnikka?
Sonnim	Mullon chongŏpwon agasshi-hant'e yaegi haetjiyo. Kurŏnde agasshi-ga pulch'inchŏlha-ndedaga che hangung mar-ul mot aradut-ket-tago ha-myŏnsŏ ŭmshig-e amu munje-ga ŏp-tago haessŏyo. Ŭmshig-i ta shig-ŏt-ko mash-i ŏmnŭnde-do mar-ieyo.

168

do you have a spare room?/
the towel is dirty and the
food is cold

12

Chibaein	A, chŏngmal choesong hamnida.
	Hangsang ch'oesŏn-uy pongsa-rul ha-ryŏgo noryŏk hanunde-do kakkum shilsu-ga palsaeng hamnida.
	Chega chŭkshi shiktang chongŏpwon-dul-ege yaegi ha-gessumnida.
Sonnim	Kŭrigo tto issŏyo. Onŭl ach'im sugŏn-ul kara-dallago haennunde sugŏn-i nŏmu tŏrŏwossŏyo.
	Kŭrigo nae adŭl pang-un ajik-kkaji ch'ŏngso-do an haessŏyo.
Chibaein	Kŭ-gŏt ch'am isang ha-gunyo.
	Sonnim ch'ŏrŏm pulp'yŏng hanun kyŏngu-ga chigŭm-kkaji ŏpsŏnnundeyo.
Sonnim	Kŭ-gŏt-ppun-i anieyo. Nae pang-uy t'ellebijyŏn-un kojang nat-ko naengjanggo mun-un yŏlli-ji-do anayo. Soljikhi mal hae-sŏ i-hot'el sŏbisu-hago shisŏr-un ŏngmang-i-neyo.
Chibaein	Choesong hamnida. Kurŏch'iman chŏhuy-do sonnim-ch'ŏrŏm pulp'yŏng manŭn saram-un p'iryo ŏps-unikka onŭl tangjang naga-juseyo. Yogŭm-un tashi hwanpul hae-dŭrigessumnida.

Phrases and expressions

. . . -e taehaesŏ ha-l mar-i issŏyo	*I have something to say about . . .*
	there's something I want to say about . . .
chŏ-hant'e malssŭm ha-shimyŏn an toelkkayo?	*wouldn't it be all right to tell me?*
	can't you just tell me?
ŏje-do mach'angaji-yŏtgoyo	*it was exactly the same yesterday as well*
mot ara-dŭt-ket-tago ha-	*say that (one) couldn't understand*
amu munje ŏp-tago haessŏyo	*(she) said that there wasn't any problem*
mashi-ŏmnŭnde-do mar-ieyo	*I'm saying (emphasis!) that the food even tasted bad*
sugŏn-ul kara-tallago haessŏyo	*I asked (her) to change the towel*
solchikhi mal hae-sŏ	*honestly speaking; to tell the truth; in fact . . .*

169

do you have a spare room?/
the towel is dirty and the
food is cold

12

chibaein 지배인	*manager* (of hotel or facility)	
sŏbisu 서비스	*service*	
(noun)-e taehaesŏ –에 대해서	*concerning* (noun), *about* (noun)	
ha-l mal 할 말	*something to say*	
malssŭm ha- 말씀하–	*speak, say* (of someone honorific, often in phrase **malssum haseyo!**)	
malssŭm haseyo 말씀하세요	*please tell me, please say it* (honorific)	
-e –에	*about, concerning*	
munje 문제	*problem*	
chigwon 직원	*employee*	
pulch'inchŏl ha- 불친절하–	*be unhelpful, be unkind, be impolite*	
muttukttuk ha- 무뚝뚝하–	*be stubborn, be blunt*	
shigŏ-iss- 식어 있–	*be bad, have gone off, cold, be stale etc.*	
mach'angaji-ieyo 마찬가지에요	*be the same, be identical*	
weit'ŏ 웨이터	*waiter*	
yaegi ha- 얘기하–	*talk, tell*	
-(n)(u)ndedaga –는데다가	*on top of* (clause ending, onto verbs, like the **-nunde** pattern)	
ara-dŭl- 알아듣–	*understand* (**l/t** verb like **tul-**, *listen*; **ara-durŏyo**, **ara-dut-ko** etc.)	
. . . tago ha- –다고 하–	*saying* (this pattern shows quoted speech; see note 4)	
-myŏnsŏ –면서	*while* (see note 5)	
shik- 식–	*get cold*	
mash-i ŏps- 맛이 없–	*be tasteless, be unpleasant* (to eat)	
noryŏk ha- 노력하–	*make effort, strive*	
shilsu 실수	*mistake*	
shilsu ha- 실수하–	*make a mistake*	
palsaeng ha- 발생하–	*occur, happen*	
chŭkshi 즉시	*immediately*	
sugŏn 수건	*towel*	
kal- 갈–	*change* (a towel, a platform, clothes etc.)	
kara-ip- 갈아입–	*change clothes*	
kara-t'a- 갈아타–	*change* (platform, trains etc.)	

170

do you have a spare room?/
the towel is dirty and the
food is cold

12

tŏrŏp-	더럽–	be dirty (polite: **tŏrŏwŏyo**, **p**-verb like **kakkap-** etc.)
ajik	아직	yet, still
ch'ŏngso ha-	청소하–	clean, clean up
ch'am	참–	very
-ch'ŏrŏm	–처럼	like
pulp'yŏng ha-	불평하–	complain
kyŏngu	경우	circumstance, situation (here: occurrence)
-ppun	–뿐	only
kojang na-	고장나–	break down
kojang nassŏyo	고장났어요	be broken down
naengjanggo	냉장고	refrigerator
mun	문	door
yolli-ji an(h)-	열리지 않–	does not open
ŏngmang	엉망	rubbish, awful, appalling
tangjang	당장	immediately
yogŭm	요금	fee
hwanpul ha-	환불하–	reimburse

Grammar

1 Concerning

You can say what you are talking, discussing, writing or reading about in Korean with the construction **-e taehaesŏ** which is added to the noun which describes what it is you are talking about. Here are some examples:

chŏngch'i-e taehaesŏ iyagi haessŏyo	*(we) talked about politics*
sŏbisu-e taehaesŏ pulp'yŏng haessŏyo	*(he) complained about the service*
nalssi-e taehaesŏ murŏ-bwassŏyo	*(he) asked about the weather*

2 The future modifier

We have already taught you a bit about the future modifier **-(u)l** and here is the opportunity to give you a few more examples, the first one taken from the dialogue. You will remember that modifiers are added to verbs which then modify or describe the noun which they precede. We've put the modifier phrase in brackets to help you spot the pattern, and likewise its literal meaning on the right-hand side:

sŏbisu-e taehaesŏ (ha-l mar-i) issŏyo	*(words to say) I've got some things to say about the service*
(ka-l shigan-i) toess ŏyo?	*(time to go) is it time to go? (lit. has it become time to go?)*
chib-e (mŏg-ul kŏsh-i) issŏyo?	*(thing to eat) is there anything to eat at home?*

3 On top of that

You have learnt the word **kedaga** which means *on top of that* and you can use a similar form to add to verbs. You use the -(ŭ)nde or -nŭnde imminent elaboration form plus -dedaga, so that the completed forms look like **cho-ŭndedaga** (*on top of being good*); **ka-nŭndedaga** (*on top of going*) and so on. Here are two examples in sentences:

I-osh-i chir-i cho-ŭndedaga ssayo
These clothes are good quality and, on top of that, they're cheap

Pi-ga o-nŭndedaga ch'uwoyo
It's raining and on top of that it's cold

4 Quotations and reported speech

This unit introduces you to the rather complicated matter of reported speech in Korean. Reported speech is when you say what someone else said to you, for example, 'He said he was going to the shops.' What the person said literally, of course, was 'I'm going to the shops', but when we report what he said we change things to something like, 'He said *he was going* to the shops.' This section is designed so that you will be able to recognize reported speech in Korean and use some of the forms yourself. It is not designed to teach reported speech comprehensively. If you wish to know more, you should consult an advanced grammar book. What we tell you here is more than you need to get by.

To report speech in Korean you use the plain style of the verb (**mŏng-nunda, sanda, kanda, chot'a** etc.), plus **ko ha-**. Remember that the plain style can be formed on any verb stem, past present or future, and honorifics. Here are three examples: the first sentence gives you what the person actually said, the second one gives the reported speech form, 'he said' or 'he says':

172

do you have a spare room?/
the towel is dirty and the
food is cold

12

na-nun chib-e kayo   *I'm going going home*
chib-e kanda-go haeyo   *he says he's going home*
(plain style of **ka-** = **kanda**)

saram-dŭr-i mansŭmnida   *there are a lot of people*
saram-dŭr-i mant'a-go haessŏyo   *he said there were a lot of*
(plain style of **man(h)-** = **mant'a**)   *people*
nalsshi-ga choassŏyo   *the weather was good*
     (Mr Kim speaking)

Kim sŏnsaengnim-i nalssi-ga   *Mr Kim said that the*
   choat-tago haessŏyo   *weather was good*
(plain style past of **cho-** = **choat-ta** (from **choass-**))

Note that suggestions and commands can be quoted in the same way:

chib-e kapshida   *let's go home*
chib-e kaja-go haessŏyo   *he suggested we go home*
(**kaja** = plain style suggestion of **ka-**)

pap mŏgŏra   *eat your food!*
pap mŏg-urago haessŏyo   *he told (him/me) to eat his/my food*

Questions are a little more complicated and you only need to be able to recognize them as having **-nya-** or **-nunya-** in them: you will then know what they are when someone uses the form.

5 While

You can say that you are doing something while you are doing something else by adding **-(ŭ)myŏnsŏ** to the 'while' clause. For example, to say that you were talking (while you watched TV), you would say: **t'ellebijyŏn-ul po-myŏnsŏ iyagi haessŏyo.** Here are a couple of other examples.

Hangung mal paeu-myŏnsŏ ŭmag-ul turŏyo
I listen to music while I study Korean

Mŏg-ŭmyŏnsŏ mal hae-boseyo
Please tell me while you're eating

6 Even though: *-nunde-do*

You have learnt the imminent elaboration form **-nunde** which indicates that you have not finished what you are saying yet and that there is more to come. You have also learned **-do**, added to the polite style minus **-yo** to mean *even though*. The combined **do** form **-nundedo** also means *even though* (*so and so*), but has a stronger emphasis than simply -do. Thus, **noryŏk ha-nunde-do kakkŭm shilsu-ga palsaeng hamnida** (from the dialogue) means *even though we (really) are trying, occasionally mistakes happen.*

The other -nŭndae-do form from the dialogue is a way of putting special emphasis on what you have just said. You saw it in the phrase **ŭmshig-i ta shig-ŏt-go mash-i ŏmnŭnde-do marieyo.** The waiter had just told Mr Lee that there was no problem with the food, and then Mr Lee adds: *even though (despite the fact that) the food was off and was tasteless.* The **mar-ieyo** bit on the end means something like *that's what I'm saying* and adds strong emphasis to what has just been said.

7 Quoted requests

Back to reported speech again. When you ask something to be done for your benefit (by using a compound verb with **chu-**, as in **hae-juseyo**, *please do it for me*) and then report what you have just said, as in *I asked him to (do it for me)*, there is a special rule to remember. Instead of saying something like (**hae-ju-rago**) **haessŏyo**, you swop the verb **chu-** and the **-ra-** which follows it with the verb **talla**, to give **hae-dallago haessŏyo** (*I asked him to do it for me*).

You saw this in the phrase **sugŏn-ul karadallago haennunde . . .** (*I asked her to change the towels for me . . .*). Do not worry about this pattern; this note is merely to explain what is going on in the dialogue and to enable you to recognize the form.

Practice

1 You are thinking of sending your children to a new school in Korea and you have a meeting with one of the teachers to chat about the school. Before you go, you jot down some questions you want to ask about the school. Can you put them into Korean in full sentences?

a How many students? (**haksaeng**: *student*)
b What facilities?
c Is it possible to study Korean and Chinese?
d How many students studying Korean? (*how many*: **myŏn-myŏng**)
e What time is lunch?
f Is it okay to go home to eat at lunchtime?

174

do you have a spare room?/
the towel is dirty and the
food is cold

12

2 You go to make a booking at a hotel with the following requirements. The receptionist asks you the following questions, for which you must prepare answers in Korean.

a Mwol towa-durilkkayo?
b Ch'imdaebang durilkkayo?
c Ai-dur-i myŏ-sar-ieyo? (ai: *child*)
d Ŏlma dongan mug-ushigessŏyo?
e Ach'im shiksa paedal hae-durilkkayo?

3 Put the following sentences into the formal style.

a Muŏs-ul hashyŏssŏyo?
b Ch'imdaebang hana chuseyo.
c Chŏ-saram-un Kim sŏnsaengnim-iseyo?
d Na-nun paekhwajŏm-e kanda.
e Radio-rul tŭr-ŭmyŏnsŏ ch'aeg-ul ilgŏyo.

4 Translate the following sentences into English.

a 일주일 이상 예약하시면 10% 할인해 드립니다.
b 솔직히 말해서 그런 사람을 싫어해요.
c 아침 벌써 먹었다고 했어요.
d 온돌방은 하루에 이만원이에요.
e 일곱시에 일어나시면 됩니다.
f 요금은 다시 환불해 드릴 수 없습니다.
g 침대방 두 개 주세요.
h 이 호텔에 대해서 할 말이 있으시면 지배인한테 말해 주세요.

175

do you have a spare room?/
the towel is dirty and the
food is cold

12

5   Ask if there are the following facilities at the hotel at which
    you are staying.

6   Translate the following into Korean.

    a   How long are you booking for?
    b   I told the bank clerk immediately.
    c   What facilities are there at the hotel?
    d   There seem to be a lot of problems with my car.
    e   My son still hasn't got up.
    f   We'll go straight to the bar and have a drink.
    g   Mr Kim is an impolite person.
    h   It would be a good idea to stay for three nights.

7   Your hotel room has a few problems, as you can see in
    the picture. Write out a series of complaints, making your
    language as strong as you can.

13

two to Taegu/ I don't want to go there!

In this unit you will learn
- how to buy train tickets
- how to ask for information about catching the train you want
- how to discuss going out for meals and drinks together

Two to Taegu

매표원	뭘 도와 드릴까요?
박선생	오늘 저녁 대구 가는 기차가 있나요?
매표원	네, 두 가지가 있는데요, 완행은 5시 30분이고 직행은 7시 45분이에요.
박선생	시간은 얼마나 걸려요?
매표원	직행은 3시간 걸리고, 완행은 4시간 30분 걸립니다.
박선생	가격은요?
매표원	완행은 팔천원이고, 직행은 만오천원입니다. 직행은 좌석이 얼마 남지 않았습니다.
박선생	네 자리를 함께 예약할 수 있을까요?
매표원	잠깐만 기다려 보세요. 확인 좀 해 보겠습니다. 아, 네. 네 자리가 있군요! 흡연석을 원하세요, 금연석을 원하세요?
박선생	금연석으로 부탁합니다.
매표원	편도를 드릴까요, 왕복을 드릴까요?
박선생	왕복으로 주세요.
매표원	언제 돌아오시겠어요?
박선생	일요일 저녁에요.
매표원	6시 30분 기차가 있는데, 완행이에요. 일요일 저녁에는 직행 기차는 없는데요.
박선생	그러면 일요일 오후에는요?
매표원	2시 30분에 직행 기차가 있어요.
박선생	그거 좋군요. 그걸로 주세요.
매표원	모두 십이만원입니다.
박선생	몇 번 홈에서 기차가 떠나지요?
매표원	아직 모릅니다. 출발 시간 전에 전광판을 봐 주세요.
박선생	네, 알겠어요. 고맙습니다.

Maep'yowon	Mwol towa-dŭrilkkayo?
Mr Pak	Onŭl chŏnyŏk Taegu kanŭn kich'a-ga innayo?
Maep'yowon	Ne. Tu-kaji-ga innŭndeyo. Wanhaeng-un tasŏ-shi samship-pun-igo chikhaeng-un ilgop-shi sashipo-pun-ieyo.
Mr Pak	Shigan-un ŏlma-na kŏllyŏyo?
Maep'yowon	Chikhaeng-un se-shigan kŏlli-go, wanhaeng-un ne-shigan samship-pun kŏllimnida.
Mr Pak	Kagyŏg-un-yo?
Maep'yowon	Wanhaeng-un p'alch'ŏn won-igo, chikhaeng-un manoch'ŏn won-imnida. Chikhaeng-un chwasŏg-i ŏlma nam-ji anassŭmnida.

Mr Pak	Ne-chari-rul hamkke yeyak ha-l su iss-ŭlkkayo?
Maep'yowon	Chamkkan-man kidaryŏ-boseyo. Hwagin chom hae-bogessŭmnida. A, ne.
	Ne chari-ga it-kunyo. Hŭbyŏnsŏg-ul wonhaseyo, kŭmyŏnsŏg-ul wonhaseyo?
Mr Pak	Kŭmyŏnsŏg-uro put'ak hamnida.
Maep'yowon	P'yŏndo-rul turilkkayo? Wangbog-ul turilkkayo?
Mr Pak	Aniyo. Wangbog-uro chuseyo.
Maep'yowon	Ŏnje tora-oshigessŏyo?
Mr Pak	Ilyoil chŏnyŏg-eyo.
Maep'yowon	Yŏsŏ-shi samship-pun kich'a-ga innunde, wanhaeng-ieyo.
	Ilyoil chŏnyŏg-enun chikhaeng kich'a-nun ŏmnundeyo.
Mr Pak	Kŭrŏmyŏn ilyoil ohu-nun-yo?
Maep'yowon	Tu-shi samship-pun-e chikhaeng kich'a-ga issŏyo.
Mr Pak	Kŭ-gŏ cho-k'unyo. Ku-gŏllo chuseyo.
Maep'yowon	Modu shibiman won-imnida.
Mr Pak	Myŏt-pŏn hom-esŏ kich'a-ga ttŏna-jiyo?
Maep'yowon	Ajik morumnida. Ch'ulbal shigan-jŏn-e chŏnkwangp'an-ul pwa-juseyo.
Mr Pak	Ne, algessŏyo. Komapsumnida.

Phrases and expressions

mwol towa-durilkkayo?	*how can I help you?*
olma nam-ji anassumnida	*there are only a few left*

Taegu 대구	a Korean city
wanhaeng 완행	*slow train (also called* **mwugwunghwa***)*
chikhaeng 직행	*fast train, express train (also called* **saemaul(ho)***)*
kagyŏk 가격	*price*
chwasŏk 좌석	*seating, places*
nam- 남–	*be left (over), remain*
chari 자리	*seat*
hamkke 함께	*together*
hwagin ha- 확인하–	*check, confirm*
hŭpyŏnsŏk 흡연석	*smoker (compartment)*
kŭmyŏnsŏk 금연석	*no smoking compartment*
wonha- 원하–	*want, require*
put'ak ha- 부탁하–	*make a request*

p'yŏndo 편도	*single*	
wangbok 왕복	*return*	
hom 홈	*platform*	
chulbal 출발	*departure*	
chulbal ha- 출발하–	*depart*	
chŏngwangp'an 전광판	*electronic notice board*	
pwa-juseyo 봐주세요	*please look at*	

Grammar

1 -*ŭlkkayo* to ask questions

In some of the earlier units of this course you learnt -ŭlkkayo as a pattern meaning *shall we?* As you will have seen in this lesson, it is also sometimes used to ask a question: ne-chari-rul hamkke yeyak ha-l su issŭlkkayo? (*is it possible to book four seats together?*). There are several patterns like this in Korean where certain verb endings do not always have their basic meaning. The context will always make clear to you which is the correct meaning and in most cases -(ŭ)lkkayo does mean *shall we?* and is used to make suggestions.

2 Making requests

Koreans have a word for *favour* (as in *do a favour for someone*), putak and you saw it used in the sentence kŭmyŏnsŏg-uro put'ak hamnida. To say *I have a favour to ask*, you say either (che-ga) put'ak issŏyo and then say what the request is or else say the request, and then add put'ak hamnida or put'ak haeyo (*please, I ask you to do it as a favour*).

3 Before and after

You have already learnt the nouns chŏn and hu which mean *before* and *after*, respectively. They can be used with nouns, as in ch'ulbal shigan-jŏn-e (*before the time of departure*), or shiksa-hu-e (*after the meal*). They can also be used with verbs, although in a slightly different way.

To say *before* (verb) you add -ki jŏn-e to the stem, as in the following examples: shijak ha-gi jŏn-e (*before we begin . . .*) or hakkyo-e ka-gi jŏn-e (*before (I/you) go to school*).

To say *after* (verb) you add -(ŭ)n hu-e (or -(ŭ)n taum-e, which has the same meaning) to the verb stem of a processive verb. This -(ŭ)n is the past modifier which you have already learnt (the present modifier, you will recall, is -nŭn, as in kanŭn), e.g. mŏg-ŭn hu-e (*after eating*); hakkyo-e ka-n taum-e (*after going to school*).

In the next dialogue there is more new grammar, but the most important thing is the colloquial language that is used. There are several examples of constructions being used in ways similar to, but not quite the same as what you have seen before and your aim should be to get the drift of what is going on, and not to be put off by the colloquialisms and (at times) seeming lack of grammar rules! This is what it will be like when you first go to Korea and listen to Koreans talking with each other. With a little practice at concentrating on the drift of what is being said, you will find that the Korean you have learnt in this course will stand you in good stead.

I don't want to go there!

Some colleagues are discussing what they will do after work.

윤선생	오늘 저녁 일 끝나고 뭐 할거에요?
백선생	일 끝나고요? 모르겠어요. 아직 계획 없어요.
윤선생	저녁이나 같이 먹으러 갈까요?
백선생	좋은 생각이네요. 그런데 우리 둘만 가요?
윤선생	다른 사람도 부르지요.
	김 선생하고 이 선생한테 얘기해 볼까요?
백선생	좋지요. 어이, 김 선생, 이 선생!
	오늘 저녁 밥 먹으면서 소주 한잔 어때요?
김선생	좋아요. 그런데 어디로 갈 거에요?
윤선생	글쎄요, 그냥 불고기하고 소주 한잔 하려고요.
	그리고 나서 노래방에도 가고요.
김선생	술 마시는 건 좋은데, 저는 불고기는 별로에요.
	그리고 노래하는 건 딱 질색이에요.
백선생	아, 그럼 불고기 말고 다른 거 먹으면
	되잖아요.
	그리고 노래하지 말고 그냥 듣기만 하세요.
김선생	그거 괜찮은 생각이네요. 그런데 오늘 돈이
	별로 없는데....
윤선생	걱정마세요. 오늘 저녁은 내가 한턱 낼께요.
김선생	아 그럼, 좋습니다.

백선생 이 선생은 어때요? 같이 가시겠어요?
이선생 글쎄요, 저도 가고 싶은데, 저는 인천에 가서
싱싱한 생선회를 먹고 싶은데요.
백선생 에이, 인천은 너무 멀어요.
그리고 생선회는 요즘 너무 비싸고요.
윤선생 게다가 저는 생선회를 못 먹어요.
이선생 좋아요, 좋아. 그냥 해 본 소리에요.
오늘은 저도 따라가서 불고기에 소주나 먹을 수
밖에 없겠네요.

Mr Yun Onŭl chŏnyŏk il kkŭnna-go mwo ha-lkŏeyo?
Mr Paek Il kkŭnna-go-yo? Morŭgessŏyo. Ajik kyehoek
ŏpsŏyo.
Mr Yun Chŏnyŏk-ina kach'i mŏg-urŏ ka-lkkayo?
Mr Paek Cho-un saenggag-ineyo. Kŭrŏnde uri tŭl-man
kayo?
Mr Yun Tarŭn saram-do purŭ-jiyo. Kim sŏnsaeng-hago
I sŏnsaeng-hant'e yaegi hae-bolkkayo?
Mr Paek Cho-ch'iyo. Ŏi, Kim sŏnsaeng, I sŏnsaeng! Onŭl
chŏnyŏk pap mŏg-ŭmyŏnsŏ soju han jan ŏttaeyo?
Mrs Kim Choayo. Kŭrŏnde ŏdi ka-lkŏeyo?
Mr Yun Kulsseyo. Kŭnyang pulgogi-hago soju han-jan
ha-ryŏgoyo. Kŭrigo nasŏ noraebang-e-do ka-go-yo.
Mrs Kim Sul mashinŭn kŏn cho-ŭnde chŏ-nun pulgogi-nun
pyŏllo-eyo. Kŭrigo norae hanŭn kŏn ttak
chilsaeg-ieyo.
Mr Paek A, kurŏm pulgogi malgo tarŭn kŏ mŏg-ŭmyŏn
toe-janayo. Kurigo norae ha-ji malgo kŭnyang
tŭt-kiman haseyo.
Mrs Kim Kŭ-gŏ koench'anun saenggag-ineyo. Kurŏnde onŭl
ton-i pyŏllŏ ŏmnŭnde . . .
Mr Yun Kŏkjŏng maseyo. Onŭl chŏnyŏg-un nae-ga han t'ŏk
nae-lkkeyo.
Mrs Kim A, kŭrŏm. Chosŭmnido.
Mr Paek I sŏnsaeng-un ŏttaeyo? Kach'i kashigessŏyo?
Mrs Lee Kŭlsseyo. Chŏ-do ka-go ship'unde, chŏ-nun Inch'ŏn-e
ka-sŏ shingshing han saengsŏn hoe-rul mŏk-ko
ship'ŭndeyo.
Mr Paek Ei, Inch'ŏn-un nŏmu mŏrŏyo. Kurigo saengsŏn
hoe-nun yojŭm nŏmu pissa-goyo.
Mr Yun Kedaga chŏ-nun saengsŏn hoe-rul mon mŏgŏyo.
Mrs Lee Choayo. Choa. Kŭnyang hae-bon sori-eyo. Onŭr-un
chŏ-do ttara-ga-sŏ pulgogi-e soju-na mŏg-ul su
pakk-e ŏpkenneyo.

Phrases and expressions

il kkŭnnago	*after finishing work*
ajik kyehoek ŏpsŏyo	*I don't have any plans yet*
cho-ŭn saenggag-ineyo	*that's a good idea*
uri tŭl-man kayo?	*is it just the two of us going?*
kŭnyang soju han jan haryŏgoyo	*we were just thinking of having a soju*
chŏnŭn pulgogi-nun pyŏllo-eyo	*I don't really like pulgogi*
norae hanŭn kŏn ttak chilsaeg-ieyo	*I really hate singing*
norae ha-ji malgo tŭt-kiman haseyo	*don't sing, just listen instead*
kŭnyang hae-bon sori-eyo	*I was just saying it (don't take it too seriously)*
soju-na mŏg-ul su pakk-e ŏp-kenneyo	*there's nothing for it (no alternative) but to eat soju*
han t'ŏk naelkkeyo	*I'll pay (for everyone); it's on me*

kyehoek 계획	*plan(s)*
purŭ- 부르–	*call*
ŏi 어이	*hey! (used to call close friends and colleagues)*
pap mŏk- 밥 먹–	*have a meal*
kŭnyang 그냥	*simply, just*
kŭrigo nasŏ 그리그 나서	*after that*
-ko nasŏ –고 나서	*after (added to verb stems)*
pyŏllo 별로	*not particularly, not really (fond of)*
ttak chilsaeg-ieyo 딱 질색이에요	*hate, is awful (to me)*
(noun) malgo 말고	*not (noun), instead of (noun) (when suggesting another alternative)*
-kiman haseyo –기만 하세요	*just do (verb)*
pyŏllo ŏps- 별로 없–	*have almost none, scarcely have any*
inch'ŏn 인천	Korean port near Seoul
sshingshing ha- 싱싱하–	*be fresh*
saengsŏn 생선	*fish*
hoe 회	*raw meat*
ei 에이	*hey, come off it!*
kedaga 게다가	*on top of that*
ttarŭ- 따르–	*follow*
-(u) su pakk-e ŏps- –(으)ㄹ 수 밖에 없–	*there is nothing for it but to (verb)*

Grammar

1 More ways of saying 'afterwards'

You can add the ending -ko na-sŏ to any present tense processive verb base to mean *after* (verb):

Il ha-go na-sŏ sul han-jan hapshida
After finishing work let's have a drink

-ko na-sŏ can be abbreviated to -kosŏ, and sometimes even to just -ko.

2 Informal sentences

This dialogue shows the way in which Koreans can add particles to the end of verbs in colloquial speech to give extra nuances to what they are saying. They can also make incomplete sentences which they complete simply by adding the polite particle -yo. You do not need to worry about learning rules for this kind of thing, since in most circumstances you will want to use a more formal and grammatical style of speaking when you first begin to speak Korean in Korea. It is very useful to recognize what is going on in colloquial speech, however, and as you spend more time speaking with Koreans you will quickly learn to do this kind of thing for yourself.

You can miss out the rest of this section if you wish, as the explanation may seem a bit complicated. Your main task should be to completely familiarize yourself with the dialogue, almost to the extent of being able to say it by heart. For the adventurous, however, here are two sentences from the dialogue with an explanation of how they have been constructed.

Soju han jan haryŏgoyo

You have previously met the -(ŭ)ryŏgo pattern, with the meaning *with the intention of*. Normally it is used in the pattern (clause A)-ŭryŏgo (clause B), as in **hangung mal paeu-ryŏgo ch'aek sassŏyo**, but here the pattern is simply (clause A)-uryŏgo-yo. Clause B has been omitted in casual speech and the polite particle added to round the construction off. The full form would have been something like **soju han jan haryŏgŏ ŏnu-sulchib-ina kalkka haeyo** (*we were thinking of going to some pub or other to have a drink*), but this is cut down to what would translate as *to have a drink* – or, in better English, *we were just thinking of going for a drink* and is made into a sentence simply be adding -yo to the -(ŭ)ryŏgo pattern.

Kŭrigo na-sŏ noraebang-e-do ka-go-yo

This means *after that (we were thinking of) going to a* noraebang *too*. The -go at the end is the clause ending -ko that normally means *and* when you are going to add another clause. However, in this case, the meaning is *as well*, *in addition*. This sentence is being added to the one that has been said previously to indicate that this is also part of the plan as well. Then the particle yo is added to round it all off.

3 Negatives with *pyŏllo*

Sentences with negative verbs in them (with an and mot) can be modified by inserting the word pyŏllo in them, to mean *not particularly*. This will be clearer with examples:

kogi-rul pyŏllo an choa haeyo   *I don't particularly like meat*
pyŏllo ka-go ship'chi anayo   *I don't particularly want to go*
pyŏllo chaemi ŏpsŏyo   *it's not particularly interesting*

The dialogue also has a pyŏllo sentence in it, which is slightly different. Chŏ-nun pulgogi-nun pyŏllo-eyo. This is a more colloquial form, putting the copula onto the end of the word pyŏllo. But you can see that it is in a sense an abbreviated form of chŏ-nun pulgogi-nun pyŏllo choa ha-ji anayo, so the pattern is essentially the same. You should stick to the full form with a negative verb most of the time and leave the colloquial, abbreviated form to native speakers.

4 Not one thing, but another instead

You can stay *instead of* (noun), or *not* (noun) by putting the word malgo after the noun, as you can see in these examples:

Sagwa-malgo kogi sa-pshida
Let's not buy apples, let's buy meat; instead of apples, let's buy meat

Chapji-malgo shinmun-ul ing-nŭn kŏ choa haeyo
It's not magazines, it's newspapers I enjoy reading

Pulguksa-malgo san-e ka-nŭn ke ŏttaeyo?
How about going to the mountain instead of Pwulguksa?

You can use a similar pattern to say *instead of* (verb). Simply add -ji malgo (this is the same -ji that you use in the long negative, or in -ji maseyo). Look at the following examples, the first is from the dialogue:

Norae ha-ji malgo tut-kiman haseyo
Don't sing (do a song), just listen (instead)

Kŏp'i mashi-ji malgo ch'a-na tuseyo
Don't drink coffee, have some tea or something instead

Wae kongbu ha-ji malgo iyagi-man hara-go haeyo?
Why are you saying just talking and not studying (instead)?

5 Just doing something

The sentence **tut-kiman haseyo** means *just listen!* The form
-kiman ha- added to processive verbs means *just* (verb) or *only*
(verb). Here are examples:

Mal ha-ji an-k'o mŏk-kiman haessŏyo
We didn't say anything, we just ate

Tŭt-kiman haeyo?
Are you only listening (rather than participating)?

6 There's nothing for it, but to . . .

When you feel you have no option but to do something or
other, or that you are obliged to do something, you can use the
pattern **-(ŭ)l su pakk-e ŏps-**. Here are examples:

Ka-l su pakk-e ŏpsŏyo.
There's nothing for it but to go; I'll have to go

Pissa-jiman sa-l su pakk-e ŏpsŏyo
Although it's expensive, there's nothing for it but to buy it

Practice

1 Translate the following sentences into English.

   a 좌석이 얼마 남지 않았어요.
   b 다른 거 먹으면 안돼요.
   c 왕복을 드릴까요?
   d 등산하는 건 딱 질색이에요.
   e 제가 갈 수 밖에 없겠네요.
   f 그냥 야구하려고요.
   g 오늘 오후 목포에 가는 기차 있어요?
   h 그거 괜찮은 생각이네요.

2 For each of the following say that you will go out *before* doing them and then that you will go out *after* doing them.

   a (Eating) lunch.
   b Telephoning your mother.
   c Having fun (**nol-**).
   d Reading the newspaper.

3 Look at the following information about train availability and then answer the questions.

열차 (기차) 시간표			
목적지	출발	도착	
서울	8:00	11:00	직행
대구	20:00	23:30	직행
부산	7:00	12:00	완행
광주	13:00	18:00	완행
서울	10:00	15:00	완행
대전	14:00	16:00	직행

   a 밤 늦게 대구에 가고 싶어요. 기차가 몇시에 출발해요?
   b 서울에 가는 직행은 몇시에 떠나요?
   c 언제 도착해요?
   d 대전에 가는 완행 있어요?
   e 부산에 가는 완행 기차 있어요?

4 Make up three sentences saying that there is nothing for it but to . . .

   a go home
   b pay the money
   c get up at six in the morning

5 Make up a set of sentences, each one using the following sets of information and using (noun)-**malgo** or (verb)-**ji malgo**. For example, for the first one you could make up a sentence which said *I want to eat fruit, not meat*.

6 Translate the following sentences into Korean.

a Buy something to eat before the departure time.
b Shall we have a talk to your parents?
c I'd like to go too, but it's a long way.
d Can I book three seats together?
e Let's go to Inchŏn, not to Seoul.
f What shall we do after finishing work?
g When are you going to come back?
h Do you like eating raw fish?

review

Introduction

So, you have virtually reached the end of this course. This unit contains more exercises which practise the situations and grammar you have been learning in the last six units. Most of these exercises are Korean to English or English to Korean translations, since that is the best way to check that you have really mastered the material in the units. Make sure you are comfortable with the topics in the list that follows and be sure to revise the grammar notes for any of the major patterns you are not quite happy with. It would be a good idea also to read through all the dialogues in the units once again. You will find there are things that you felt a bit uneasy about at the time that are now clearer to you and you are sure to understand more fully what is going on grammatically in the dialogues. Even though you have reached the end of the course, you will find that simply reading through the dialogues every so often will help you to retain the things you have learnt.

Topic revision

The following list shows the main topics that have been covered in the last six units. You should feel capable of handling these topics at a simple level should you need to when you are in Korea. If you feel unsure about a particular topic, you should go over the dialogue again more thoroughly, and should revise the expressions and vocabulary that go with it. Of course there will still be many things that you are not able to say in Korean, but with the tools we have given you you should be able to succeed in carrying out many language tasks, some at quite a high level, and should have a more fascinating and enjoyable experience as a result whenever you visit Korea or communicate with Korean people.

- advanced phone conversations
- cancelling appointments
- dating and talking about other people
- describing what you did
- buying presents
- retorting
- policemen and traffic offences
- lost property
- describing objects
- feeling ill
- getting medicine
- buying and comparing clothes
- trying on clothes
- booking in a hotel and asking about facilities
- complaining
- train journeys
- arranging to go out

Practice

1 Translate the following into English.

a Ŏmŏni-ga yŏnghwa-rul choa ha-nikka abŏji taeshin bidio po-myŏn toeyo.
b Sut'uresu-ga wonin-in kŏt kat'ayo.
c Sashil aju chungyo han sŏryu-ga tŭrŏ-issŏyo.
d Ch'ŏngpaji-ga mot ssŭge toeŏssŏyo.
e Uri chipsaram-i ama al-go iss-ulkŏeyo.
f Naeil chŏnyŏk il kkŭnnago san-e ka-l kyehoek issŏyo?
g Tangshin-un nae ŭygyŏn-ul hangsang choa ha-ji anayo.
h Uri pang mun-un yŏlli-ji-do anayo.
i Tosŏgwan-i ŏdi-inji chom karŭch'yŏ-jushigessŏyo? (tosŏg-wan = *library*)
j Kŭrŏk'e sur-ul mani mashyŏssŏyo?
k Yŏjŭm aju yuhaeng ha-nun sut'ail-ieyo.
l Myŏnhŏcchŭng chom poyŏ-juseyo.

2 For each of the following pictures make up a question which asks if someone has ever tried doing them. Then make up an answer which says *yes, I have* and another which says *you did it yesterday, as a matter of fact.* (*dance*: **ch'um ch'u-**)

3 Make up an appropriate response to the following questions or requests.

  a 김선생님 좀 바꿔 주세요.
  b 영화구경을 좋아하세요?
  c 데이트할 때 보통 어디 가세요?
  d 이 청바지 질이 어때요?
  e 약속을 자주 취소하는 사람이세요?

4 Translate the following into Korean.

  a I really didn't see the sign.
  b You can wear it with jeans.
  c I'm ringing to cancel my appointment.
  d Is there a telephone and TV in the room?
  e The service is rubbish!
  f We bought him socks last year.
  g It looks a bit small.
  h I thought so.
  i I'd like to go to Inchŏn and eat raw fish.
  j What does your car look like?
  k Would you write a letter for me?
  l My head hurts so much I can't sleep.

5 Your friend has a new girlfriend and you quiz him about her. Make up questions to fill in the following fact file:

Name _____

Age _____

Occupation _____

Father's name _____

How met? _____

What do together? _____

Likes/Dislikes _____

6 Translate the following into English.

a 잘못하면 아주 위험해요.
b 복동씨한데 전할 말이 있어요?
c 손님 방까지 배달해 드립니다.
d 어제 여기 왔었는데요. 잠바를 놓고 갔어요.
e 아가씨가 질이 좋다고 했어요.
f 여자 친구 생겨서 매일 나가는 것 같아요.
g 이야기하지 말고 듣기만 하세요.
h 식후에 한 알씩 하루 두 번 드세요.
i 이거 봐. 질이 별로 안 좋아.
j 혹시 어디 갔는지 아세요?
k 새 텔레비젼은 어떨까요?
l 남대문에서는 비슷한 게 두 배나 더 싸요.

7 Complete the following dialogue.

A Naeil chŏnyŏg-e shigan-i issŏyo?
You (No, an urgent matter has come up. Why?)
A Kŭnyang naga-go ship'ŏnnŭndeyo.
You (How about Monday?)
A Wolyoil-lar-un abŏji-ŭy saengshin-ieyo.
You (Really? Will there be a party?)
A Aniyo. Kŭnyang shiktang-e ka-sŏ kach'i chŏnyŏk ha-nŭn kŏ-eyo.
You (What are you going to buy for him?)
A Yangmal-yo. Hangsang yangmal sayo.
You (How about Tuesday? Do you have time then?)
A Ne, choayo. Nait'-u ka-lkkayo? (nait'u: night club)
You (That's a good idea.)

8 Rewrite the dialogue in question 7 using the informal and plain styles of speech.

9 Put the following sentences into the formal style.

   a Chigŭm ŏdi kaseyo?
   b Chumun haessŏyo?
   c Ilgop-shi-e irŏnayo.
   d Ppalli hae-juseyo.
   e Chŏ-saram-un pulch'injŏl han saram-ieyo.

10 The following pictures tell what you did last Saturday. Write an account of what you did, putting in as many details as you can according to what the pictures suggest.

11 Translate the following into Korean.

   a I started meeting her often from that time.
   b Don't be surprised even if you have no energy (strength).
   c You help this time.
   d Although it might look similar, it isn't.
   e Be (more) careful from now on.
   f We'll go straight to the restaurant and eat.
   g It's turned out well then. Goodbye!
   h This evening I'll pay.
   i What time did you leave our department store?
   j Mistakes do happen.
   k Shall I introduce you?
   l Would you like to try it on?

translation of dialogues

Unit 1

Where are you off to?

Sangmin	Jaemin! Hello/How are you!
Jaemin	Hello! How have you been getting along?
Sangmin	Fine, fine. Where are you going?
Jaemin	Right now I'm off to the city centre.
Sangmin	What are you going to do in the city centre?
Jaemin	I'm going to buy some bread.
Sangmin	I'm also going to buy bread in the city centre.
Jaemin	Let's go together!
Sangmin	Yes, let's.

Cheers!

Sangmin	Excuse me/Waiter! Do you have any soju?
Ajŏssi	Yes, yes. We have. Soju, beer, western spirits – all of them.
Sangmin	Well then, give us a beer and one soju, please.
Ajŏssi	Yes. I understand.
Sangmin	And we also need some snacks/side dishes. What do you have?
Ajŏssi	Fruit, squid, dry snacks, p'ajon – we've got all of those.
Sangmin	Then give me some fruit and some squid, please.
Ajŏssi	Here you are.
Sangmin	Thank you. Enjoy it! (Good appetite!)
Sangmin	Cheers!

Unit 2

Long time, no see!

Mr Pak	Mr Kim! How are you?
Mr Kim	Ah, Mr Pak! Hello there!
Mr Pak	Long time, no see!
Mr Kim	Yes, that's right. It's really been a long time.
Mr Pak	How have you been getting along?
Mr Kim	Yes, fine. How's business these days?
Mr Pak	It's so-so. This is my wife.
Mr Kim	Oh, really? Pleased to meet you. I've heard a lot about you.
Mr Pak's wife	Pleased to meet you. I'm Yunhuy Jang.
Mr Kim	I'm Jinyang Kim. I'm pleased that I've met you.

It's not me!

Mr O	Excuse me!
Mr Lee	Yes?
Mr O	Are you the Korean language teacher?
Mr Lee	No. I'm not a Korean language teacher. I'm a Japanese language teacher.
Mr O	Ah, I'm sorry. Isn't this the Korean department's office?
Mr Lee	No, this isn't the Korean department. This is the Japanese department.
Mr O	Right. Where is the Korean department office, please?
Mr Lee	It's over there.
Mr O	Excuse me, is this the Korean department's office?
Mr Kim	Yes. What brings you here? (Can I help you?)
Mr O	I've come to meet the Korean language teacher.

Unit 3

Sorry, wrong number!

Tony	Hello? I'm sorry, but can I speak to Mr Kim, please?
Mr Pak	There is no such person here.
Tony	Isn't that 389 2506?

Mr Pak	No. You've dialled the wrong number.
Tony	I'm sorry.
Tony	Hello? I'm sorry, but can I speak to Mr Kim, please?
Mr Kim's wife	Wait a moment, please.
Mr Kim	Yes? Speaking.
Tony	Ah, hello. I'm Tony from the British embassy.
Mr Kim	Ah, hello! Long time, no see!
Tony	Do you have any free time this lunchtime?
Mr Kim	Yes, I do.
Tony	Then I'd like to buy you lunch.
Mr Kim	Yes, fine. Let's meet at 12 in front of Lotte Hotel.
Tony	Great. So, I'll see you in a little while.

Are you ready to order yet?

Waiter	Welcome! Please take a seat over here.
Mr Kim	Thank you.
Waiter	Would you like anything to drink?
Mr Kim	We'll have some beer first, please.
Mr Kim	Do you like Korean food?
Tony	Yes, I like it a lot, but I can't eat spicy food so well.
Mr Kim	Then let's eat pulgogi or kalbi.
Tony	Yes, fine. And I'd like to eat some naengmyon as well.
Waiter	Would you like to order?
Tony	Pulgogi for two people and two dishes of naengmyon, please.
Waiter	Would you like water naengmyon or pibim naengmyon?
Tony	Water naengmyon, please.
Waiter	Enjoy your meal!
Tony	Waitress! More water and more kimchi, please.

Unit 4

How much is it all together?

Assistant	What are you looking for?
Chris	Do you have dictionaries?

Assistant	Yes. A Korean dictionary?
Chris	Yes, I'd like both a Korean–English dictionary and an English–Korean dictionary.
Assistant	Here you are.
Chris	How much is it?
Assistant	Each volume is 10,000 won; 20,000 won all together.
Chris	Do you have Chinese character dictionaries also?
Assistant	We have three kinds of Chinese character dictionary.
Chris	The cheapest one, please.
Assistant	Just a moment . . . here it is.
Chris	Thank you. How much is it all together?
Assistant	The Chinese character dictionary is 30,000 won . . . therefore all together it's 50,000 won.
Chris	The cheapest one is 30,000 won? How much is the most expensive one, then?! 100,000 won?!
Assistant	Oh, I'm sorry; I've made a mistake. It's 30,000 won all together. Would you like a receipt?
Chris	Yes please.
Assistant	OK. Here it is. Goodbye!
Chris	Goodbye.

Finding the way

Mr Pak	Excuse me, can you tell me where the bank is around here?
Bank Clerk A	If you go left at that post office over there, there is the Sango'p bank.
Mr Pak	Thank you.
Mr Pak	I'd like to change some English money into Korean money.
Bank Clerk B	We don't deal with foreign currency at this bank. Please go to the Korea Exchange Bank.
Mr Pak	Where is there a Korea Exchange Bank?
Bank Clerk B	Cross over the road and go towards Chongno. At the crossroads in Chongno, if you go right there is a Korea Exchange Bank.
Mr Pak	Is it far from here?
Bank Clerk B	No. It's about five minutes on foot.

Unit 5

Is this the bus for Tongdaemun market?

Mr Kim	Excuse me, is there a bus for Tongdaemun market here?
Mr Lee	I don't have a clue, I'm not from Seoul.
Mr Kim	Excuse me, is there a bus to Tongdaemun market from here?
Mrs O	No. You can't get a bus to Tongdaemun market from here. But if you get bus number 20 it will take you to Namdaemun market.
Mr Kim	Namdaemun market? What is there at Namdaemun market?
Mrs O	What is there? There's nothing they don't sell at Namdaemun market.
Mr Kim	Are there more goods than at Tongdaemun market?
Mrs O	In my opinion Namdaemun market has more goods than Tongdaemun, and is more interesting. However, they don't sell monkeys at Namdaemun market. They do sell them at Tongdaemun.
Mr Kim	Is that true?! Although . . . I don't need a monkey.
Mrs O	Then take the number 20 bus.
Mr Kim	Where do I get it?
Mrs O	Take it at the stop straight across the road.
Mr Kim	How much is the fare?
Mrs O	My, you must be a real stranger here (country bumpkin)! It's 400 won.
Mr Kim	Thank you.
Mrs O	Hurry up. The bus is coming!

This fruit doesn't look too good!

Minja	How much are the apples here?
Chŏmwon A	One box is 30,000 won.
Minja	That's too expensive. Will you cut the price a bit?
Chŏmwon A	OK, you can take a box for 28,000 won.
Minja	It's still expensive.
Chŏmwon A	Then go and try somewhere else! Bad luck all morning (today, since the morning)!

Minja	These apples don't look too good (fresh). Some of them have gone bad.
Chŏmwon B	Really? Then I'll cut the price a bit for you.
Minja	How much will you give me them for?
Chŏmwon B	Just give me 31,000 won.
Minja	What?! That's even more expensive than the stall next door!
Chŏmwon B	All right. Then just give me 27,000 won.
Minja	Please cut me a bit more off the price.
Chŏmwon B	All right, then! Just pay 25,000 a box.
Minja	Thank you. Three boxes please.

Unit 6

Off to the mountains

Mr Kim	The weather's really good today.
Tony	Yes. The weather's better in Korea than England.
Mr Kim	What are you going to do tomorrow? If you don't have anything on, shall we go to the mountains?
Tony	I do want to go, but tomorrow I decided to go shopping at Tongdaemun market with my wife.
Mr Kim	How about next Sunday, then?
Tony	Next Sunday I'm thinking of going to Pulguksa with some friends from university.
Mr Kim	Next Sunday won't do either, then. When would be okay?
Tony	The Sunday after that would probably be fine.
Mr Kim	All right. Then let's go that following Sunday.
Tony	I like mountain climbing too. But there aren't many mountains in Britain so I haven't been able to do much. By the way, which mountain shall we go to?
Mr Kim	Tobongsan mountain would be convenient.
Tony	Then shall we meet at the entrance to Tobongsan mountain?

I've got a nasty headache!

Jaehoon	I'm going into town. Shall we go together?
Yongt'ae	I don't know . . . I don't feel too good.
Jaehoon	You don't feel well *again*? You're always pretending to be ill!
Yongt'ae	No I'm not. That's not true. Today I really am ill.

Jaehoon	What is it this time?
Yongt'ae	I've got a nasty headache. My head hurts.
Jaehoon	Is that all? Don't worry – it's perhaps because the weather is hot.
Yongt'ae	I don't think so. I have stomach ache as well.
Jaehoon	Is it bad?
Yongt'ae	Yes. It hurts a lot.
Jaehoon	Then let's go to the chemist to buy some medicine.
Yongt'ae	I can't. I have no energy (strength). Besides, my legs hurt.
Jaehoon	Your legs, too? It seems like your whole body hurts! Is there anywhere that doesn't hurt?
Yongt'ae	Shut up! Don't make fun of me. I need some medicine.
Jaehoon	I've got a cure-all medicine here – it's alcohol! It's better than medicine, you know!
Yongt'ae	Don't make jokes. I can't drink alcohol. I really need to go to the hospital.

Unit 8

She's just gone out

Mr Yun	Hello?
Jaemok	Hello. Can I speak to Chongmin, please?
Mr Yun	Yes, hold on please. I'm sorry, she was here until a little while ago, but she has just gone out.
Jaemok	Oh dear. Have you any idea where she might have gone?
Mr Yun	I don't have a clue. Just a moment. Maybe my wife will know.
Wife	Tonight Chongmin has gone out to see a movie with her boyfriend.
Jaemok	Really? That's strange, she was supposed (lit: *decided*) to meet me this evening . . .
Wife	Oh dear. Well, she's gone out on a date with a different guy and she won't be back until late.
Jaemok	Oh well, it's turned out well then – I was just ringing up to cancel. Something came up today.
Wife	Oh really? It has turned out well. Do you have a message for Chongmin?
Jaemok	No, I don't. Goodbye.

What did you do last night?

Yongt'ae	Taegyu, how are you doing?!
Taegyu	Hi there! How are things?
Yongt'ae	Nowadays I'm a bit busy. I've (just) got a girlfriend, so I'm even more busy!
Taegyu	I thought so. What's her name?
Yongt'ae	She's called Kim Chongmin. She graduated last year from Seoul National University. Now she's working for Hyundai cars.
Taegyu	How did you meet?
Yongt'ae	My friend did an introduction for me. At first I didn't like her that much, but a month later we met by chance at a party. We started meeting regularly from then on.
Taegyu	And now you're meeting her and dating nearly every day, are you?
Yongt'ae	More or less!
Taegyu	I tried to ring you last night, but you'd gone out then too. Where did you go last night?
Yongt'ae	Last night? I don't remember. I expect we went somewhere or other.
Taegyu	You don't remember?! Had you drunk so much?!
Yongt'ae	You mean *me* drinking? (lit. *who was drinking?*) You're the one who drinks every day (on the contrary).
Taegyu	Anyhow, where did you go?
Yongt'ae	We went to a noraebang, my girlfriend really likes noraebangs.
Taegyu	Where did you go after coming out of the noraebang?
Yongt'ae	We played a bit of table tennis.
Taegyu	Is that all? Tell me honestly!
Yongt'ae	It's true! Nothing happened!

Unit 9

We bought him that last year!

Wife	It's granddad's birthday tomorrow.
Husband	What, already?
Wife	Yes. We're going to have to decide what to buy him.
Husband	Can't you decide? I'm busy.
Wife	I always decide. Please help this time.

Husband	All right. Why don't we buy him a jumper?
Wife	He's got ten already. He doesn't need another one.
Husband	What about a shirt then?
Wife	He doesn't need a shirt either.
Husband	A book?
Wife	You know he doesn't like reading.
Husband	Since grandma likes reading it would be OK if she read it instead!
Wife	Don't joke. Try making a better suggestion.
Husband	What about an umbrella?
Wife	He doesn't go out when it rains.
Husband	Some socks, then?
Wife	We bought him that last year.
Husband	How about a new electric razor?
Wife	We bought him that the year before. Besides, he doesn't shave himself properly (*frequently*).
Husband	You see?! You don't like my suggestions. You'd better decide, like I said at first!

I'm sorry, I really didn't know!

Policeman	Excuse me. Please show me your driving licence.
Driver	Why? What's the matter?
Policeman	You really don't know?
Driver	What are you talking about?
Policeman	Just look at the cars parked here. The cars have all been parked in the same direction.
Driver	So what?
Policeman	OK then, didn't you see that red one-way signpost over there?
Driver	Ah, it's a one-way street! I'm sorry. I really didn't know.
Policeman	You've committed a serious offence. It's very dangerous and there is a large fine if you go into a one-way street the wrong way.
Driver	I really didn't see the sign. Please let me off this once.
Policeman	Be careful from now on. The fine is 50,000 won.
Driver	Thank you very much and keep up the good work.

Unit 10

What did you do with it?

Sonnim	Excuse me, I was here yesterday with some friends and I left my bag behind.

Chongŏpwon	Just let me go and have a look. Can you describe your bag?
Sonnim	Yes . . . it's very big, black and made of leather.
Chongŏpwon	There's a briefcase. Is that it?
Sonnim	No, it's not a briefcase.
Chongŏpwon	No, we don't seem to have anything. Was there anything important inside?
Sonnim	Yes, actually. There were some important documents, some books and my bank cards.
Chongŏpwon	Please wait a moment. I will ask the manager.
Sajang	Hello, how can I help you?
Sonnim	I've lost my bag – yesterday I ate here and left it behind (*put it down and left*).
Sajang	What time did you leave the restaurant?
Sonnim	About 11 p.m., I think.
Sajang	Around closing time . . . Ah yes, I remember now. There was a bag when we were cleaning this morning.
Sonnim	What did you do with it?
Sajang	I sent it to the police station. They are keeping it there.
Sonnim	Can you tell me where the police station is?
Sajang	Yes, go out of the restaurant and turn left and it's on the third (*small*) street on your right.
Sonnim	Thank you very much. Goodbye.

Nasty headaches

Yaksa	Hello, can I help you?
Mr Pak	Yes, I've got a very bad headache; I wonder if you could give me some medicine.
Yaksa	Yes, certainly. When did you get it?
Mr Pak	It came yesterday. I've been working very hard at work and have had a lot of stress – probably overwork and stress is the reason.
Yaksa	It could be. Do your eyes hurt at all?
Mr Pak	Yes, they do a bit.
Yaksa	Have you been able to sleep?
Mr Pak	No, my head hurts too much, and so I can't sleep.
Yaksa	I see. It's probably linked to stress, then. I recommend these tablets.
Mr Pak	How often should I take them?

Yaksa	You can take one every four hours while it's very bad. When it gets a bit easier, then just take one tablet after meals three times a day.
Mr Pak	Are there any side-effects?
Yaksa	When you take the medicine you will feel drowsy so take care. Don't be surprised if you feel tired easily.
Mr Pak	OK. Thank you very much.

Unit 11

Would you like to try it on?

Minho	Look at that shirt; it's really nice.
Pyŏngsu	Well, I think the design is a bit old-fashioned.
Minho	No, I like them. Agassi, how much are those shirts?
Chŏmwon A	8,000 won.
Minho	Wow, that's really cheap.
Pyŏngsu	Yeah, but look at it, the quality's not very good.
Minho	Oh, I don't know. Shall we go and look somewhere else then?
Chŏmwon B	Welcome! What are you looking for?
Minho	Yes, I'm looking for casual shirts. (*Something in*) a bright colour. Something stylish and good quality which I can wear with jeans.
Chŏmwon B	What about these? This style is very popular at the moment.
Minho	What is it made of?
Chŏmwon B	100% cotton. Would you like to try one on?
Minho	Yes, please . . . Does it suit me?

Do you think it suits me?

Chŏmwon	Ah, that looks very nice.
Minho	Do you think it suits me?
Pyŏngsu	Yes. But it seems/looks a bit small.
Chŏmwon	Would you like to try a bigger one?
Minho	Yes, please.
Chŏmwon	Here you are.
Pyŏngsu	That looks a bit better.
Chŏmwon	Ah, that looks super.
Minho	By the way, how much is it?

Chŏmwon	32,000 won.
Minho	What?
Chŏmwon	Why? That's a very good price. Only 32,000 won.
Pyŏngsu	It sounds a bit expensive to me!
Minho	At Namdaemun they had a similar one for only 8,000 won.
Chŏmwon	Ah yes, at Namdaemun. It looks the same, but the quality is very different. If you buy clothes at Namdaemun, they become unusable in just two or three months, so you have to buy new ones.
Pyŏngsu	Well, I don't know. Do you reckon this shirt will last four times as long, then?
Chŏmwon	Oh, at least. And it will be a much better fit.
Minho	Mmm. I'll go and think about it, I think.

Unit 12

Do you have a spare room?

Sonnim	Do you have any free rooms, please?
Chuin	Yes, we do. Would you like beds or sleeping on the floor?
Sonnim	One with bed and one with floor sleeping.
Chuin	Certainly. It will be 50,000 won for the room with a bed, and 40,000 for the room with floor sleeping. How many nights are you staying?
Chuin	Three nights, please. We may stay a little longer than that (I don't know).
Sonnim	If you book for five nights or more, we offer a 5% discount.
Chuin	Oh, I'll talk about that with my wife. Is breakfast included in the price?
Sonnim	Yes, breakfast is included. Between 7 and 10 a.m. please go to the basement restaurant. Or you can have breakfast brought to your room for 2,000 won extra per person.
Chuin	No, we'll go to the restaurant, thank you. What other facilities does the hotel have?
Sonnim	We have a swimming pool, a sauna, a games room, a noraebang, a bar, a Korean restaurant and a western one.
Chuin	Is there a TV and a phone in the rooms?
Sonnim	Of course, and there is also a mini-bar.

| Chuin | Oh, that's excellent. It would be better to book for five nights, then. My wife will probably like that. |

The towel is dirty and the food is cold

Sonnim	Excuse me, I'd like to speak to the manager, please.
Chongŏpwon	Excuse me, but is there a problem?
Sonnim	Yes, I have something to say about the hotel service.
Chongŏpwon	Is there any chance you can tell me what the problem is?
Sonnim	I'd like to speak to the manager direct about it.
Chongŏpwon	Very well, sir. Hold on a moment please.
Chibaein	Hello, I'm the manager what is the problem?
Sonnim	It seems that there are many problems with the service at this hotel. The staff are unfriendly and unhelpful; this morning we went in for breakfast and the food was cold. Yesterday it was the same.
Chibaein	Really? I'm very sorry to hear that. Did you speak to the waiter about it?
Sonnim	Of course I spoke to the waitress! She was impolite, and while saying that she couldn't understand my Korean, she said that the food was fine. It wasn't; it was cold and the taste was awful.
Chibaein	I'm extremely sorry, sir. We always try to do our best, but sometimes mistakes happen. I'll make sure that I speak to the kitchen staff right away.
Sonnim	And that's not all. This morning I asked for my towel to be changed and the new towel was very dirty and they still haven't cleaned my son's room.
Chibaein	This is strange. We don't usually get any complaints like this.
Sonnim	Even that is not all. The television in our room has broken down and the fridge door won't even open. I have to say that quite frankly the service and facilities are rubbish.
Chibaein	I'm sorry but we also don't need guests like you who complain so much in our hotel. Please leave right away. We will refund your money.

Unit 13

Two to Taegu

Maep'yowon	Can I help you?
Mr Pak	Are there any trains to Taegu this evening please?
Maep'yowon	Yes, there are two trains, a slow one at 5.30, and a fast one at 7.45.
Mr Pak	How long do they take?
Maep'yowon	The fast one takes three hours, the slow one four hours 30 minutes.
Mr Pak	What about the price?
Maep'yowon	Yes, the slow one is 8,000 won, the fast 15,000, and we only have a few seats left for the fast one.
Mr Pak	Can we book four seats together?
Maep'yowon	Please wait a minute. Just let me check . . . yes, that's fine. There are four seats available. Non-smoking or smoking?
Mr Pak	Non-smoking, please.
Maep'yowon	Would you like single tickets or return?
Mr Pak	No, return please.
Maep'yowon	When are you coming back?
Mr Pak	Sunday evening.
Maep'yowon	There's a train at 6.30; but it's a slow one. There is no fast train on Sunday evening.
Mr Pak	What about Sunday afternoon?
Maep'yowon	Yes, there's one at 2.30.
Mr Pak	That'll be okay. We'll take the fast one, please.
Maep'yowon	That will be 120,000 won altogether, please.
Mr Pak	What platform does the train go from?
Maep'yowon	I don't know yet. Before the time of departure look at the electronic notice board.
Mr Pak	Okay, thank you very much.

I don't want to go there!

Mr Yun	What are you doing after work this evening?
Mr Paek	After work? Don't know. I haven't got anything planned.
Mr Yun	What about going out for a meal?
Mr Paek	Sounds a good idea. Just the two of us?
Mr Yun	We could invite some others. What about Mr Kim and Mr Lee?

Mr Paek	Yeah, sure! Hey, Mrs Kim, Mrs Lee! Do you fancy going out for a meal tonight?
Mrs Kim	OK, but where are we going to?
Mr Yun	We could go and eat pulgogi, and of course we could drink soju and then go out to a noraebang or something.
Mrs Kim	I like drinking, but I don't particularly like pulgogi, and I hate singing.
Mr Paek	Well *you* don't have to eat pulgogi, you can have something else. And you can just listen instead of singing.
Mrs Kim	Yeah, that's fair enough. But I don't have much spare cash right now.
Mr Yun	Don't worry. I'll buy.
Mrs Kim	Yes, okay then. That's nice of you.
Mr Paek	What about you, Mr Lee, would you like to come?
Mrs Lee	I would like to go, but I'd prefer to go out to Inchŏn and eat raw fish, though.
Mr Paek	No, it's too far and it's too expensive.
Mr Yun	Besides, I can't eat raw fish.
Mrs Lee	OK, OK, it was only an idea. I guess I'll just have to come and eat pulgogi and soju!

Exercises on Korean alphabet

Exercise 3

1	Pakistan	2	Mexico
3	New Zealand	4	The Netherlands
5	Sweden	6	Denmark
7	Indonesia	8	Poland
9	Canada	10	America

Exercise 4

1	hotel	2	piano
3	computer	4	television
5	radio	6	taxi
7	lemon	8	ice cream
9	hamburger	10	sandwich
11	orange juice	12	tennis
13	camera	14	tomato

Exercises on romanization

Exercise 1

1	재민	2	가요
3	지금	4	양주
5	마른 안주	6	중국
7	마시다	8	밥
9	진짜	10	우리

Exercise 2

1	Ŏttaeyo?	2	Saram
3	Sŏnsaengnim	4	Aniyo

5   Samushil   6   Mannada
7   Miguk   8   Hakkyo
9   Taesagwan   10 Chŏmshim

Unit 1

Exercise 1

a   Chigŭm ilbon-e kayo.
지금 일본에 가요.
b   Ajŏssi, maekju issŏyo?
아저씨, 맥주 있어요?
c   Mwo sa-rŏ kage-e kayo?
뭐 사러 가게에 가요?
d   Yangju-hago ojingŏ chuseyo.
양주하고 오징어 주세요.
e   Kŭrigo anju-do chuseyo.
그리고 안주도 주세요.
f   Na-do kage-e kayo.
나도 가게에 가요.
g   Maekju-hago marŭn anju-hago pap ta issŏyo.
맥주하고 마른 안주하고 밥 다 있어요.
Or, Marun anju-hago maekju-hago pap ta issŏyo.
마른 안주하고 맥주하고 밥 다 있어요.

Exercise 2

a   Ppang issŏyo.
b   maekju issŏyo.
c   sulchip issŏyo.
d   kwail issŏyo.

Exercise 3

1   Hakkyo-e kayo.
2   Kamsa hamnida.
3   Annyŏng haseyo!
4   Ne, chal chinaessŏyo.
5   Maekju mashi-rŏ sulchib-e kayo.
6   Kŭrŏm, maekju-hago soju chuseyo.

Exercise 4

a   kayo   Chigŭm hakkyo-e kayo.
b   issŏyo   Soju issŏyo?
c   sayo   Mwo sayo?

d mŏgŏyo   Kim sŏnsaengnim ppang mŏgŏyo.
e ŏpsŏyo   Ojingŏ ŏpsŏyo.
f haeyo   Mwo ha-rŏ sulchib-e kayo?
g anjayo   Anjayo!

Exercise 5

a Kage-esŏ mwo sayo? Or
   Mwo sa-ro kage-e kayo?
b Kim sŏnsaengnim, annyŏng haseyo!
c Ku-daum-e mwo haeyo?
d Chigum shinae-e kayo?
e Ŏdi kayo?
f Maekju-hago kwail-hago ppang – ta issŏyo!
g Pap-do chwuseyo.
h Ojingŏ yŏgi issŏyo. Mashikke tuseyo!
i Yangju ŏpsŏyo. Kurŏm maekju hana chuseyo.
j P'ajŏn-hago soju-hana chuseyo.

Exercise 6

a Ajŏssi, ojingŏ chuseyo.
b Ajŏssi, wisk'i chuseyo.
c Ajŏssi, mul chuseyo.

Exercise 7

a One soju, one beer and some dry snacks.
b Octopus, fruit, western spirits and one beer.

Exercise 8

a A: Annyŏnghaseyo? Ŏdi kayo?
   B: Ne. Annyŏnghaseyo? Kage-e kayo.
   A: Na-do kage-e kayo. Kach'i kayo.
   B: Ne. Kach'i kayo. Kŭrigo sul mashi-rŏ sulchip-e kayo.

b A: Chal chinaessŏyo?
   B: Ne. Chal chinaessŏyo.
   A: (to the waiter) Ajŏssi, maekju hana hago soju hana
      chuseyo.
   Waiter: Ne. Algessŏyo.
   A: Kŭrigo anju-do chuseyo. Mwo issŏyo?
   Waiter: Kwail hago ojingŏ hago marŭn anju issŏyo.
   A: Kŭrŏm kwail chuseyo.

Unit 2

Exercise 1

a ssi, do, e d ga
b rŏ, e, yo e nun, I
c un

Exercise 2

a O sŏnsaengnim annyŏng haseyo! Hoesa-nun ŏttaeyo?
b Misisu Cho annyŏng haseyo! Saŏb-un ŏttaeyo?
c Pak sŏnsaengnim puin annyŏng haseyo! Kajog-un ŏttaeyo?
d Taegyu-ssi annyŏng haseyo! Hakkyo-nun ŏttaeyo?
e Misu Pak, annyŏng haseyo? Kŏngang-un ŏttaeyo?

Exercise 3

Ne, oraeganman-ieyo. Chal chinaessŏyo?
Yojŭm choayo [=it's good at the moment].
Samushir-e kayo.
Chŏgi-eyo.
Kim sŏnsaengnim manna-rŏ kayo.

Exercise 4

a I-gŏsh-i ojingŏ-eyo.
b I-gŏsh-i chaeg-ieyo.
c I-gŏsh-i sagwa-eyo.
d I-gŏsh-i shinmun-ieyo.
e I-gŏsh-i chapchi-eyo.

a I-gŏsh-i ojingŏ-ga anieyo.
b I-gŏsh-i chaeg-i anieyo.
c I-gŏsh-i sagwa-ga anieyo.
d I-gŏsh-i shinmun-i anieyo.
e I-gŏsh-i chapchi-ga anieyo.

Exercise 5

a Excuse me, are you Mr Pak?
b No, I'm not Mr Pak. Mr Pak is the Chinese teacher.
   This is the Chinese department office.
a Ah, I'm sorry. Excuse me, but could you tell me where the
   Korean department is?
b It's over there. I'm going to see (meet) a teacher (someone) at
   the Korean department also.
a Let's go together then.

Exercise 6

a Miguksaram-iseyo?
   Ne, miguksaram-ieyo.
   Aniyo, miguksaram-i anieyo.
b I sŏnsaengnim-iseyo?
   Ne, I sŏnsaengnim-ieyo.
   Aniyo, I sŏnsaengnim-i anieyo.
c Chungguk sŏnsaengnim-i aniseyo?
   Ne, chungguk sŏnsaengnim-ieyo.
   Anio, chungguk sonsaengnim-i anieyo.
d Paek sŏnsaengnim adur-i anieyo? (or, aniseyo)
   Ne, Paek sŏnsaengnim adur-ieyo.
   Anio, Paek sŏnsaengnim adur-i anieyo.
e Hakkyo sŏnsaengnim aniseyo?
   Ne, hakkyo sŏnsaengnim-ieyo.
   Anio, hakkyo sŏnsaengnim-i anieyo.

Exercise 7

a Pak Sangmin-ieyo. A, kuraeyo? Mannasŏ pangapsumnida.
b Yojum hakkyo-nun ŏttaeyo?
c Sillye hamnida. Ilbonmal sŏnsaengnim-iseyo?
d Ajŏssi, ojingŏ issŏyo? Ojingŏ ŏttaeyo? Choayo.
e Hankuk hakkwa samushir-i anieyo? Ne. Anieyo.
f Chŏ-nun Woo sŏnsaengnim-i anieyo. A, kŭraeyo?
   Choesong-hamnida.
g Uri chungguk mal sŏnsaengnim-iseyo. Kŭraeyo? Malssŭm
   mani tŭrŏssŏyo.
h Ilbon kage-eyo?
i Na-do hanguk sŏnsaengnim manna-rŏ kayo.
j Pak sŏnsaengnim puin manna-rŏ wassŏyo.
k Hanguk hakkwa-ga ŏdi-eyo?
l Hakkyo samushir-i ŏdi-eyo?

Exercise 8

A Annyŏng haseyo?
B A! Annyŏng haseyo?
A Oraeganman-ieyo.
B Ne. Kuraeyo. Chinccha oraeganman-ieyo.
A Chal chinaessŏyo?
B Ne. Chal chinaessŏyo. Yojŭm saŏb-un ŏttaeyo?
A Kujŏ kuraeyo.
   (signalling to his son) Uri adur-ieyo.
B A! Kŭraeyo. Pangapsŭmnida.

Exercise 9

Yŏgi-nun chunguk hakkwa samushir-i anieyo.
Chunguk mal sŏnsaengnim-i ŏpsŏyo.

Unit 3

Exercise 1

a Pak sŏnsaengnim-hago Misisu Kim manna-go ship'ŏyo.
b Ppang-hago kwail sa-go ship'ŏyo.
c Pulgogi-hago kalbi mŏk-ko ship'ŏyo.
d Yŏngo sŏnsaengnim-hago ilbonmal sŏnsaengnim kidari-go
    ship'ŏyo.
e Maekju-hago wisk'i mashi-go ship'ŏyo.
f Ojingŏ-hago naengmyŏn chumun ha-go ship'ŏyo.
    Second part: Pak sŏnsaengnim-ina Misisu Kim manna-go
    ship'ŏyo; ppang-ina kwail sa-go ship'ŏyo, etc.

Exercise 2

김 선생님: 오팔이-오구이공
(Kim sŏnsaengnim: o-p'al-i-o-gu-i-gong.)
재민: 이구일-육사팔이
(Chaemin: i-gu-il-yuk-sa-p'al-i.)
의사: 육육육-공이삼일
(Uysa: yuk-yuk-yuk-gong-i-sam-il.)
피터: 공일육이삼-이구육공
(P'it'ŏ: kong-il-yuk-i-sam-i-gu-yuk-kong.)
박 선생님: 공일오일육팔칠구일공이
(Pak sŏnsaengnim: kong-il-o-il-yuk-p'al-ch'il-gu-il-gong-i.)

Exercise 3

a Hanguk ŭmshik choa haseyo?
b Chŏ-nun Hilton Hotel-uy Sangmin-ieyo.
c Yŏlshi-e hakkyo ap'esŏ mannapshida.
d Onŭl chŏmshim-e shigan-i issŏyo?
e Usŏn mul chom chuseyo.
f Maeun kŏ chal mot (pron: mon) mŏgŏyo.
g Kalbi saminbun-hago naengmyŏn tu-kurut chuseyo.

Exercise 4

a Na-nun Ilbon taesagwan-e mot kayo.
b Chigum chŏmshim mŏg-uro shiktang-e mot kayo.
c Jaemin-ssi-nun Sangmin-ssi mot kidaryŏyo (or, kidariseyo).
d Sangmin-ssi maeun kŏ mon mŏgŏyo.

e (Chungguk taesagwan-ap'esŏ) Misisu Jang mon mannayo.
f Paekhwajŏm-e mot kayo.

Exercise 5

a kaseyo   kapshida
b chumun haseyo   chumun hapshida
c poseyo   popshida
d anjŭseyo   anjupshida
e kidariseyo   kidaripshida
f saseyo   sapshida
g mannaseyo   mannapshida

E.g. Kim sŏnsaengnim chamkkan kidariseyo. Yŏlshi-e hakkyo-e kapshida.

Exercise 6

The first sentence says something is good (irrespective of whether or not you personally like it) and the second says that you like it (irrespective of its quality).

Exercise 7

a Chunguk mal-lo malhapshida.
b Paekhwachŏm-e kapshida.
c Maekju-na wain mashipshida.
d Mikuk-e kago ship-jiman, mot kayo.
e Wiski cho-ch'iman, mon mashyŏyo.
f Kim sŏnsaengnim-hant'e chŏnhwa hago ship-jiman, chalmot kŏrŏssŏyo.

Exercise 8

a 97   d 867
b 53   e 34495
c 207

Exercise 9

a I like spicy food, but I can't eat Korean (well). Or, Although I like spicy food, I can't eat Korean.
b Excuse me, where is the British embassy?
c Please sit down over here (at this side). Would you like anything to drink?
d Do you have (some/free) time? Let's meet later, then.
e Mr Kim? Just a moment . . . I'm sorry, but there is no such person here. You've misdialled.
f Is that 863-0542?

Exercise 10

Yŏl-tu-shi-e hakkyo ap'-esŏ mannapshida.

Unit 4

Exercise 1

a kurŏn tarun kaseyo
b kamyŏn
c jiman sajŏn
d yŏgisŏ oshippun
e chŏ-nun uy
f uch'eguk orun unhaeng
g chongnyu-ga
h modu turilkkayo
i ieyo saŏp
j pissan ship'ŏyo

Exercise 2

a movie
b what (him)
c none
d word
e bread

Exercise 3

a Yŏboseyo. Kim sŏnsaengnim chom pakkwo chuseyo.
b Naeil shigan issuseyo?
c Kŏgi Hankuk taesakwan anieyo?
d Wuri chip saram-ieyo.
e Yŏngo sajŏn issŏyo?
f Hanguk umshik choahaseyo?
g Maekju mashi-go ship'ŏyo?

Exercise 4

a Han-gwon-e paek won-ssig-ieyo.
   Kurŏnikka modu sa-baek won-ieyo.
b Han-jan-e ch'il-paek won-ssig-ieyo.
   Kurŏnikka modu ch'ŏn-sa-baek won-ieyo.
c Han-gae-e i-ch'ŏn won-ssig-ieyo.
   Kurŏnikka modu man-i-ch'ŏn won-ieyo.´
d Han-byŏng-e ch'ŏn-o-baek won-ssig-ieyo.
   Kurŏnikka modu sa-ch'ŏn-o-baek won-ieyo.
e Han-sangja-e yuk-ch'ŏn won-ssig-ieyo.
   Kurŏnikka modu man-p'al-ch'ŏn won-ieyo.

Exercise 5

a sŏ uro I
b I e esŏ
c ul uro
d un/i rul
e nun ul na
f nun I
g ul ina
h ga
i e ieyo

Exercise 6

a Chaek se kwon, chaek yŏdŏl kwon, chaek sumul-du kwon.
b ir-il, sam-il, yukship-ch'il-il.
c Han saram, ilgop saram, sŏrŭn-ne saram.
d Ojingŏ se mari, ojingŏ ahop mari, ojingŏ yŏl-ne mari.
e Tu pyŏng, yŏl pyŏng.
f Kae ahop mari, kae han mari.
g Chŏn won, man won.

Exercise 7

a Marun anju an chumun haeyo.
b O-bun an kŏllyŏyo.
c Maekju an tuseyo.
d Sŏnsaengnim an kidariseyo.
e Chaek an ilgŏyo.

Exercise 8

a Sillye-jiman, yŏgi shiktang issŏyo?
b Naengmyŏn mon mŏgŏyo. Kalbi-do mon mŏgŏyo.
c Ŏlma-eyo? Han chŏpshi-e i-ch'ŏn won . . . ,
    kurŏnikka modu yuk-ch'ŏn won-ieyo.
d Yŏgisŏ oencchog-uro kaseyo. O-bun kamyŏn, Chongno
    sagŏri-ga issŏyo.
    Oencchog-uro kaseyo. Ŭnhaeng-i orŭncchog-e issŏyo.
e Cheil ssan ke ŏlma-eyo?
f Kŏrŏsŏ ship-pun cchŭm kŏllyŏyo.
g Yŏgi Hanguk oehwan ŭnhaeng chijŏm-i ŏpsŏyo.
h Ton-ul chom pakku-go ship'ŏyo. O-man won cchŭm issŏyo.
i Hanguk-e yŏl-kachi chongnyu-uy kimch'i-ga issŏyo.
j Hanguk mal sajŏn-ul turilkkayo?
k Ŏttŏn chongnyu-rul turilkkayo?
l Cheil ssan kŏ chuseyo.

m Kim sŏnsaengnim-i nappun saram-ieyo?
n Uch'egug-e kaseyo? Choayo. Annyŏnghi kaseyo.

Exercise 9

Clerk   Mwol ch'asuseyo?
Child   Uyu issŏyo?
Clerk   Ne, issŏyo.
Child   Uyu tu pyong hago ppang chom chuseyo.
Clerk   Yogi issŏyo.
Child   Ŏlmaeyo?
Clerk   Sam ch'ŏn won-ieyo.
Child   Maekju hago kogi hago sagwa hago kimch'i-do issŏyo?
Clerk   Ne, issŏyo.
Child   Ŏlmaeyo?
        etc., etc., etc.

Unit 5

Exercise 1

a 아니요. 남대문 시장이 동대문 시장보다 더 재미있어요.
b 동대문 시장에서 원숭이는 안 팔아요.
c 이십 번 버스를 타면 남대문 시장에 가요.
d 네. 남대문 시장에는 안 파는 게 없어요.
e 바로 길 건너편 정류장에서 타요.

Exercise 2

a Aniyo. Na-nun mot kayo.
b Namdaemun shijang-ap'esŏ Kim sŏnsaengnim mannayo.
c Kurŏm tarun te-e ka-boseyo.
d Sambaek oship won-ieyo.
e Hanguk choa ha-jiman hangungmal chaemi ŏpsŏyo.

Exercise 3

a Kim sonsaengnim(uy) kae-igunyo!
b O sŏnsaengnim puin-ishigunyo!
c Ilbon ch'aeg-igunyo!
d Hanguk oehwan unhaeng-igunyo!
e Hyŏngjun-igunyo!
f Chunggungmal sŏnsaengnim-ishigunyo!

Exercise 4

a Hanguk ŭmshig-i ilbon ŭmshik-poda tŏ mashi issŏyo.
b Yŏgi-nun kŏgi-poda tŏ man(h)ayo.

c Kich'a-nun bǒsu-poda tǒ pallayo.
d Kim sǒnsaengnim-i Pak sǒnsaengnim-poda chaesu tǒ man(h)ayo.
e Namdaemun shijang-i Tongdaemun shijang-poda pissayo.

Exercise 6

a Wow, it's expensive here! Let's go and try next door (at the next door shop).
b They do sell them here, but if you go somewhere else (to a different place) it's cheaper.
c Where do you catch a bus for (going to) Seoul city centre?
d I haven't had any luck all morning!
e Japan is more expensive than Korea. Mind you (however . . .), Korea is expensive too.
f There are more English people in Korea than I thought.
g I'll cut the price for you. You can take a box for 13,000 won.
h Would you like to order?
i Since this isn't Korea (since we're not in Korea) there are few places selling kimchi.
j You want to know if we've got monkeys? Go and try at Tongdaemun market!

Exercise 7

The acceptable sequences are: a, c, d, h.

Exercise 8

a I sajǒn-i pissa-neyo.
b Taegyu-ga o-neyo.
c Mwo ha-neyo?
d I shinmun-i chǒngmal chaemi in-neyo.

Exercise 9

a I saram-i Pak sǒnsaengnim-igo chǒ saram Kang sǒnsaengnim-ieyo.
b Ǒmǒni ch'aek ilk-ko abǒji t'ellebi-rul pwayo.
c Kogi(-do) mon mǒk-ko sagwa-do mon mǒgoyo.
d Shibil pǒn bǒsu-ga Namdaemun shijang-e ka-go iship pǒn bǒsu-nun Tongdaemun shijang-e kayo.
e Sangjun(-do) bǒsu t'a-go Myǒngt'aek-do bǒsu t'ayo.

Exercise 10

O-ship-ch'il pǒn bǒsu-ga hakkyo-e kanun bǒsu-eyo.
Ship-p'al pǒn bǒsu-nun shinae-e kayo.

Unit 6

Exercise 1

a ap'ŭlkŏeyo
b mŏgŭlkŏeyo
c ŏpsŭlkŏeyo
d ka-giro haessŏyo
e sa-giro haessŏyo
f mŏk-kiro haessŏyo
g polkka haeyo
h halkka haeyo
i kalkka haeyo
j kalkkayo?
k mannalkkayo?
l t'alkkayo?

Exercise 2

Naeil-un shyop'ing halkka haeyo.
Hal ir-i manasŏ nŏmu pappayo.
Taehak tongch'ang-hago golf hagiro haessŏyo.
Tŭngsan-ul an choa haeyo.

Exercise 3

A Mŏri-ga ap'ayo.
B Mani ap'ayo?
A Kŭraeyo. Mani ap'ayo.
B Kŭrŏm yag-ul sarŏ yakkug-e kapshida.
A Na-nun mot kayo. Tari-do ap'ayo.
B A! Yŏgi twut'ong yag-i issŏyo.
A Kuraeyo? Komawoyo.

Exercise 4

a nolliji maseyo (or, shikkurŏwoyo)
b an doegennneyo (or, chaesu ŏmneyo!)
c chŏnshin-i ta ap'ugwunyo
d mworaguyo? (or, shikkurŏwoyo)
e shikkŭrŏwoyo
f ch'akkak haessŏyo
g kŭrŏch'i anayo
h anin kŏt kat'ayo
i kŏkjŏng haji maseyo
j mworaguyo?

Exercise 5

a ppalli t'apshida
b Shigan-un in-
c an choayo
d kach'i kalkkayo?
e kǔ saram puin-i an choayo

Exercise 6

a kedaga
b kǔlsseyo
c kǔrǒch'iman (kuraedo would be even better)
d kǔrǒch'iman
e kǔrigo

Exercise 7

a Kogi-rul choa haji anayo.
b Chigǔm kaji mot haeyo.
c Chumun haji anayo.
d I sagwa-ga shingshing haji anayo.
e Bǒsu t'aji mot haeyo.

Exercise 8

Mǒri-ga ap'-ayo. Tari-do ap'-ayo. Umshig-ul mot mǒg-ǒyo.

Unit 7

Exercise 1

a Then let's go together.
b Do you have (free) time today lunchtime?
c It's really been a long time (since we've seen each other).
d I'm not the Japanese language teacher.
e I'm sorry. I made a mistake.
f Next Monday will perhaps be OK.
g Since I'm not from Seoul either, I really don't know.
h So your whole body hurts, then?! Is there anywhere that doesn't hurt?
i I'd like to change English currency into Chinese.
j And I'd like to eat some naengmyon as well.
k Give us some dried snacks and some Korean pancake, please.
l You can take them for 20,000 won a box.

Exercise 2

a Se-shi-eyo.
b Yŏdŏl-shi pan-ieyo. Or, Yŏdŏl-shi sam-ship-pun-ieyo.
c Yŏl-shi sa-ship-o pun-ieyo.
d Ilgop-shi i-ship pun-ieyo.
e Yŏsŏt-shi ship pun-ieyo.
f Yŏdŏl-shi ship-o pun-ieyo.

Exercise 3

a haeyo,   ha-go,   ha-pshida.
b tadayo,   tat-ko,   tat-upshida.
c p'arayo,   p'al-go   p'a-pshida.
d pappayo,   pappu-go,   pappu-pshida.
e umjigyŏyo,   umjigi-go,   umjigi-pshida.

Exercise 4

a San-e kapshida.
b Undongha-rŏ san-e kayo.
c Yu-wol ship-i ir-e kapshida.
d Yŏdŏl-shi-e mannapshida.
e Kyohoe ap'-esŏ mannapshida.

Exercise 6

E.g. Ŏdi kayo?
     Kage-e kayo.
     Mwo sa-rŏ kage-e kayo?
     Ojingŏ sa-rŏ kayo.

Exercise 7

a 박 선생님은 7시 30분에 일어나요.
b 힐튼 호텔에서 이 선생님의 부인을 만나요.
c 중국 음식을 먹어요.
d 영화 보러 극장에 가요.
e 11시에 자요.

Exercise 8

a Chukku-rul choa ha-ji anayo. T'enisu choa haeyo.
b Aniyo, maeun kŏ chal mon mŏgŏyo. Kalbi mŏg-ul swu
   issŏyo.
c Aniyo, manhi an pwayo. Kurŏch'iman radio-rul manhi
   turŏyo.
d Chal mot pwullŏyo. Umag-ul (music) chal turŏyo.
e Aniyo, chunggungmal paeu-ji anayo. Yŏngŏ paewoyo.

Exercise 9

a Kyohoe-esŏ yŏngguk taesagwan-un mŏl-ji anayo.
b I kunch'ŏ-e hanguk oehwan unhaeng-i ŏpsŏyo. Sangŏp unhaeng-un issŏyo.
c Hakkyo-ga ŭnhaeng yŏp'-ieyo.
d Chegwajŏm-i mŏrŏyo.
e Ne. Uch'egug-un taesagwan-poda tŏ mŏrŏyo.
f Hakkyo-e karyŏmyŏn, kŏrŏsŏ saship-o pun cchum kŏllyŏyo.
g Uch'egug-un chegwajŏm yŏp'-ieyo.

Exercise 11

a 나도 영어를 공부하러 학교에 가요.
b 가게 밖에서 만납시다. 나중에 봐요.
c 맛있게 드세요. (많이 드세요)
d 정말 병원에 가야겠어요.
e 그럼 만오천원만 내세요.
f 십오분 쯤 걸려요.
g 요즘 사업은 어때요?
h 제일 싼거 주세요.
i 요즘 날씨가 좋아요.
j 한국 대사관에서 박 선생님을 만나러 왔어요.
k 매운 거 못 먹어요.
l 우체국 가는 버스가 여기 서요?

Unit 8

Exercise 1

a Hakkyo-e kassŏyo.
b Maekju mani mashyŏssŏyo.
c Yaksog-ul mot chik'yŏssŏyo.
d Ch'ingu-rul mannassŏyo.
e Yŏnghwa-rul po-go ship'ŏssŏyo.
f Tobongsan-e kalkka haessŏyo.

Exercise 2

a Hae-juseyo.
b Shyop'ing hae-juseyo.
c Chŏmshim sa-juseyo.
d Kim sŏnsaengnim-hant'e chŏnhwa hae-juseyo (or better, hae-jwushigessoyo).
e Yag-ul sa-juseyo.
f Shijak hae-juseyo.

Exercise 3

ach'im-e . . . -kiro haessŏyo . . . kurŏch'iman . . . saengyŏso . . .
kurŏnikka . . . ha-ryŏgo . . . haessŏyo . . . chik'yŏssŏyo

Exercise 4

a 오늘 학교에 못 가요. 머리가 아프거든요.
b 일요일 날에 시내에 못 가요. 다른 약속이 있거든요.
c 오늘 밤 탁구 못 쳐요. 팔이 아프기 시작했거든요.
d 노래방에 가요? 나는 안 가요. 노래방을 싫어하거든요.
e 재민씨 못 가요? 그럼 잘 됐네요. 나도 못 가거든요.

Exercise 5

a Taehak tongch'anghoe-ga issŏyo.
b Friday, 10th, June.
c Chipsaram hago shyop'ing haryŏgo haeyo.
d Tobongsan-e karyŏgo haeyo.
e From Friday, 17th, June
f Tony hago chŏmshim-ul mŏgŏssŏyo.

Exercise 6

a Please try the soup! (Have a taste of . . .)
b Pulguksa han bŏn ka-boseyo.
c Even though you're busy, go and see.
d Have you never tried playing table tennis? Then have a go!
e Jaemin-ssi ajik an wassŏyo? Kurŏm chogum tŏ kidaryŏ-boseyo.

Exercise 7

a Pappŭn ir-i saengyŏ-sŏ, mot kayo. (Or, kal su ŏpsŏyo).
b Chib-e ŭmshig-i ŏpsŏ-sŏ, shiktang-e kayo.
c Saŏp-i an choa-sŏ, ton-i ŏpsŏyo.
d Pakk-e naga-sŏ kidari-pshida.
e Sangmin-ssi chib-e ka-sŏ mwol halkkayo?
f Sinae-e ka-sŏ kwail chom sa-o-seyo.

Exercise 8

a Yaksog-ul ch'wisoha-ryŏgo chŏnhwa haess-ŏyo. Ir-i
   saenggyŏt-kŏdunyo.
b Sangmin-ssi-nun t'akku ch'i-rŏ panggum nagass-ŏyo.
c Chŏum-enun Kimch'i-ga kurŏk'e maum-e tul-ji anan-nunde
   (Or, Kimch'i-rul pyŏllo choaha-ji anan-nunde), iksuk
   haejyŏss-ŏyo.
d Ŏnje chorŏphaess-ŏyo?
e Sulchip-esŏ uyŏnhi manass-ŏyo.

f Isangha-neyo! K'urisu-nun pŏlssŏ torawass-ŏyo.
g Ŏje pam-e mwo haess-ŏyo? Solchikhi mal hae-boseyo.

Exercise 9

T'enisu hae bo-ass-ŏyo?
Nonggu hae bo-ass-ŏyo?
Sinmun ilg-ŏ bo-ass-ŏyo?
Yŏngguk umshik mŏg-ŏ bo-ass-ŏyo?

Unit 9

Exercise 1

a P'at'i-e nuga olkka kŏkjŏng-ieyo.
b Umshig-i mojaralkka(-bwa) kŏkjŏng-ieyo.
c Kim sŏnsaengnim-i an oshilkka(-bwa) kŏkjŏng-ieyo.
d Yŏja ch'ingu-ga tangshin-ul an choahalkka(-bwa) kŏkjŏng-ieyo.
e Pi-ga olkka(-bwa) kŏkjŏng-ieyo.

Exercise 2

김선생님 대학교 선생님이세요. 런던 대학교에서 한국말을 가르치시고 일본말도 가르치세요. 매일 아침 공원에 가서서 산책하세요. 개하고 같이 가세요. 공원은 아주 좋아요. 김선 생님의 개는 고기를 잘 먹어요. 작년부터 부인도 가끔 산책 하시기 시작하셨어요. 부인도 가시면 둘이 식당에 가서서 커 피 한잔 마시세요.

Exercise 3

a Yag-ul sa-yagessŏyo.
b Chwiso ha-ryŏgo chŏnhwa hae-yagessŏyo.
c Sajŏn-ul sa-yagessŏyo.
d Tora-ga-yagessŏyo.
e Shinmun-ul pwa-yagessŏyo.

Exercise 4

a Muŏs-ul salkka kyŏlchŏng hae-yagessŏyo.
b Muŏs-ul ibulkka kyŏlchŏng hae-yagessŏyo.
c Ŏdi anjulkka kyŏlchŏng hae-yagessŏyo.
d Muŏs-ul chumun halkka kyŏlchŏng hae-yagessŏyo.
e Chumar-e ŏdi kalkka kyŏlchŏng hae-yagessŏyo.

Exercise 5

a Na-do o-l su issŏyo?
b I kŏ mŏg-ul su issŏyo?

c   Na-rul naeil manna-l su issŏyo?
d   Ilbonmar-ul mal ha-l su ŏpsŏyo.
e   Ton-i ŏps-ŏsŏ sa-l su ŏpsŏyo.
f   Yŏgi chuch'a ha'l su ŏpsŏyo.

Exercise 6

a   Ŏje sat-janhayo.
b   Aniyo, pŏlssŏ kyŏrhon haet-janhayo!
c   Pŏlssŏ haet-janhayo.
d   Ilkki shirŏ ha-janhayo.
e   Wuri chipsaram-ieyo. Ŏje mannat-janhayo.

Exercise 7

A   Naeir-i oppa saengir-ieyo.
    Mwol sa-dŭrilkka chŏng haeyagessŏyo.
B   Ch'ŏngbaji-rul sa-dŭrilkkayo?
A   Ch'ŏngbaji-nun pŏlssŏ yŏl pŏl-ina kat-ko issŏyo.
B   Kŭrŏmyŏn chaeg-un ŏttŏlkkayo?
A   Oppa-nun chaeg-ul sirŏhaeyo.
B   Kurŏm mannyŏnp'ir-unyo?
A   Mannyŏnp'il-do tŏ isang p'iryo ŏpsŏyo.
B   Kurŏm CD-nun?
A   Changnyŏn-e sa juŏt-janayo.

Unit 10

Exercise 1

a   Naeil shigan issŏyo?
b   Yŏnggug-esŏ wan-nŭndeyo.
c   Ŏje chŏnhwa haen-nŭndeyo.
d   kabang-ul nok'o kassŏyo.
e   Sajŏn-ul sa-go ship'-undeyo.
f   Kim sŏnsaengnim ŏdi kasyŏssŏyo?

Exercise 2

a   Pi-ga o-nun kŏt kat'ayo.
b   Ku saram-un Pak sŏnsaengnim-i-n kŏt kat'ayo.
c   Toksŏ-rul shirŏ ha-nun kŏt kat'ayo.
d   Jaemin-ssi Tongdaemun shijang-e ka-n kŏt kat'ayo.
e   Kim sŏnsaengnim naeil oshi-nun kŏt kat'ayo.
f   Kabang-ul yŏgi noh-un kŏt kat'ayo.

Exercise 3

Aju k'ugo kŏmjŏng saeg-igo kajug-uro madurŏssyo.

Exercise 4

a Umshig-ul mŏg-ul ttae iyagi (mal) ha-ji maseyo.
b Chuch'a ha-l ttae choshim haseyo.
c Shinae-e ka-l ttae na-hant'e chŏnhwa hae-juseyo.
d Yŏnghwa-ga kunna-l ttae shiktang-e kapshida.
e Toch'ak haess-ul ttae maekju hana mashyŏssŏyo.
f Naga-l ttae kach'i kapshida.

Exercise 5

a Anyhow, what have you decided to do now?
b Didn't you see my girlfriend? If you see her (please) give me a call.
c If you get a bit better don't take the medicine any more.
d When will you graduate? What plans have you got after that?
e Are these papers important? Of course they're important! It's my driving licence, stupid!
f When we have a date, we often go to see a movie.

Exercise 6

a K'un shilsu-rul hasyŏssŏyo.
b Pam nutke toshi-e kamyŏn wihŏmhaeyo.
c Ku sajŏn chom poyŏ jushigessŏyo?
Igŏ ŏdi-sŏ sashyŏssŏyo?
d Musun munje-ga innayo?
Ne. Nae yag-ul irŏbŏri-n kŏt kat'ayo.
e Yojum st'uresu-rul nŏmu mani pada-sŏ,
pam-e cham-ul chal su ŏpsŏyo.
f Kabang-ul irŏbŏri-syŏssŏyo? Mwo-ga turŏ innayo?
g Nae saenggag-ul choaha-ji anch'anayo.
h Kuraesŏ mwol hashyŏssŏyu?

Exercise 7

Take two tablets every three hours while it's very bad.
When it gets a bit better, then take one tablet before meal only at lunchtime.

Unit 11

Exercise 1

a 이 웃이 정말 좋다.
b 비가 온다.
c 뭘 하니?

d 밥을 먹고 있다.
e 걱정하고 있니?
f 조금 더 기다리면 버스가 올 거다.
g 밥 먹는다.
h 어제 밤 어디 갔니?
i 조심했니?

Exercise 2

a Myŏn-uro mandŭn ot.
b Ŏje uri-ga mashin maekju.
c Kim sŏnsaengni-i il-ko innŭn chaek.
d Ku saram-i ip-ko innŭn shyŏch'u.
e Changnyŏn-e uri-ga pon yŏnghwa.
f Nae-ga shirŏha-nŭn ŭmshik.

Exercise 3

a Choa poyŏ-do, an choayo.
b Pissa-do, mash-i issŏyo.
c Pi-ga wa-do, naga-go ship'ŏyo.
d Ku saram-ul choaha-ji ana-do, manna-yagessŏyo.
e Palgun saeg-ira-do, ŏulli-ji anayo.
f Mŏri-ga ap'a-do, noraebang-e kalkka haeyo.

Exercise 4

A Musŭn yŏnghwa-rul polkkayo?
B ——rul popshida.
A Kŭ-gŏn uri-ga changnyŏn-e pon yŏnghwa-janayo.
—— rul popshida.
B Kŭ-gŏn shigan-i nŏmu nujoyo.
A Yŏldu-shi-ga nŏmu nujŏyo? Musun mar-ieyo?!
B Kŭraedo ku yŏnghwa-nun chŏngmal chaemi ŏmnun kŏt kat'ayo.
A Musŭn yŏnghwa-rul polkka?
B ——rul poja.
A Kŭ-gŏn uri-ga changnyŏn-e pon yŏnghwa-jana.
—— rul poja.
B Kŭ-gŏn shigan-i nŏmu nujo.
A Yŏldu-shi-ga nŏmu nujo? Musun mar-iya?!
B Kŭraedo ku yŏnghwa-nun chŏngmal chaemi ŏmnun kŏt kat'a.

Exercise 5

a Hangugmar-ul chal hanun saram-i wayo.
b Ŏje san os-ul choaha-ji anayo.
c Kŭ saram-un mŏshinŭn saram-ieyo.

d Chir-i tŏ choa-do ne bae-na pissayo.
e Tangshin-i ip-go innun os-ul ibŏ pol su issŏyo?
f Mworaguyo?
g Sul mashi-ji anass-ŏdo, pam-e unjŏnhal ttae choshimhaseyo.
h Pisut han kŏ issŏyo?

Unit 12

Exercise 1

a Haksaeng-i myŏnmyŏng-imnikka?
b Musun shisŏl-dur-i issumnikka?
c Hangungmal hago chunggungmar-ul kongbu hal su issumnikka?
d Myŏnmyŏng-i hangungmar-ul kongbu hamnikka?
e Chŏmshimshigan-un myŏ-shi-imnikka?
f Chŏmshimshigan-e pap mŏg-urŏ chip-e ka-do toemnikka?

Exercise 2

a Pin pang issŏyo?
b Ne. Ch'imdae-bang chuseyo.
c Ilgop-sal hago tasŏt-sar-ieyo.
d Sam-il tongan-iyo.
e Anio. Chikchŏp shiktang-e kasŏ mŏkkessŏyo.

Exercise 3

a Muŏs-ul hashyŏsssumnikka?
b Chimdaebang hana chushipshio.
c Chŏ saram-un Kim sŏnsaengnim-ishimnikka?
d Na-nun paekhwajŏm-e kamnida.
e Radio-rul tur-umyŏnsŏ ch'aeg-ul ilksumnida.

Exercise 4

a If you book for more than a week, we'll give you a 10% discount.
b To be (perfectly) honest, I hate people like that.
c He said that he had (or, he has) already eaten breakfast.
d A room with a floor mattress is 20,000 won per day.
e It will be okay if you get up at 7 o'clock.
f We can't give you a refund (of the fare).
g Two rooms with (western) beds, please.
h If you've got something to say (comments to make) about this hotel, please speak to the manager.

Exercise 5

a I hot'er-e sauna shisŏr-i issumnikka?
b Ach'im shiksa-rul paedal hae-jumnikka?
c I hot'er-e suyŏngjang-i issumnikka?

Exercise 6

a Myŏch'il tongan yeyak hasyŏssumnikka?
b Chukshi unhaengwon-hant'e yaegi haessumnida.
c I hot'er-e musun shisŏl-dur-i issumnikka?
d Nae ch'a-e munje-ga manun kŏt kat'-ayo.
e Nae adur-un aji-kkaji irŏna-ji anassŏyo.
f Uri-nun chukshi ba-e kasŏ sul mashil kŏeyo.
g Kim sŏnsaengnim-un pulch'injŏl han saram-ieyo.
h Sam-il tongan mungnun ke chok'essŏyo.

Unit 13

Exercise 1

a There are not many seats left.
b You can't eat something different.
c Would you like a return ticket?
d Mountain climbing is really awful. (*I really hate it . . .*)
e It looks like I'll have to go, then.
f We were just going to have (*intending to have*) a game of baseball.
g Is there a train going to Mokp'o this afternoon?
h That's a decent idea (surprise!).

Exercise 2

a Chŏmshim mŏk-ki chŏn-e.
Chŏmshim mŏg-un taum-e.
b Ŏmŏni-hant'e chŏnhwa ha-gi chŏn-e.
Ŏmŏni-hant'e chŏnhwa ha-n taum-e.
c Nol-gi chŏn-e.
No-n taum-e.
d Shinmum-ul ilk-ki chŏn-e.
Shinmun-ul ilk-un taum-e.

Exercise 3

a 20.00 (10.00 p.m.)
b 8.00
c 11.00
d No, there isn't.
e Yes, there is.

Exercise 4

a Chib-e toraga-l su pakk-e ŏpsŏyo.
b Ton-ul nae-l su pakk-e ŏpsŏyo.
c Ach'im yŏsŏ shi-e irŏna-l su pakk-e ŏpsŏyo.

Exercise 5

a Na-nun kogi malgo kwail mŏk-ko ship'-ŏyo.
b Na-nun swuyŏng malgo nonggu ha-go ship'-ŏyo.
c Na-nun shinmun malgo sosŏl chaek ilk-ko ship'-ŏyo.
d Na-nun norae ha-ji malgo umak tut-ko ship'-ŏyo.

Exercise 6

a Ch'ulbal shigan chŏn-e (or, Ch'ulbal ha-gi chŏn-e),
   mŏg-ul kŏ-rul saseyo.
b Pumonim-hant'e yaegi halkkayo?
c Na-do ka-go ship-chiman, nŏmu mŏrŏyo.
d Se chari-rul hamkke yeyak hal su issŏyo?
e Sŏul malgo Inch'ŏn-e kapshida.
f Il kkunna-n daum-e mwol halkkayo?
g Ŏnje tora-o-shigessŏyo?
h Saengsŏnhoe choaha-seyo?

Unit 14

Exercise 1

a Since Mum likes watching movies, she can watch the video
   instead of Dad.
b It's probably due to stress.
c In fact (actually) there were some very important papers
   inside.
d (My) jeans have worn out (become unusable).
e My wife will perhaps know.
f Tomorrow evening after work I'm planning to go to the
   mountains.
g You never like my ideas (or, opinions).
h The door to our room doesn't even open.
i Could you tell me where the library is, please (lit:, could you
   teach me . . .).
j Did you drink so much alcohol (as that)?
k It's a very popular style nowadays.
l Show me your driver's licence please.

Exercise 2

a Yagu hae boshyŏssŏyo?
   Ne. Hae bwassŏyo. Sashir-un ŏje hae bwassŏyo.
b Suyŏng hae boshyŏssŏyo?
   Ne. Hae bwassoyo. Sashir-un ŏje hae bwassŏyo.
c T'aku hae boshyŏssŏyo?
   Ne. Hae bwassŏyo. Sashir-un ŏje hae bwassŏyo.
d Ch'um ch'wo boshyŏssŏyo?
   Ne. Hae bwassŏyo. Sashir-un ŏje hae bwassŏyo.

Exercise 3

a Shillye-jiman yŏgi kurŏn saram ŏpsŏyo.
b Aniyo, shirŏ hamnida.
c Deit'u ha-l ttae-nun pot'ong nait'u-na shiktang-e kayo.
   (=nightclub)
d Pyŏllo cho-ch'i an-un kot kat'ayo.
e Aniyo, yaksog-ul chal chik'yŏyo.

Exercise 4

a Chŏngmallo p'yojip'an-ul mot pwassŏyo.
b Ch'ongbaji hago kach'i ibul swu issŏyo.
c Yaksog-ul ch'wiso ha-ryŏgo chŏnhwa haessŏyo.
d Pang-e chŏnhwa hago t'erebi-ka issŏyo?
e Sŏbisu-ga ŏnmang-ieyo.
f Changnyŏn-e ku saram-hant'e yangmar-ul sa juŏssŏyo.
g Chom chag-un kŏt kat'-ayo.
h Kurŏn chul arassŏyo.
i Inch'ŏn-e kasŏ saengsŏnhoe-rul mŏk-ko ship'-ŏyo.
j Cha-ga ŏttŏk'e saenggyŏssŏyo?
k P'yŏnji han-jang ssŏ jushigessŏyo?
l Mŏri-ga nŏmu ap'asŏ cham-ul mot chayo.

Exercise 5

Name:	Irŭm-i mwo-eyo?
Age:	Myŏt-sar-ieyo?
Occupation:	Chigŏb-i mwo-eyo?
Father's name:	Abŏji irum-i mwo-eyo?
How met:	Ŏttŏk'e mannass-ŏyo?
What do together:	Hamkke (Kach'i) mwol haeyo?
Likes/dislikes:	Mwol choahaeyo?
	Mwol sirŏhaeyo?

Exercise 6

a If you do it wrong (*if you don't do it properly*) it's very dangerous.
b Do you have a message for Poktong?
c We deliver it to your room (lit:, the guest's room).
d I was here yesterday. I left my jumper.
e The girl said that it was good quality.
f I've got a new girlfriend and it seems like we're out every day.
g Don't talk; just listen.
h Take one tablet twice a day after meals.
i Look at this! The quality's pretty bad.
j You wouldn't know where he/she has gone, would you?
k How would a new television be?
l A similar thing is about twice as cheap at Namdaemun.

Exercise 7

Anio, pappŭn ir-i issŏyo. Waeyo?
Wolyoir-un ŏttaeyo?
Kuraeyo? P'at'i-ga issŏyo?
Abŏji-hant'e mwol sa-durilkkŏeyo?
Hwayoir-un ŏttaeyo? Ku ttae-nun shigan issŏyo?
Cho-un saenggag-ieyo.

Exercise 8

Informal style:

A   Naeil chŏnyŏg-e shigan-i issŏ?
You Ani, pappun ir-i issŏ. Wae?
A   Kunyang naga-go ship'ŏnnunde.
You Wolyoir-un ŏttae?
A   Wolyoil-lar-un abŏji saengshin-iya.
You Kurae? P'at'i-ga issŏ?
A   Ani. Kunyang shiktang-e kasŏ kach'i chŏnyŏk hanun kŏ-ya.
You Abŏji-hant'e mwol sa-durilkkŏya?
A   Yangmal. Hangsang yangmal sa.
You Hwayoir-un ŏttae? Ku ttae-nun shigan issŏ?
A   Ung, choa. Naitu kalkka?
You Cho-un saenggag-iya.

Plain style:

A   Naeil chŏnyŏg-e shigan-i iss-ni?
You Ani, pappun ir-i iss-ta. Wae?
A   Kŭnyang naga-go ship'ŏnnunde.
You Wolyoir-un ŏttŏ-ni?

A   Wolyoil-lar-un abŏji saengshin-ida.
You   Kurae? P'at'i-ga iss-ni?
A   Anida. Kunyang shiktang-e kasŏ kach'i chŏnyŏk hanun
      kŏ-da.
You   Aboji-hant'e mwol sa-durilkkŏ-ni?
A   Yangmal. Hangsang yangmal sa-nda.
You   Hwayoir-un ŏttŏ-ni? Ku ttae-nun shigan iss-ni?
A   Ung, cho-t'a. Naitu kalkka?
You   Cho-un saenggag-ida.

Exercise 9

a Chigŭm ŏdi kashimnikka?
b Chumun haesssumnikka?
c Ilgop shi-e irŏnamnida.
d Ppalli hae-jushipshio.
e Chŏ saram-un pulch'inchŏl han saram-imnida.

Exercise 10

Ach'im igop-shi-e irŏnassŏyo.
Ach'im-ul mŏg-un daum-e ahop-shi-e kyohoe-e kassŏyo.
Yŏl-du-shi-e   yŏja   ch'ingu   hago   kach'i   chŏmshim-ul
mŏgŏssŏyo.
Se-shi-e kich'a-ul t'ago Pusan-e kassŏyo.
Ilgop-shi-e yŏnghwa-rul pwassŏyo.

Exercise 11

a Kŭ ttae-but'ŏ ku yŏja-rul chaju manna-gi shijak haessŏyo.
b Him-i ŏpsŏ-do nolla-ji maseyo.
c I-bon-e-nun tangshin-i towa jwuseyo.
d Pisut hae poyŏ-do pisut ha-ji anayo.
e Chigŭm-but'ŏ tŏ choshim haseyo.
f Chigŭm (chukshi) shiktang-e kasŏ pap mŏg-ul kŏeyo.
g Kurŏm chal toenneyo. Annyŏnghi keseyo.
h Onul chŏnyŏg-un nae-ga nae-lkkeyo.
i Uri paekhwajŏm-ul myŏ-shi-e ttŏna-shyŏssŏyo?
j Shilsu-ga palsaeng hamnita.
k tangshin-ul sogae halkkayo?
l Ibŏ boshigessŏyo?

Korean–English vocabulary

aa!	*ah!*
ach'im	*morning; breakfast*
	(abbreviated form)
ach'im ha-	*have breakfast*
ach'imshiksa	*breakfast*
adul	*son*
agassi	*waitress!, lit. = girl, unmarried*
	woman
ajik	*yet, still*
ajŏssi	*waiter!*
aju	*very*
al	*tablet*
algesssŭmnida	*I understand; OK, right, fine*
	(formally)
ama	*perhaps, probably*
an	*not* (used to make verbs negative)
anj-	*sit*
an p'anŭn ke	*something which is not sold,*
	not available
anieyo	*is not* (opposite of *-(i)eyo*,
	negative copula)
aniyo	*no*
anj-	*sit* (stem)
anju	*snacks or side dishes for drinks*
annyŏnghi kaseyo	*goodbye* (to someone who is
	leaving)
annyonghi kyeseyo	*goodbye* (to someone who is
	staying)
ap'esŏ	*in front of*
ap'ayo	*hurts* (polite style)
ap'ŭ-	*hurts* (stem)

ap'ŭn	*hurting, painful* (adjective)
ara-dŭl-	*understand* (l/t verb like *tul-*, listen; *ara-duroyo, ara-dut-ko* etc.)
bae	*double, (two) times*
bŏsu	*bus*
cchae	*number* (time)
cchok	*side*
ch'a	*car* (short form)
ch'aj-	*look for*
ch'aja po-	*to have a look, to look for*
ch'am	*very*
ch'anggu	*window, cashier window*
ch'i-	*to play (tennis, table tennis etc.)*
ch'imdae	*bed*
ch'imdaebang	*room with bed*
ch'ŏngbaji	*blue jeans*
ch'ŏngso ha-	*clean, clean up*
-ch'ŏrom	*like*
ch'onsaram	*country bumpkin, yokel*
ch'ŏŭm	*at first*
ch'ulbal	*departure*
ch'ulbal ha-	*depart*
cha-	*sleep*
chadongch'a	*car*
chaejangnyŏn	*the year before last year*
chaemi iss-	*is interesting, is fun*
chaeryo	*stuff, (raw) material*
chaesu	*luck*
chaesu ŏps-	*have no luck, have bad luck*
chaju	*often, frequently*
chal	*good, well* (adverb)
chalmot	*wrongly, mis-*
cham	*sleep* (noun)
chamba	*jumper*
chamkkan	*a little (while)*
chamkkan kidariseyo	*please wait a moment*
chan	*cup*
changnyŏn	*last year*
chapchi	*magazine*
chapswo po-	*try eating* (honorific form)
chapsushi-	*eat honorific equivalent of mok-*

chari	*seat*
che	*my* (humble form)
che saenggag-enun	*in my opinion*
cheil	*the most*
chegwajŏm	*bakery*
chibaein	*manager (of hotel or facility)*
chigŭm	*now*
chigwon	*employee*
chiha	*basement*
chiha shiktang	*basement restaurant*
chijŏm	*branch*
chikchŏp	*direct(ly)*
chikhaeng	*fast train, express train (also called saemaul(ho))*
chil	*quality*
chilsaeg-i-	*(really) hate*
chinccha	*really*
chip	*house*
chipsaram	*wife*
chŏ	*me*
chŏ-	*that one (a long way away, old English 'yon')*
cho-ch'i anh-	*is not good (from choh-)*
cho-un saenggag-ineyo	*that's a good idea*
chŏ . . .	*er . . . , hmm . . .*
choa ha-	*like (stem)*
choayo	*good, fine, OK (polite style)*
choesong ha-jiman	*I'm sorry, but; excuse me, but . . .*
choesong hamnida	*I'm sorry; I apologize; excuse me*
chŏgi	*(over) there*
chŏgŏ-do	*at least*
chogum	*a little, a bit*
chogum chŏn	*a little while ago*
choh-	*good (stem)*
chohŭy	*humble form of wuri 'our, my'*
chom	*a little; please*
chŏmshim	*lunch*
chŏn	*before*
chŏn ha-	*communicate*
chŏn ha-l mal	*something to say/pass on/ communicate*
chŏn-e	*previously*

chŏng ha-	decide
chŏngdo	extent, about (approximately)
chŏngi myŏndogi	electric shaver
chŏngmal	really
Chongno	Chongno (one of the main streets in Seoul, north of the Han river)
chongnyu	type, sort, kind
chŏngnyujang	bus stop
chongŏpwon	waiter, assistant
chŏngwangp'an	electronic noticeboard
chŏnhwa	telephone
chŏnhwa ha-	telephone (verb stem)
chŏnshin	the whole body
chŏnyŏk	evening
chŏrŏn	oh dear!, o my!
chorŏp ha-	to graduate
chorum	sleepiness, drowsiness
choshim ha-	be careful, be cautious
chu-	give (stem)
chuch'a han	parked
chuch'a ha-	to park
chukshi	immediately
chumushi-	sleep (honorific equivalent of cha-)
chumun ha-	order (stem)
chungguk	China
chungyo ha-	be important
chungyo han	important (modifier form, like an adjective)
chuseyo	please give (polite request form)
chwahoejŏn	left turn
chwahoejŏn han taum-e	after doing a left turn
chwasŏk	seating, places
chwiso ha-	cancel
deit'u ha-	to date
dijain	design
-do	too, also (particle, attaches to nouns)
-dongan	during
du	two (pure Korean number)

-e	*at (a certain time)*
-e	*each, per*
-e	*to (preposition, attaches to nouns)*
-e	*about, concerning*
-e taehaesŏ	*about, concerning*
-ege	*to*
ei	*hey, come off it!*
-esŏ	*location particle (place in which something happens); from*
ha-	*do (verb stem)*
ha-l mal	*something to say*
ha-rŏ	*in order to do*
haessŏyo	*did (past tense form of ha- do)*
haeyo	*do (stem plus polite ending -yo, irregular form)*
-hago	*and*
hakkwa	*department (of college/ university)*
hakkyo	*school*
halmŏni	*grandma*
hamkke	*together*
han	*one (pure Korean, when used with a counter or measure word)*
han (number/time) cchŭm	*about, around, approximately*
-hant'e	*to, for (a person)*
han-yŏng	*Korean–English*
hana	*one*
hangsang	*always*
hangungmal	*Korean language*
hanguk	*Korea(n) (pronounced hanguk)*
hanja	*Chinese characters*
hanshiktang	*Korean restaurant (serving Korean food)*
-hant'e	*to (a person)*
harabŏji	*grandfather*
harin	*discount*
harin ha-	*give a discount*
haru	*one day (duration)*
haru-e	*per day*
him	*strength, energy*
hoe	*raw meat*
hoesa	*company*

hokshi	*maybe, perhaps, possibly*
hom	*platform*
honja	*alone, on one's own*
hot'el	*hotel*
hupyŏnsŏk	*smoker (compartment)*
hwagin ha-	*check, confirm*
hwaldongjŏg-in	modifier form of the below (like an adjective)
hwaldongjŏk	*casual, active*
hwanpul ha-	*reimburse*
hwolsshin	*by far, far and away*
hu	*after*
hullyung ha-	*is excellent, great*
Hyŏndae chadongch'a	*Hyundai car (company)*
i	*two*
i-	*this one (+ noun), this noun*
i-bŏn	*this time*
il	*matter, business, work*
il ha-	*work (verb stem)*
il kkŭnnago	*after finishing work*
ilbang t'onghaeng	*one way*
ilbang t'onghaengno	*one-way street*
ilbon	*Japan*
ilbonmal	*Japanese language*
ilcchik	*early*
ilk-	*read*
ilyoil	*Sunday*
ilyoillal	*Sunday (longer form)*
Inch'ŏn	*Korean port near Seoul*
-inbun	*portion*
ipku	*entrance*
-irang	*with (-rang after vowel)*
irŏbŏri-	*lose*
irŏk'e	*like this*
irŭm	*name*
isang	*more than*
isang ha-	*is strange, bizzare*
isang ha-ne(yo)	*(it is) strange!*
iss-	*1 exist, there is/are (stem)* / *2 have (stem)*
issŏyo	as above, polite style
issushi-	*have (honorific of iss- in its meaning of possession)*

ittaga	*in a little while*
-iyo	(used to check information, 'you mean?')
-ji maseyo	*please don't*
k'adu	*a card*
k'ŭn	*big*
ka-	*go (verb stem)*
kabang	*a briefcase, a bag*
kabo-	*go and see, visit (a place)*
kach'i	*together*
kage	*shop*
kagyŏk	*price*
kaji	*kind, example (counter for the noun chongnyu)*
kajok	*family*
kajuk	*leather*
kajyŏga-	*take*
kal-	*change (a towel, a platform, clothes etc.)*
kalbi	*marinated and fried meat, usually beef or pork*
kanŭn	*going to, bound for*
kara-ip-	*change clothes*
kara-t'a-	*change (platform, trains etc.)*
karŭch'i-	*teach*
kat'-	*be the same, be similar; seem like*
katko kyeshi-	*have, possess (for honorific person; polite style = katko kyeseyo)*
kat'ŭn	*same*
kat'ŭn kŏt	*(a) similar thing, something similar*
kayo	*go (stem plus polite ending -yo)*
kedaga	*on top of that*
kidari-	*wait*
kil	*road, route*
-ki-man haseyo	*just do (verb)*
kimch'i	*classic Korean side dish, marinated cabbage*
kiŏk	*memory*

-kiro haessŏyo	*decided to*
-kkaji	*until*
kkakka-ju-	*cut the price (for someone's benefit)*
kkoebyŏng-ul purijiyo	*you're making it up! (feigning an illness)*
kkok	*exactly, certainly, precisely*
kkok	*without fail, definitely*
kkunna-	*finish*
kkunnae-	*finish (verb stem, to finish something)*
kkwoebyŏng	*a feigned illness*
kŏ	*thing, object, fact* (abbreviation of *kot*, spelt *kos*)
-ko	*and* (to join clauses)
-ko naso	*after* (added to verb stems)
-kŏdunyo	(see page 110)
kŏgi	*over there* (nearer than *chogi*)
kojang na-	*break down*
kojang nassŏyo	*be broken down*
kŏkchŏng ha-ji maseyo	*don't worry!* (colloquial form: *kokjong maseyo*)
kŏkjŏng	*worry, concern*
kŏkjŏng ha-	*be worried*
kŏlli-	*takes* (time duration)
kŏllyŏyo	*it takes* (polite style)
kolmog	*alley, small road*
komapsumnida	*thank you*
kŏmjŏng	*black*
kŏn	*thing, object* (abbrev of *kot* + topic particle)
kŏngang	*health*
kŏnnŏp'yŏn	*opposite side*
kŏrŏsŏ	*on foot*
kŏrŏssŏyo	*dialled* (past tense of *kol-*, irreg. verb)
kos	*place*
kŏuy	*nearly, almost*
kŭ-	*that one* (nearer than *cho*)
kŭ-daum-e	*after that*
kŭ-gŏn	*that thing* (topic)
kŭ-gŏt poragu!	*you see!*
kŭjŏ kuraeyo	*so-so*
kuk	*soup*

kŭlsseyo	*I dunno, I'm not sure, who knows?*
kŭmyŏnsŏk	*no smoking compartment*
kŭnch'ŏ	*district, area, vicinity*
kŭnsa ha-	*look super, look good*
kŭnyang	*simply, just*
kŭraedo	*however, nevertheless, but still*
kŭraesŏyo?	*so what?*
kŭraeyo (?)	*really (?), is it / it is so (?)*
kŭrigo	*and (also) (used to begin a sentence)*
kŭrigo nasŏ	*after that*
kŭrŏhch'i anhayo	*of course not*
kŭrŏk'e	*like that*
kŭrŏm	*then, in that case*
kŭrŏn	*such a, that (particular)*
kŭrŏn p'yŏn-ieyo.	*(we) tend to be so / do so (it's usually like that, etc.)*
kŭrŏnikka	*therefore, because of that*
kŭrŭt	*dish*
kushik	*old style, old fashioned*
kwail	*fruit*
kwaro	*overwork*
kwallyŏn	*relation, link*
kwon	*volume (measure word)*
kyehoek	*plan(s)*
kyeshi-	*exist (honorific of iss- in its existential there is/are meaning)*
kyohoe	*church*
kyŏljŏng ha-	*decide*
kyŏngch'al	*policeman*
kyŏngch'alsŏ	*police station*
kyŏngu	*circumstance, situation*
kyŏu	*only*
mach'angaji-ieyo	*be the same, be identical*
-mada	*each, every*
maeil	*everyday*
maekju	*beer*
maeun	*spicy*
maj-	*to fit well (maj + nunda = man-nunda)*
mal	*language*
mal ha-	*speak, say*

mal han daero	*as (I) said, like (I) said*
malssŭm	*words, speech*
malssŭm ha-	*speak, say (of someone honorific, often in phrase malssŭm haseyo!)*
malssŭm haseyo	*please tell me, please say it (I'm listening!) (honorific)*
malssŭm mani turŏssŏyo	*I've heard a lot about you*
man	*10,000*
-man	*only*
man(h)-	*is many (h is not pronounced, polite style = manayo)*
man(h)i	*much, many, a lot*
man-ch'i anasŏ	*since there aren't many (written manh-ji anhaso)*
man-e	*within, in only (2 or 3 months)*
manbyŏngt'ongch'iyak	*cure-all medicine, miracle cure*
mandul-	*make (l- irregular verb like p'al, nol- etc.)*
mandurŏssŏyo	*be made of (past tense of mandul-, l- irregular verb)*
manna-	*meet (stem)*
mannasŏ pangapsumnida	*pleased to meet you*
marun anju	*dried snacks*
mash-i ŏps-	*be tasteless, be unpleasant (to eat)*
mashi-	*drink*
mashi-ŏmnunde-do mar-ieyo	*I'm saying (stress) that even the food tasted bad*
maum	*mind, heart*
maum-e (kkok) turŏyo	*I (really) like it*
maum-e tul-ji anayo	*I don't like (her) (maum-e an turoyo)*
miguk	*America*
miniba	*mini-bar*
modu	*all together, everything, everyone*
mollayo	*I don't know*
mom	*body*
mŏri	*head*
mŏrŏyo	*is far (polite style, irregular stem)*
morŭ-	*not know (stem)*
morŭgessŏyo	*I don't know*
mŏshiss-	*be stylish, be handsome*

mot	*cannot (nb mot + m- = mon m-)*
mot ara-dŭt-ket-tago ha-	*say that (one) couldn't understand*
mŏk-	*eat*
muk-	*stay, lodge, spend the night*
mul	*water*
mul naengmyŏn	*thin noodles in cold soup, spicy and refreshing!*
mulgŏn	*goods*
mun	*door*
munje	*problem*
muŏs	*what (full form of mwo)*
murŏ-bo-	*ask*
musŭn	*what (kind of), what, which*
muttukttuk ha-	*be stubborn, be blunt*
mwo	*what?*
mwol	*what (object form)*
-myŏn	*if*
myŏn	*cotton*
myŏndo(-rul) ha-	*shave*
myŏnhŏcchung	*(driving) licence*
-myŏnsŏ	*while (see p. 172)*
myŏt (myoch')	*what (number)?*
myŏt shi	*what time*
na	*I/me*
-na	*approximately, about; or*
naaji-	*get better*
nae	*my*
nae-	*pay*
naeil	*tomorrow*
naengjanggo	*refrigerator*
naengmyŏn	*thin noodles with vegetables*
naga-	*go out*
nalssi	*weather*
nam-	*be left (over), remain*
Namdaemun	*Great South Gate (in Seoul), Namdaemun*
namja ch'ingu	*boyfriend*
namp'yŏn	*husband*
nao-	*come out*
ne	*yes*
nŏ(h)-	*put down, leave*
nolla-	*to be surprised, be shocked*

nolli-	*make fun of*
nolli-ji maseyo	*don't joke, don't kid me, don't tease*
nŏmu	*too (much)*
nongdam	*joke (noun)*
nongdam ha-	*jokes (verb)*
norae	*a song*
noraebang	*'karaoke' singing room*
noraeha-	*sing*
noryŏk ha-	*make effort, strive*
nŭkki-	*to feel*
nŭtke	*late*
nuga	*who? (subject form)*
nugu	*who?*
nun	*an eye*
o-	*come (stem)*
ŏcchaettun	*anyway*
ŏdi	*where?*
ŏdi kannunji aseyo?	*do you know where (she) has gone?*
ŏdinga	*somewhere or other*
oehwan	*exchange*
oehwan unhaeng	*Korea Exchange Bank*
oen	*left*
ohiryŏ	*rather, on the contrary*
ŏi	*hey! (used to call close friends and colleagues)*
ŏje-do mach'angaji-yŏtgoyo	*it was exactly the same yesterday as well*
ojingŏ	*squid*
ŏlma	*how much*
ŏlma nam-ji anassumnida	*there are only a few spaces left*
ŏlma-dongan	*how long*
ŏlma-dongan mwug-ushigessŏyo?	*how long will you be staying?*
ŏmmu	*business, service*
ŏmnun kŏt kat'unde	*it doesn't look as though there is anything / are any*
ondolbang	*room with bed on floor*
ŏngmang	*rubbish, awful, appalling*
ŏnje	*when*
ŏnu	*which one*
onŭl	*today*

orae	*long*
oraeganman-ieyo	*long time no see!*
orakshil	*amusements (electronic games, etc.)*
orŭn	*right*
ŏsŏ oseyo	*welcome!*
ŏttaeyo?	*how is it?*
ŏttŏlkkayo?	*how would it be?*
ŏttŏk'e	*how?*
ŏttŏk'e saenggyŏssŏyo?	*what does it look like?*
ŏttŏn	*certain, some* (as a question word = *which?*)
ŏulli-	*suit (a person)*
p'iryo ha-	*is needed (p'iryo ha- also exists but is less common)*
p'oham doeŏ-iss-	*be included*
p'yŏndo	*single (ticket, way)*
p'yŏnji	*letter*
p'ajŏn	*Korean-style pancake*
p'aljiman	*they sell, but . . .*
p'anŭn ke	*item for sale, items sold*
p'arayo	*sell (polite style form, stem is irregular)*
p'at'i	*party*
p'iro	*fatigue, weariness*
p'iryo iss-	*is necessary, is needed*
p'iryo ŏps-	*is not necessary, is not needed, has no need of*
p'ŏsent'u	*per cent*
p'yo	*ticket*
p'yoji	*a sign, a signpost*
p'yojip'an	*a signpost*
p'yŏn ha-	*is comfortable, is convenient*
pae	*stomach*
paedal ha-	*deliver*
paekhwajŏm	*department store*
pakku-	*change*
palgŭn	*bright*
palsaeng ha-	*occur, happen*
pam	*night*
pang	*room*
pangapsŭmnida	*pleased to meet you*
panggŭm	*just now*

panghyang	*direction*
pap	*rice (cooked rice)*
pap mŏk-	*have a meal*
pappŭ-	*is busy*
pappŭn	*busy*
paro	*directly*
pat-	*to receive*
pi-ga o-	*rains, is raining*
pibim	*mixed*
pilli-	*borrow*
pillyŏ-ju-	*lend*
pin	*empty, vacant, free (of seats and rooms)*
pissa-	*is expensive*
pissan	*expensive* (adjective)
pisŭt ha-	*look similar*
po-	*see, look (sometimes = meet)*
-poda	*more than*
pogwan ha-	*keep*
pŏl	*(counter for clothes)*
pŏlgŭm	*a fine, a penalty*
pŏn	*number*
pŏn	*time (as in first time, second time, many times)*
ponae-	*send*
pŏri-	*throw away*
poyŏ-ju-	*to show*
ppalgan	*red*
ppalli	*quickly*
ppang	*bread*
-ppun	*only*
pujagyong	*a side-effect*
pulch'injŏl ha-	*be unhelpful, be unkind, be impolite*
pulgogi	*Korean spiced marinated beef*
Pulguksa	*Pulguksa (Korean Buddhist temple, near Kyongju)*
pulp'yŏng ha-	*complain*
pun	*minute*
purŭ-	*call*
put'ak ha-	*make a request*
-put'ŏ	*from*
pwa-juseyo	*please look at*
pwayo	*see, look (polite style, irregular)*

pyŏlil	*a special matter, something particular*
pyŏlil ŏpsumyŏn . . .	*if you don't have anything special on . . .*
pyŏllo	*not particularly, not really (+ negative)*
pyŏllo ŏps-	*have almost none, scarcely have any*
pyŏngwon	*hospital*
-rŏ	*in order to*
sa-	*buy* (verb stem)
saek	*colour*
saenggak	*thought*
saenggak	*idea*
saenggang na-	*remember, it comes to mind*
saenggi-	*to occur, happen, take place; look like*
saengil	*birthday* (normal form)
saengshin	*birthday* (honorific form)
saengson	*fish*
sagŏri	*crossroads*
sagwa	*apple*
sai-e	*between*
sajang(nim)	*manager* (honorific form)
sajŏn	*dictionary*
samushil	*office*
san	*mountain*
sangja	*box*
sangŏp	*trade*
Sangŏp ŭnhaeng	*Commercial Bank* (literally, trade bank)
saŏp	*business*
saram	*person*
sarang ha-	*love*
sashil	*fact (the fact is . . .)*
sauna	*sauna*
sayo	*buy* (stem plus polite ending -yo)
se	*three* (pure Korean)
shi	*o'clock*
shigan	*time, hour*
shigŏ-iss-	*be bad, have gone off, be stale*
shijak ha-	*begin, start*

shijang	*market*
shik-	*get cold*
shikhu	*after meal*
shikkurŏwoyo!	*shut up!, be quiet!*
shiksa ha-	*have meal*
shiktang	*restaurant*
shillye hamnida	*excuse me, please*
shillye-jiman ...	*excuse me, but ...*
shilsu	*mistake*
shilsu ha-	*make a mistake*
shim ha-	*be serious*
shinae	*town centre*
shinmwun	*newspaper*
shirŏ ha-	*to dislike*
shisŏl	*facility*
shwipke	*easily*
shyŏch'u	*shirt*
shyop'ing (ha-)	*shopping (do/go shopping)*
sŏ-	*stop (stem)*
sŏbisu	*service*
sogaeha-	*to introduce*
soju	*soju, Korean wine/vodka*
solchikhi	*frankly, honestly*
solchikhi mal hae-boseyo	*tell me the truth!*
solchikhi mal hae-sŏ	*honestly speaking; to tell the truth; in fact ...*
sonnim	*customer*
sŏryu	*document*
Sŏul	*Seoul*
ssa-	*is cheap*
ssan	*cheap (adjective)*
-sshik	*each, per (see notes)*
ssŏgŏssŏyo	*has gone bad, has gone off (polite style, past tense)*
ssŭ-	*write*
ssŭ-ge	*usable*
sŭt'enduba	*bar (standing bar)*
sŭt'ail	*style*
sŭt'uresu	*stress*
sugo haseyo	*work hard!* (said to someone doing their job)
sugŏn	*towel*
sugŏn-ul kara-tallago haessŏyo	*I asked (her) to change the towel*

sulchip	*pub*
suyŏng ha-	*swim*
suyŏngjang	*swimming pool*
t'a-	*take (transport), travel on (transport)*
t'akku	*table tennis*
ta	*all, everything*
Taegu	*Korean city*
taehaesŏ	*about, concerning* (noun *e taehaeso*)
taehak	*university*
taehakkyo	*university*
taesagwan	*embassy*
taeshin	*instead, on behalf of*
tal	*month*
tangjang	*immediately*
tangshin	*you* (often between husband and wife)
tari	*leg*
tarŭ-	*be different* (polite style = *tallayo*)
tarŭn	*another, different*
tashi	*again*
taŭm (daum)	*after, next*
te	*place*
tŏ	*more*
tŏ isang	*any more*
Tobongsan	*Tobongsan (Korean mountain in Seoul)*
toe-	*become*
toksŏ	*reading*
ton	*money*
tongch'ang	*colleague* (fellow student in this case)
Tongdaemun	*Great East Gate (in Seoul), Tongdaemun*
torao-	*come back, return*
tŏrŏp-	*be dirty* (polite = *torowoyo*, *p*-verb like *kakkap*- etc.)
towa-ju-	*to help*
tŏwosŏ	*because it is hot, because you're hot*
ttae	*time (when)*

ttak chilsaeg-ieyo	*hate, is awful (to me)*
ttara-	*follow*
tto	*again; moreover, also*
ttok	*exactly, precisely* (often used with *kat'*-)
tu	*two* (pure Korean number)
tul	*two* (when you mean 'the two of them', 'both')
tŭngsan	*mountain climbing*
tŭrilkkayo	*would you like?* (lit., shall I give you?)
tŭrŏ iss-	*be contained, be included*
tŭrŏ o-	*to enter*
tut'ong	*headache*
uch'eguk	*post office*
uhoejŏn	*right turn*
uhoejŏn han taum-e	*after doing a right turn*
ŭmryosu	*drink*
ŭmryosu hashigessŏyo?	*would you like something to drink?*
ŭmshik	*food*
ŭng	*yes* (casual form)
ŭnhaeng	*bank*
ŭnhaengwon	*bank clerk*
unjŏnsu	*a driver*
uri	*we/our*
uri tul-man kayo?	*is it just the two of us going?*
-uro	*towards, in the direction of* (-ro, after vowels)
usan	*umbrella*
usŏn	*first*
-ŭy	*belonging to*
ŭygyŏn	*suggestion, opinion*
ŭynon	*discussion*
ŭynon ha-	*discuss*
ŭyŏnhi	*by chance, coincidentally*
wa!	*wow!*
waeyo	*why?*
wain	*wine*
wangbok	*return*
wanhaeng	*slow train*
wassŏyo	*came* (past tense form)

wayo	*come* (polite style form)
weit'ŏ	*waiter*
wihŏm ha-	*be dangerous*
won	*won* (unit of Korean currency)
won ha-	*want, require*
wonin	*reason, cause*
wonsungi	*monkey*
yaegi ha-	*talk, tell*
yag-ul mŏgŏyagessŏyo	*I'll have to take some medicine*
yak	*medicine*
yakkuk	*chemist, drugstore*
yaksa	*pharmacist, chemist*
yaksok	*appointment*
yangju	*spirits, western liquor*
yangmal	*socks*
yangshiktang	*western restaurant*
ye	*yes* (politer form of *ne*)
yeyak ha-	*reserve, book*
yŏboseyo	*hello* (on the telephone)
yŏgi	*here*
yŏgi-so	*from here* (abbrev of *yogi-eso*)
yogŭm	*fee, fare*
yŏja ch'ingu	*girlfriend*
yojŭm	*nowadays*
yojŭm chaemi-ga ŏttŏseyo?	*how are you doing?, how are things these days?*
yojŭm saŏb-un ŏttaeyo?	*how is business these days?*
yŏl	*ten* (pure Korean number)
yŏldu	*twelve* (pure Korean number)
yŏlli-ji an(h)-	*does not open*
yŏng-han	*English–Korean*
yŏngguk	*England/ish, Britain/ish*
yŏnghwa	*film, movie*
yŏngŏp	*business*
yŏngsujung	*receipt*
yŏp'	*next door*
yuhaeng ha-	*be popular, be in vogue*

English–Korean vocabulary

about, concerning	-e; -e taehaeso
about/around, approximately	han (*number/time*) cchŭm
after (after, next)	hu (taum/daum)
again (moreover, also, furthermore)	tashi, tto
all, everything	ta
almost, nearly	kŏŭy
alone	honja
altogether, everything, everyone	modu
always	hangsang
and	-hago
and (to join clauses)	-ko
and (also) (used to begin a sentence)	kŭrigo
apple	sagwa
appointment, promise	yaksok
area, district, vicinity	kŭnch'o
at (a certain time)	-e
bag, briefcase	kabang
bank (bank clerk)	ŭnhaeng (unhaengwon)
basement	chiha
bed; (room with a bed) (– on the floor, Korean style)	ch'imdae; ch'imdae bang, ondolbang
beer	maekju
before	chŏn
begin, start	shijak ha-
big	k'ŭn
birthday (honorific form)	saengil (saengshin)
black	kŏmjŏng

blue jeans	ch'ŏngbaji
body	mom
borrow	pilli-
boy/girlfriend	namja/yŏja ch'ingu
bread	ppang
break down	kojang na-
breakfast	ach'imshiksa
breakfast (abbreviated form); (to have breakfast)	ach'im; ach'im mŏk-
bus	bŏsu
bus stop	chŏngnyujang
business	saŏp
busy	pappŭ-
buy (verb stem)	sa-
by far, far and away	hwolssin
call	purŭ-
cancel	ch'wiso ha-
car	chadongch'a
car (short form)	ch'a
careful/cautious	chŏshim ha-
change (clothes/trains etc.)	pakku- (kara-ip-/t'a-)
cheap	ssa-
check, confirm	hwagin ha-
China	chungguk
Chinese character	hanja
church	kyohoe
clean, clean up	ch'ongso ha-
colour	saek
come (out)	o- (nao-)
comfortable/convenient	p'yon ha-
company	hoesa
complain	pulp'yong ha-
cotton	myon
country bumpkin, yokel	ch'onsaram
cup	chan
customer	sonnim
dangerous	wihom ha-
decide	chŏng ha-
deliver	paedal ha-
depart	ch'ulbal ha-
department (store)	hakkwa (paekhwajom)
departure	ch'ulbal

design	dijain
dictionary	sajŏn
different	tarŭ-
directly	chikchŏp/paro
discount	harin
dish	kŭrŭt
dislike	shirŏ ha-
district, area, vicinity	kŭnch'ŏ
do (verb stem)	ha-
document	sŏryu
door	mun
double, times	bae
drink	mashi-
driver	unjŏnsu
during	-dongan
each, every (each, per)	-mada, (-sshik)
early	ilcchik
easy, easily	shwip-, shwipke
eat	mŏk-
eat (honorific, equivalent of *mok-*); (*try eating*) (honorific form)	chapsushi-; chapswo po-
effort, strive	
embassy	taesagwan
employee	chigwon
empty	pin
energy, strength	him
England, Britain	yŏngguk
English–Korean	yŏng-han
entrance	ipku
everyday	maeil
everything, everyone, altogether	modu
eye, snow	nun
exactly, certainly, precisely	kkok, ttok
exchange (*Korea Exchange Bank*)	oehwan (unheng)
excuse me, sorry, but . . .	choesong ha-jiman
excuse me, please	shilye hamnida
exist, there is/are (honorific) (stem)	iss- (kyeshi-)
expensive	pissa-
express train	chikhaeng
evening (time as well as meal)	chŏnyok
everything, all	ta

family	kajok
feel	nŭkki-
film, movie	yŏnghwa
(at) first	ch'ŏŭm
fish	saengsŏn
food	ŭmshik
(on) foot	kŏrŏsŏ
frequently, often	chaju
(in) front of	ap'esŏ
from (location particle, place in which something happens)	-put'ŏ, (-esŏ)
fruit	kwail
give	chu-
go (out)	ka- (naga-)
good (stem)	choh-
good, fine, ok (polite style)	choayo
good, well (adverb)	chal
goodbye (to someone who is leaving)	annyŏnghi kaseyo
goodbye (to someone who is staying)	annyŏnghi kyeseyo
graduate	cholŏp ha-
grandfather, old men in general	harabŏji
grandma, old women in general	halmŏni
handsome	mŏshiss-
have (stem)	iss-
have (honorific form)	issŭshi-
head	mŏri
health	kŏngang
hello (on the telephone)	yŏboseyo
help	towa-ju-
here (from here)	yŏgi (yogi-so)
hospital	pyŏngwon
house	chip
how?	ŏttŏlkk'e
how is it?	ŏttaeyo?
however, nevertheless, but still	kŭraedo
how much, long	ŏlma, -dongan
hurts (polite style)	ap'ayo
hurts (stem)	ap'ŭ-
hurting, painful (adjective)	ap'ŭn
husband	namp'yŏn

if	-myŏn
important	chungyo ha-ha-rŏ
in order to do	ha-rŏ
interesting, fun	chaemi iss-
introduce	sogae ha-

Japan (Japanese language)	ilbon (mal)
joke	nongdam (ha-)
jumper	chamba
just, simply	kŭnyang
just now	panggŭm

kind, type, example	kaji
Korea	hanguk
Korean–English	han-yŏng
Korean language	hangungmal

language, word (to speak/say)	mal (mal ha-)
last year	changnyon
lately, nowadays	yojŭm
least	chŏgo-do
left	oen
leg	tari
lend	pillyŏ-ju
letter	p'yŏnji
like (adjective)	-ch'ŏrom
like (stem), I like (polite form)	choa ha-, maŭm-e tŭrŏyo
like that	kŭrŏk'e
like this	irok'e
little (while, time); in a little while	chamkkan; ittaga
little, a bit (quantity)	chogŭm
little, please	chom
look, see (sometimes = to meet)	po-
look for	ch'aj-
look, to look for	ch'aja po-
lose	irŏbŏri-
love	sarang ha-
lunch	chŏmshim

magazine	chapchi
make (l- irregular verb like p'al, nol etc.)	mandŭl-
manager (honorific form)	sajang (nim)
many (h is not pronouced)	man(h)-

market	shijang
maybe, perhaps	hokshi
me (humble form)	na (chŏ)
medicine (pharmacist), (drugstore)	yak (yaksa) (yakkuk)
meet (stem) (pleased to meet you)	manna- (mannaso pangapsŭmnida)
mind, heart	maŭm
minute	pun
mis-, wrongly	chalmot
mixed	pibim
money	ton
month	tal
more (any more)	to
more than	isang, -poda
morning	ach'im
most	cheil
mountain (climbing)	san (tungsan)
my (humble form)	che
name	irŭm
needed (not needed)	p'iryo ha-/iss- (ops-)
nevertheless, however, but still	kŭraedo
newspaper	shinmun
next	yŏp'
night	pam
no	aniyo
noodles in cold soup	mul naengmyŏn
not (opposite of -(i)eyo)	anieyo
not available, something which is not sold	an p'anŭn ke
not know (stem)	morŭ-
now	chigŭm
nowadays, lately	yojŭm
number (times)	-cchae
number (time as in 'first time', etc.)	pon, (pon)
o'clock	-shi
office	samushil
often, frequently	chaju
OK, right, fine (formal)	algessŭmnida
one	hana
one day	haru
only	-man, -ppun
opinion (in my) (humble form)	che saenggag-enŭn

opposite side	kŏnnŏp'yŏn
order; would you like to order?	chumun ha-; chumum hashigessŏyo?
our, we	uri
our, we (humble form of *wuri*)	chŏhŭy
over there	kogi
park	chuch'a ha-
particularly (not), (not) really (negative)	pyŏllo
per, each	-e
perhaps, probably	ama
person	saram
place	kos
plan	kyehoek
play (tennis, piano etc.)	ch'i-
please don't . . .	-ji maseyo
please give (polite request form)	chuseyo
police (man/station)	kyŏngch'al/-sŏ
portion	-inbun
post office	uch'eguk
previously	chŏn-e
price	kagyŏk
problem	munje
promise, appointment	yaksok
pub	sulchip
quality	chil
quickly	ppalli
rains, is raining	pi-ga o-
really (colloquial)	chinccha
really	chŏngmal
really(?), is it(?), is that so(?)	kŭraeyo(?)
read	ilk-
reason, cause	wonin
receipt	yŏngsujŭng
receive	pat-
red	ppalgan
refrigerator	naenjanggo
request	put'ak ha-
reserve, book	yeyak ha-
restaurant	shiktang

return (tickets)	wangbok
rice, cooked (uncooked)	pap (ssal)
right (direction)	orŭn
road	kil
room	pang
same/identical	mach'angaji
school	hakkyo
seat	chari
see, look (sometimes = to meet)	po-
shave	myŏndo (-rul) ha-
shop	kage
sit	an
sit (stem)	anj-
side	cchok
side dish for drinks or snack	(marŭn) anju
simply, just	kŭnyang
single (ticket, way)	p'yŏndo
sleep	cha-
sleep (honorific)	chumushi-
smoker (compartment);	hŭpyŏnsŏk; kŭmyŏnsŏk
non-smoking compartment	
snow	nun
socks	yangmal
soft drinks	ŭmryosu
something to say	ha-l mal
son	adŭl
song, 'karaoke' singing room	norae (ha-), noraebang
(I'm) sorry, I apologize, excuse me	choesong hamnida
so-so	kŭjo kŭraeyo
soup	kuk
spicy	maeun
spirits, western liquor	yangju
squid	ojingŏ
start, begin	shijak ha-
stay, lodge, spend the night	muk-
stomach	pae
stop (verb stem)	sŏ-
strange, bizarre	isang ha-
strength, energy	him
stylish/handsome	mŏshiss-
suit (a person)	ŏulli-
Sunday	ilyoil
swim (swimming pool)	suyŏng ha- (suyŏngjang)

take (time duration)	kŏlli-
take, travel on (transport)	t'a-
talk, tell	yaegi ha-
tasty/tasteless	mash-i iss-/ŏps-
teach	karŭch'i-
telephone	chŏnhwa
telephone (verb stem)	chŏnhwa ha-
thank you	kamsahamnida/
	komapsumnida
that one (long way away)	chŏ-
that one (nearer than *cho-*)	kŭ-
(over) there	chŏgi
therefore, because of that	kŭronikka
thing, object, fact (abbreviation	kŏ
of *kot* spelt *kos*)	
thought, idea (remember,	saenggak (na-)
it comes to mind)	
three (pure Korean)	se
this one (+ noun), *this noun*	i-
ticket	p'yo
time, hour	shigan
times/double	bae
to (preposition, attaches to nouns)	-e
to	-ege
to/for (a person)	-hant'e
today	onŭl
together	hamkke
together	kach'i
tomorrow	naeil
too, also (particle, attaches	-do
to nouns)	
too (much)	nŏmu
towards, in the direction of	ŭro
towel	sugŏn
town centre	shinae
turned out well, it's all for	chal toenneyo
the best	
two	du, i
umbrella	usan
understand (1/t verb like	ara-dŭl-
tul- listen; *ara-duroyo*)	
unfortunately	an toegenneyo
university	taehak, taehakkyo

until	-kkaji
USA	miguk
very	aju, ch'am
vicinity, area, district	kŭnch'o
wait	kidari-
wait a moment (please)	chamkkan kidariseyo
waiter!	ajŏssi
waitress! (lit. = girl, unmarried woman)	agassi
want, require	won ha-
water	mul
we, our	uri
weather	nalssi
welcome!	ŏsŏ oseyo
well, good (adverb)	chal
what (object form) (full form)	mwo (mwol) (muos)
what (kind of, which) (number)	musun, myŏt/myŏch'
when	ŏnje
where	ŏdi
which one?	ŏnŭ
while, a little	chamkkan
who? (subject form)	nugu(nuga)
wife (not a polite form)	chipsaram
window	ch'anggu
with (*irang* after consonants)	-rang
word, language (to speak/say) (polite form)	mal (mal ha-); malssŭm
work, matter, business	il
worry (to)	kŏkchŏng (ha-)
write	-ssŭ
wrongly, mis-	chalmot
yes	ne
yet, still	ajik
year before last	chaejangnyŏn
you (often between married couples)	tangshin

taking it further

Websites that can be used for learning Korean:

- Korean@Monash: http://www.arts.monash.edu.au/korean/
- Korean studies at Sogang University:
  http://korean.sogang.ac.kr/
- *An Introduction to Korean* by J. David Eisenberg:
  http://langintro.com/kintro/
- Korean through English with the Korean Ministry
  of Culture and Tourism:
  http://www.mct.go.kr/hangeul/index.html
- Korean Language Institute at the University of Bridgeport:
  http://www.bridgeport.edu/Indexhtml/Centers/Disted/
  crsmaterials/korn101/
- Mr Oh's learnkorean.com: http://www.learnkorean.com/
- Korea for kids:
  http://www.curriculum.edu.au/accessasia/korea/kids.htm
- Snapshots of Asia (Korea) at Access Asia:
  http://www.curriculum.edu.au/accessasia/snapshot/korea/
  korea.htm
- Learning hangul with Soyongdori:
  http://library.thinkquest.org/20746/
- Audio files of Korean conversations and narrations
  at Indiana University:
  http://languagelab.bh.indiana.edu/korean101.html
- Korean folk tales for kids at the Korean LG company
  website. This is not designed for language learning, but it
  has an English version as well as a Korean one. Go to
  http://www.lg.co.kr/english/ and click on 'LG Korean
  Folk Tales'.

index of grammatical terms